PERESTROIKA: SOVIET DOMESTIC
AND FOREIGN POLICIES

Perestroika: Soviet Domestic and Foreign Policies

edited by

Tsuyoshi Hasegawa and Alex Pravda

The Royal Institute of International Affairs · London

SAGE Publications · London · Newbury Park · New Delhi

First published 1990

SAGE Publications Ltd
28 Banner Street
London EC1Y 8QE

SAGE Publications Inc
2111 West Hillcrest Drive
Newbury Park, California 91320

SAGE Publications India Pvt Ltd
32, M-Block Market
Greater Kailash – I
New Delhi 110 048

British Library Cataloguing in Publication Data

Perestroika: Soviet domestic and foreign policies. — (Royal
    Institute of International Affairs)
    1. Soviet Union. Government Policies
    I. Hasegawa: Tsuyoshi, *1914*– II. Pravda, Alex, *1947*–
    III. Series
    354.4702

    ISBN 0–8039–8289–5
    ISBN 0–8039–8308–5 Pbk

Library of Congress catalog card number 89–064218

Phototypeset by Input Typesetting Ltd, London SW19 8DR
Printed in Great Britain by Billing and Sons Ltd, Worcester

Contents

vi   *Contents*

List of Contributors

Japanese Contributors

Yutaka Akino	Associate Professor, University of Tsukuba
Tsuyoshi Hasegawa	Professor, Slavic Research Centre, Hokkaido University
Akio Kawato	Director, Division of Eastern Europe, Japanese Ministry of Foreign Affairs
Naomi Koizumi	Research Fellow, Japan Institute of International Affairs, Tokyo
Nobuo Shimotomai	Professor, Hosei University

European Contributors

Hannes Adomeit	Stiftung Wissenschaft und Politik, Ebenhausen
Archie Brown	St Antony's College, Oxford
Julian Cooper	University of Birmingham
Philip Hanson	University of Birmingham
Neil Malcolm	Royal Institute of International Affairs, London
Marie Mendras	Université de Paris I and Centre National de la Recherche Scientifique
Alex Pravda	St Antony's College, Oxford, and formerly Royal Institute of International Affairs, London

Preface

Almost one and a half centuries after Marx wrote *The Communist Manifesto*, another spectre is haunting Europe and the entire world. This spectre, perestroika, is likely to change fundamentally the future development of the world, but not in the way Marx predicted. Whereas Marx was confident about the demise of capitalism and history's inevitable march forward to socialism, perestroika's main impetus comes from the recognition that the communist system as it now exists has spent its historical usefulness. Whereas Marx was categorical about the fundamental irreconcilability of the two systems – a principle on which the system of East–West relations was built – perestroika calls for all-human values to transcend differences between socialism and capitalism. While Marx saw in communism the only possibility for world integration, it is primarily the economic and technological integration in the capitalist world that has alerted the backward socialist economies to the need for integration with the world economy. In other words, the spectre of perestroika is not a threat to our survival; it is a challenge to the system we have created to protect ourselves from that threat, because it is changing the very nature of the threat itself.

There can be no doubt that fundamental changes are taking place in the Soviet Union. These changes encompass the economy, the political system, social relations and attitudes to the outside world, and amount to no less than a revolution. This revolution is not only changing the nature of the communist system from within, but also beginning to undermine the very foundations of the postwar international system. At no time in postwar history has Soviet foreign policy been so integrally connected with domestic change, nor have the reactions of the outside world ever constituted such a critical factor in determining the direction of change within the Soviet Union.

Moreover, perestroika is not an isolated phenomenon limited only to the Soviet Union. The winds of change and reform have been blowing in Eastern Europe, China, Vietnam and even North Korea. Will these reforms succeed? If so, what kind of socialist systems are likely to emerge? If not, what will be the outcome of their failure? What are the roots of these changes and what factors shape their dynamics? Most importantly perhaps for outside observers, what are the connections between reforms within communist states and their attitudes and policies towards the rest of the world? What are the implications of these reforms for the world as a whole? Are they likely to move in a direction to end the cold war, facilitate East–West cooperation, help resolve regional conflicts in the Third World and create a new international security system? Without a good understanding of such implications and of the reforms themselves it is difficult to formulate effective policies on such fundamental issues as arms control, Sino-Soviet detente, Vietnamese policies in Indochina, or new prospects for collaboration across the divide in Europe.

In order to further our understanding of the policy changes taking place in the communist world, Japanese and European specialists, under the sponsorship of the Sasakawa Peace Foundation, in 1988 launched a three-stage project on foreign policy and domestic politics in communist states. The overall aim of the project is to produce a systematic comparative analysis of the relationship between domestic developments and foreign policy reforms in communist states. An important part of the first stage of the project, focusing on the USSR, was a conference held at Chatham House in December 1988 at which European and Japanese members of the project team presented papers on major domestic and international dimension of perestroika. This was the first time that Soviet specialists from Europe and Japan had met to discuss the reforms under Gorbachev. The conference successfully produced a fruitful exchange of views that brought out subtleties of regional perspectives rarely found at conferences on the Soviet Union.

Lively discussion revealed a greater commonality of views between Japanese and European participants than the organizers had anticipated. In fact, differences of opinion tended to cut across rather than follow regional groupings. At the conference as in this volume, differences in interpretation between Japanese and European analysts are perhaps less marked than a shared outlook on the origins, nature and the significance of the remarkable changes taking place in the Soviet Union. The chapters, which are derived from papers presented at the conference, cover major dimensions of perestroika that bear on the relationship between Soviet domestic and foreign policy reform under Gorbachev, a theme reviewed in the introduction. The chapter by Tsuyoshi Hasegawa sets into historical context the nature and significance of perestroika. The remarkable reforms and developments associated with political perestroika are examined by Archie Brown in Chapter 3, while Nobuo Shimotomai (Chapter 4) chronicles the key role played by intellectuals in the development and use of glasnost to foster reform and a climate conducive to the growth of 'civil society'.

The economic problems and remedies that lie at the basis of perestroika are reviewed by Philip Hanson in Chapter 5; the external dimensions of economic perestroika form the subject of Akio Kawato's critical assessment of the Soviet Union's chance of playing a new role in the world economy (Chapter 6). Julian Cooper (Chapter 7) then considers the attempts to make better civilian use of the resources of the defence industries, while Naomi Koizumi in Chapter 8 examines the military and their policy role.

The last four chapters in the volume deal with key aspects of change in external policy and relations. In Chapter 9 Neil Malcolm traces the postwar evolution of innovative thinking on international issues, while Marie Mendras (Chapter 10) assesses the critical elements in current 'new thinking'. The practical policy produced by 'new thinking' in the two major regions of most direct concern to the project, Asia and Europe, are examined by Yutaka Akino (Chapter 11) and Hannes Adomeit (Chapter 12).

The editors of any collective volume owe a debt to a large number of people; editors managing the first product of a collaborative project involving participants from two continents are all the more heavily indebted. We would like to take this opportunity to thank those who provided such useful comments on the original papers and helped to create an atmosphere of lively and creative academic discussion at the conference: Motofumi Asai, Brian Bridges, Bryan Cartledge, Irene Commeau-Rufin, Peter Duncan, James Eberle, Ferdinand Feldbrugge, Peter Ferdinand, Michael Kaser, Hiroshi Kimura, Malcolm Mackintosh, Laura Newby, John Roper, Seizaburo Sato, Tsuneaki Sato, Gerald Segal and Akihiko Tanaka.

Our thanks go also to the staff of Chatham House for their support, primarily Peter Duncan and Dawn Margrett in connection with conference arrangements, and Pauline Wickham and Leonard Geron for assistance in producing this volume. Shyama Iyer provided invaluable help on both conference and volume throughout this first stage of the project. The organization of this stage would not have been possible without the support of the Economic and Social Science Research Council (Grant No. EOO 22 2011) for the

Soviet foreign policy programme at the Royal Institute of International Affairs. We would like to acknowledge the co-sponsorship of the conference by the Asia Pacific Association of Japan. This volume and the project as a whole owe their existence to the sponsorship and financial support of the Sasakawa Peace Foundation. We gratefully acknowledge the support of the Foundation and the advice and help of its staff, especially Programme Officer Toshihiko Okoshi and Programme Director Kazuo Takahashi.

The support, help and collaboration forthcoming from the Foundation and our academic colleagues throughout this stage of the project make us confident that the next two stages will prove to be as enjoyable and fruitful as this initial phase.

Tsuyoshi Hasegawa
Alex Pravda

1

Introduction: Linkages between Soviet Domestic and Foreign Policy under Gorbachev*

Alex Pravda

Domestic and foreign policy are more closely connected under perestroika than at any previous stage in Soviet development. Gorbachev has himself highlighted the unprecedented priority of internal factors: 'Our foreign policy today stems directly from our domestic policy to a greater extent than ever before.'[1] Soviet leaders have, of course, always placed domestic needs first, yet the weight accorded them in the last four years is certainly greater than at any time since the early Khrushchev period. Arguably, domestic considerations have figured more prominently under perestroika than in any peacetime period since the years immediately following the Revolution. Indeed, Soviet observers have drawn parallels between the domestic priorities under Gorbachev and those that led to the Treaty of Brest-Litovsk and later the New Economic Policy (NEP).[2]

If the Gorbachev years stand out in the salience of domestic factors in foreign policy, they are even more remarkable for congruence between the thrust of change on internal and external policy fronts. In previous periods of major change in Russian and Soviet history (patterns of which are discussed by Tsuyoshi Hasegawa in the next chapter), domestic and foreign policies have been inconsistent and even divergent. Even those periods which at first glance appear to be similar in congruence to perestroika, prove on closer consideration to have been less congruent. Take NEP for instance: moves towards greater involvement in the international system in the early twenties corresponded to domestic economic reform but were at odds with political centralization. This partial incongruity helped to weaken what was anyhow a temporary rather than permanent strategy of development.

Any serious assessment of the correlation between domestic and foreign policy strategies at different stages in Soviet development would require the elaboration of a complex set of criteria.[3] For our present purposes we can use the rather crude, though helpful, criteria of tendencies towards 'open' or 'closed' policy strategies at home and abroad. 'Closed' policies in the domestic setting are associated, self-evidently, with conservation of the concentration of economic and political power within few institutions; 'open' strategies strive to introduce economic decentralization and wider political participation and accountability. On the security and foreign policy front, the terms are self-explanatory, denoting on the 'closed' side tendencies towards isolationism and autarky and on the 'open' side efforts towards greater economic and political interaction with the Western world. Using these rough yardsticks, policy in the Stalin period tended to consistency at the 'closed' end of the spectrum (with obvious exceptions in foreign policy in the mid to late 1930s and in both contexts during the war). Under Khrushchev the picture is predominantly one of striving towards greater 'openness' on both fronts, notably in the first de-Stalinization period (1953–7), which laid the basis for many of the reforms which perestroika has taken far further. It was only the last years of Khrushchev's rule that saw retreat from reform on both fronts. Inconsistency between domestic and foreign policy became the hallmark of the Brezhnev era, in which strategies appeared to diverge. A 'closing' of political and economic reform went hand in hand with a foreign policy of detente which opened up contacts with the West. In fact the disquieting influences involved in the detente policy probably reinforced the natural inclination of a conservative and cautious regime to maintain tough controls over political developments, particularly dissidence. Incongruity and tension between the two sets of policies reflected and deepened the general incoherence in policy which Neil Malcolm sees in Chapter 9 as characterizing the end of the Brezhnev period. Fear of change paralysed movement on both domestic and foreign policy fronts from the late 1970s (except for the short Andropov interregnum) to Gorbachev's accession. Reluctance to tackle mounting problems at home and abroad associated with 'stagnation' (*zastoi*) compounded the tensions within and between domestic and foreign policies in the late 1970s and early 1980s.

Since assuming office and assessing the legacy of *zastoi* in terms of systemic crisis, Gorbachev has pursued a comprehensive, radical and highly activist policy of 'opening up' on both domestic and international fronts – the strategy of perestroika. Gorbachev is the first Soviet leader to see the salvation of the Soviet Union in a strongly Westernizing strategy rather than temporary tactic. He is the first to consider the USSR to be in a systemic crisis sufficiently grave to warrant revolutionary change and at the same time the first to have sufficient confidence to attempt this by exposing the Soviet Union to outside influences and involvement. The Gorbachev years have thus seen a stronger and, most notably, more dynamic and proactive congruence of movement towards 'open' domestic and international policies than at any time in the Soviet period. Domestic and foreign policy perestroika form integral and interactive parts of an ambitious strategy of modernizing the Soviet Union, bringing the system into the twenty-first century, through opening up politics to the population and the Soviet Union to the developed world.

Gorbachev's references to the 'organic unity' of perestroika should thus not be seen merely as an effort to create the image of policy consistency.[4] They reflect what amounts to a general strategic concept of perestroika, one developed in the process of practical change yet one that from the outset has stressed the close connections between internal and external reform.[5] As the process of perestroika has developed in ever more radical directions, so the links between its domestic and external components have thickened. Domestic perestroika has broadened from economic to political reform (and reform on both those fronts has become progressively more radical), while foreign policy has gone from efforts to re-establish detente to the determined pursuit of entente and a qualitatively new involvement in the international system. All this does not mean that there is any *absolute* correlation between progress of perestroika at home and abroad (Marie Mendras in Chapter 10 rightly rejects any 'automatic' synchronization). Yet the processes of internal and external perestroika are symbiotically connected both in terms of policy impetus and policy momentum. The interconnections are complex, and influence flows in both directions. On the one hand, declining international standing certainly contributed to the initial decision to undertake radical domestic change, which in turn required a neo-detentist policy in order to obtain international tranquillity. On the other hand, democratizing reforms within the Soviet Union have contributed substantially to the creation of a non-threatening and more acceptable image abroad which remains essential to the successful pursuit of Gorbachev's more cooperative foreign policy strategy. To complete the internal–external policy circle, as it were, a successful international strategy of this kind is in turn the key to creating a climate favourable to economic interaction with the West that can provide the Soviet Union with both the short-term material aid and longer-term cooperation which many see as important to the success of perestroika.

The close interaction and interdependence of domestic and foreign policy developments over the last four years is the reason why this volume brings together analyses of both the internal and international dimensions of perestroika. Most chapters examine major aspects of change in particular policy areas; those by Neil Malcolm and Marie Mendras (Chapters 9 and 10) look more specifically at the interaction between domestic and foreign policy. Neither attempts comprehensively to assess the weight of domestic and international factors in shaping the overall strategy in process of perestroika, an objective which is part of a major cooperative project of which the present volume represents a preliminary publication. The project will explore the whole complex relationship between domestic politics and foreign policy reform in communist states. This volume seeks simply to examine developments in major domestic and foreign policy areas under perestroika; this introduction seeks merely to map some of the contours of the linkages between them. To do this we discuss linkages under three broad headings: resources, policy thinking and domestic politics.[6]

Resources

Resource-based linkages provide the most direct and palpable connection between domestic and foreign policy since they self-evidently involve basic questions of allocation of priorities between guns and butter, or more accurately between developing different dimensions of security and economic capabilities. Two sets of resource linkages have proved particularly critical under perestroika. The first may be labelled 'harnessing the military', and has involved efforts to reduce the security burden and make more effective use of military resources for domestic economic development. The second may be summarized as greater interaction with the world economy, and relates to maximizing the domestic benefits of external economic ties. Whereas foreign policy considerations have played an important part in resource allocation decisions, particularly in the first area, domestic priorities have largely driven policy change.

Harnessing the Military

A close policy connection between security demands and domestic economic development has long figured prominently in the Soviet

Union. For the most part leaders, notably Stalin, have invoked security imperatives in order to justify domestic privation. An awareness of the need to reduce the military burden emerged, however, under Khrushchev, who attempted to cut back – ultimately unsuccessfully – on military size and expenditure. Although this policy was reversed through the late 1960s and 1970s, debates around this issue resurfaced in the late Brezhnev period which saw a slowdown in military spending. While the Brezhnev leadership undoubtedly regarded the attainment of military parity with the United States as a major achievement, some realized the costs of such sustained defence priorities for civilian economic development in general and consumption in particular.[7]

Under Gorbachev, concern about the costs of established policy with its high military priority has stemmed from anxiety both about military performance as well as about the development of the economy in general. Many in the defence establishment have from the late 1970s realized that Soviet technological capabilities would not easily be able in future to compete with Western weapons development, notably in the area of emerging technologies. The threat of the United States racing ahead in this field was intensified by the appearance of the SDI programme. Hence Gorbachev's early emphasis on using vigorous arms control policy to try and slow down the pace and scope of American military technological development. The emphasis on the ABM treaty, and Soviet willingness to consider deep cuts in strategic arsenals, as well as the unsuccessful effort to bring about a test moratorium through unilateral moves, all underscored the policy urgency of constraining the technological arms race and taking pressure off the Soviet defence industry. As well as contributing to the reinvigoration of its arms control policy, the problem of keeping technological military pace with the West has reinforced the case for radical economic reform in the Soviet Union. Even in the late Brezhnev years the military began to realize that they needed a more dynamic and innovative economy in order to generate the advanced technologies vital to maintain parity with the United States in a qualitative rather than the traditional quantitative sense. Gorbachev has taken account and also possibly full political advantage of this realization and used the qualitative-based technology security argument to strengthen the case for a more efficient and integrated economy, one that eliminates what he has dubbed the 'internal Cocom' which confines the development of key technologies largely to the defence sector.[8] The perestroika leadership have shown keen appreciation of the crucial importance to national security of the economic and technological capability to innovate. 'Today what is instrumental to the security of a country', Shevardnadze told a foreign ministry meeting in July 1988, 'is not so much its stockpiles as its capacity to develop and produce new things.'[9] The case for radical economic reform is thus strengthened by a wider security argument which depicts such change as the only way to prevent the Soviet Union from sliding further down the international league table and losing its standing as a superpower or even a great power. As Japan and West Germany show, the path to world status and influence lies increasingly through developing economic and civilian technology rather than military strength.

To some extent, therefore, the rationale of perestroika serves mid-term security purposes. On the other hand, perestroika also involves a reduced emphasis on the overall importance of defence priorities in overall Soviet development. The main thrust of this emphasis is for a reduction in the defence burden and a reallocation of scarce resources to the civilian sector. Ryzhkov and others have stressed the enormous burden imposed upon the economy by the yoke of military expenditure, a burden both in financial, and perhaps more importantly, in general resource terms – scarce materials and skills.[10] Indeed a major case for the pursuit of radical disarmament policies – aside from the much vaunted danger of nuclear conflict – is couched in terms of releasing Soviet economic development from the narrow confines of the arms race and allowing it to evolve in more diverse and profitable civilian directions, thus improving living standards and raising the economic and general standing of the USSR in the world.[11] That domestic economic pressures have themselves played a key role in driving the policy to reduce military expenditure (and press for disarmament) is suggested by the growing emphasis placed on defence cuts since 1987 as the economic situation has worsened. Public admission of a deficit of over 100 billion roubles, slowing growth rates and deteriorating supplies, was the background for the announcement in December 1988 of unilateral troop cuts and in January 1989 of a 14.2 per cent cut in military expenditure[12] which is now officially estimated at approximately 80 billion roubles per year.[13] Deeper cuts of up to 50 per cent in defence expenditure are planned by 1995[14] as long as progress is maintained towards ambitious objectives in conventional arms reductions.

The onslaught on the defence burden has several external and domestic policy ramifications. On the foreign policy front it obviously increases the credibility of Soviet disarmament intentions. It also clearly provides the main driving force to pursue further arms cuts, particularly in conventional forces. The INF treaty, while a major political and psychological breakthrough, involves considerable verification costs and relatively small direct savings. A START agreement would save on future expenditure but only far-reaching conventional cuts can make a really useful contribution in the economic sense. It is perhaps the general thrust of disarmament policy rather than its specific components that matters, for it creates a political climate that facilitates a downgrading of military priorities. On the domestic front targeting military expenditure for cuts may well help to show that the leadership is doing something to try and improve the general economic situation, something that is politically useful at a time when other economic reform measures seem to be making little if any impact on living standards. In fact a direct connection is frequently made between reductions in defence and benefits in the civilian sector – witness the support of the Minister of Health for lower military spending.[15] More importantly, subordinating military to civilian priorities has helped substantially to shift resources towards the civilian sector. In Chapter 7 Julian Cooper examines the moves made since 1988 to convert more military production facilities to civilian use, to transfer light industrial enterprises to military management and expose the defence industry to economic reform. As he argues, these moves represent not merely a tactic to ease economic pressures and build up technological strength but also a 'historic and long-term shift of priorities from military to civilian purposes'. This shift stems from the twin imperatives of maintaining technological parity and modernizing the domestic economy, both of which require demilitarization of security and of the domestic economic system. The complex of interconnected security and domestic factors involved in harnessing the military thus constitutes a very strong resource linkage between internal and external policy under perestroika.

Interaction with the World Economy

A less dramatic yet in the long term arguably a more important resource linkage involves Soviet external economic relations. If one part of the perestroika argument is that Soviet development has been diverted and handicapped by excessive military contest with the United States, another is that the USSR has been weakened by insufficient contact and economic competition with the advanced industrial world. Awareness of the decline of the Soviet Union by world economic standards undoubtedly helped to increase the sense of impending crisis that informed the decision to embark on perestroika. For not only had the Soviet Union slipped in its share of world product, it also occupies a lowly (fiftieth to sixtieth) position in world per capita consumption and compared badly in some basic respects even with tsarist Russia.[16] Such international comparisons continue to be used to point up the urgency of persisting with economic reform. Awareness of international decline might not have resulted in perestroika had it not been coupled with a conviction that isolation is partly responsible for Soviet backwardness and that the only way to close the widening gap and modernize the economy lay in closer long-term economic interaction with an increasingly interdependent global economy. As Shevardnadze told a Ministry of Foreign Affairs audience in July 1987, 'we have to become a more organic part of the world economic system'.[17] This conviction lies at the heart of the 'open' strategy that distinguishes perestroika from many previous Soviet attempts at reform, and, if anything, its centrality has become more apparent since 1987. 'Our restructuring', Gorbachev told the Supreme Soviet in August 1989, 'is inseparable from a policy of full-blooded participation in the international distribution of labour.'[18]

At present participation is far from being full-blooded. The Soviet Union has a meagre 4 per cent share in world trade. As Chapter 6 makes clear, the structure of that trade makes USSR a very weak player of the world economic stage. The composition of trade is reminiscent of a Third World country, with energy accounting for over 60 per cent of exports. Despite the evident difficulties of increasing economic involvement, more rigorous interaction is seen as an important aid to domestic economic perestroika in at least three respects. Most clearly the improvement of foreign trade performance is the only way to repay existing hard currency debts, which in 1989 stood at around 34 billion roubles. More importantly, it is essential for purchase of technology necessary for modernization. Even if the leadership is anxious to avoid the mistakes of the 1970s, when too much emphasis was placed on importing capital goods, it sees Western technology as a vital component of effective modernization. Export earnings are also important for purchases of foodstuffs and perhaps increasingly of manufactured consumer goods economically and politically necessary in the short term at least to buoy up perestroika.

The most important function of increased economic involvement with the advanced world lies in stimulating and promoting radical reform and efficiency within the Soviet economy. (For a review of the current stage of reform, see Chapter 5.) Unlike Brezhnev, who used foreign trade as a kind of substitute for domestic reform,

Gorbachev seeks to help shake up and modernize the economy by exposing the Soviet Union to world involvement. The decentralization of the foreign trade system is intended to help break down ministerial and departmental power and foster a sense of independence and initiative as well as to boost export capabilities and educate Soviet managers. 'Know how' has made its way into the Russian language yet has still not penetrated Soviet economic and managerial culture. To try and remedy this Moscow has signed training agreements with major Western states including Britain, France, the United States and West Germany. Inculcation of Western managerial techniques is also one of the objectives behind the policy of joint ventures with capitalist partners. From a slow start in 1987 this policy had resulted by mid-1989 in 685 agreements on joint ventures with the West.[19] Although joint ventures and other production cooperation schemes are unlikely to make a major economic impact on Soviet performance, they could act as catalysts of wider domestic economic modernization both by means of incentives and competitive pressures.

Neither joint ventures nor the foreign trade system can make much headway, however, unless domestic economic reforms make real progress, allowing the new decentralized trade system to operate effectively and steps to be taken towards currency convertibility which remains essential to any substantial growth in inward investment and trade. As Philip Hanson and Akio Kawato argue (in Chapters 5 and 6), the obstacles and problems remain formidable and there is only a slim chance of the Soviet Union becoming anything like internationally competitive before the early years of the next century. Most Soviet economists would concur with this assessment; even Gorbachev has become increasingly sober since 1988 about overcoming the knot of linked domestic and international economic problems. As he told the new Soviet parliament in summer 1989: 'Whereas at the start it appeared as if change in human rights and arms control would be difficult to implement and economic relations looked relatively simple, it now seems to be the other way round.'[20]

Despite, or perhaps because of, the fact that the problems appear more formidable, economic objectives have come to figure increasingly importantly in Soviet foreign policy. Shevardnadze has called on Soviet diplomats to 'economize' Soviet foreign policy[21] and Soviet relations with all major Western states have placed economic agreements high on the agenda. Interest has also been expressed in joining international economic organizations such as GATT, and Gorbachev has made clear, most directly in his message to the G7 meeting in Paris in July 1989, that the Soviet Union wishes to be more fully involved in international economic affairs. This policy is driven by a mixture of motives. On the one hand Soviet interest flows from a concern to use economic channels to become more involved in the established international system and stabilize relations with its key actors. 'Doing business' rather than competing militarily with the rest of the world, Gorbachev seems convinced, is an important way of getting the Soviet Union accepted as a 'normal' member of the international community. Economic motives are equally or more important. Doing business, Soviet leaders hope, may help them in modernizing the Soviet economy; as realists they understand that future Soviet standing and international influence will depend increasingly on how the country performs economically by world standards. This element, and, indeed, the entire nexus of resource issues, thus provide an ever more important and complex linkage connecting the domestic and international dimensions of perestroika.

Policy Thinking

The scope and depth of the connection between the domestic and international dimensions of perestroika emerges more clearly when we turn to the area of policy thinking. We are concerned here with policy approaches and frameworks of analysis as well as policy values, common norms and perspectives shaping strategy and tactics. The perspectives and prescriptions associated with Soviet foreign policy under perestroika go under the official label of 'new thinking'. Possibly more coherent a body of policy principles than its domestic equivalent, 'new thinking' intersects to a remarkable degree with innovative thinking on domestic affairs. Both share a pool of central ideas, beliefs, principles and perspectives that bestride the domestic and foreign policy spheres. Gorbachev has described 'new thinking' as 'in essence the ideology and theory of restructuring as a whole and not only in foreign policy'.[22] This common pool of ideas may for the sake of convenience be called 'perestroika thinking'. Its sources and major elements are sketched in the following section.

One of the reasons for the emergence of perestroika thinking has been the rise to influence of a number of policy specialists who advise and write on both domestic and international issues. These 'dual policy influentials' include people such as Bovin, Burlatsky, Butenko, Frolov, Primakov, Shmelev and Shakhanazarov. Academics, journalists and commentators who have often spent time in official academy and party think-tanks, these 'dual specialists' share key formative political experiences with many of their reformist colleagues in either the international or the domestic operating policy fields. These experiences have given them an antipathy towards Stalinism and a favourable memory of Khrushchev's efforts at de-Stalinization, coupled with a vivid experience of the negative aspects of the Brezhnev period as well as of the more positive specialist discussions of the 1970s that produced and reinforced many of the ideas that now form the basis of perestroika thinking. (In Chapter 4 Nobuo Shimotomai discusses the role of specialists in perestroika, while in Chapter 9 Neil Malcolm examines the evolution of the ideas in 'new thinking'.) These 'dual specialists' share with one another the additional experience of living abroad (in the West or Eastern Europe) or at least enjoying extensive international contacts which have often informed and radicalized the ideas they derived from domestic sources. To some extent, therefore, they have injected Western, as well as East European and Chinese, perspectives into perestroika thinking (their colleagues specializing solely in international affairs are often more strongly Westernized) and stand in contrast to the more closed, Russian-centred commentators and theorists who typically take a more conservative line.

The overlap found among 'dual specialists' is paralleled and reinforced by the dual domestic/foreign policy orientation among progressive members of the top leadership. Foreign Minister Shevardnadze retains a strong interest in domestic policy as he spent his entire previous career in that area, and continues to play an important role at home (as in the aftermath of the Tbilisi clashes of spring 1989). Medvedev, now in charge of ideology, for a time oversaw relations with socialist states. His predecessor as Secretary for Ideology, Yakovlev, plays a key role in internal and external affairs, being both one of Gorbachev's closest associates in the general area of ideology and head of the new International Affairs Commission of the Central Committee, thus effectively in charge of coordinating foreign policy strategy. Gorbachev himself started with little or no international experience (though he had visited Canada and Eastern Europe), but since becoming General Secretary has of course devoted a remarkable amount of time and energy to foreign affairs.

To do justice to the connections between policy thinking in the domestic and international field would require a comprehensive analysis of recent theoretical innovations in both areas as well as their interplay. The aim of this paper is simply to sketch some of the main traits of 'perestroika thinking'. Most of these traits amount to perspectives and tendencies of analysis rather than specific recommendations, even if some do suggest and are closely associated with clear policy strategies and tactics.

The first trait is analytical eclecticism, a strong tendency away from circumscribed Marxist-Leninist approaches to analysing policy problems to one employing wide-ranging social science theories and methods. As realistic and pragmatic politicians, out to modernize the entire Soviet system, Gorbachev, Yakovlev and Shevardnadze have called for innovative approaches in the analysis of international as well as domestic developments. Rather than asking social scientists in traditional style to spin new variations on ideological themes, they now urge them to use any kind of analysis that will produce penetrating assessments of key policy problems.[23] After all, in many instances, Western literature is of infinitely more use than the works of Marx or Lenin for dealing with critical domestic problems, such as bureaucratic inefficiency, or foreign policy ones like regional conflicts or arms control. The fact that the political leadership now apply criteria of effectiveness in problem solving rather than doctrinal orthodoxy has cleared the way for a whole spectrum of new policy ideas and concepts derived from Western specialist literature. In the security policy area these include the action–reaction process of the arms race, the role of enemy images, non-provocative defence, reasonable sufficiency, mutual security and interdependence. In the domestic context, as Archie Brown details in Chapter 3, many of the concepts once rejected as bourgois have now been given authoritative endorsement. He also notes how some Western states, including Switzerland, have recently come to qualify as models for socialist development. And indeed many of the key reform policies have drawn heavily on the experience of both socialist and capitalist states. As economic perestroika has become more radical, so the focus of 'learning' has shifted – differently in various policy spheres – from the GDR and China, to Hungary, Japan and Sweden.[24]

The approach to analysis promoted by policy specialists and encouraged by the reform leadership effectively involves the de-ideologization or at least the de-dogmatization of policy thinking. Even if Gorbachev may wish ideally to build a new Marxist-Leninist framework to explain and legitimate perestroika policies, his priority as a pragmatic politician is to encourage innovative thinking which produces policies that will work rather than be doctrinally acceptable. Such pragmatic realism has strongly come to the fore on the domestic and foreign policy fronts. Gorbachev has, for instance, defined socialist quality (*sotsialistichnost*) in terms of effectiveness, while Shevardnadze in similar vein has made 'profitability' the key yardstick of foreign policy.

This eclectic problem-solving approach has raised to prominence two analytical perspectives that figure importantly in perestroika thinking: recognition of the legitimacy of diverse interests and of the need to reconcile these for the general rather than class good. The lifting of doctrinal constraints has made possible shifts in policy views of the nature of interests both within Soviet society and in the world at large. Rather than trying to fit domestic and international interests into the Procrustean bed of class analysis, perestroika thinking acknowledges that the situation is far more complex and that interests have deep historical, national, psychological roots which are as, or possibly more important than, their traditional class dimensions.

The same approach sheds doubts on traditional assumptions about ineluctable historical tendencies either within Soviet society or the international community. To assume inexorable progress towards 'new Soviet man', a predominant Soviet identity for ethnic groups in the USSR or towards the socialist commonwealth of nations and an international communist movement is now seen as an unrealistic base for the conduct of domestic and foreign policy. Given the failure of past Soviet efforts to mould opinion at home and impose frameworks of development on other countries, it is hardly surprising that the present leadership has far less confidence in domestic or international 'social' engineering. Pluralism as diversity and complexity is accepted as a normal and almost natural feature of domestic and international life.

At the same time pluralism does not mean irreconcilable conflict. Emphasis on diversity of interests as normal goes hand in hand with stress on interdependence. Gorbachev and others have emphasized the harm of thinking in old zero-sum terms of *kto kogo* (who overcomes whom). Rather than focusing on the essential conflictual class nature of differences, 'perestroika thinking' highlights the over-arching importance of common 'all human' interests and values that link all members of domestic and international communities (see Chapter 10). The primacy of such 'all human' values and interests over those of class means that policy must be directed not towards emerging victorious in a struggle but towards bringing about agreement and reconciliation. In the domestic context this has meant greater efforts to recognize rather than confront minority interests – whether in the case of the Baltic republics or the miners. Internationally it has involved seeking to reconcile what were previously considered antagonistic forces, whether in Afghanistan or, as Yutaka Akino notes, in Kampuchea. In the East–West context this reconciliation approach is evident in Moscow playing down military, political and ideological conflict and pointing up the need to go beyond peaceful coexistence towards co-development.[25]

This de-ideologized approach to interests involves important shifts in policy tactics and methods towards accommodation, compromise and more political and legalistic means of managing domestic and international problems. Rather than being seen as a sign of weakness, concessions made to secure agreement are now lauded as a mark of political maturity: Gorbachev takes every opportunity to stress the virtues of 'sensible compromise' (partly, of course, in order to defend himself against criticism).[26] The use of force, on the other hand, is seen as a last resort in both the domestic and international arena. At home vigorous criticism of Stalinism has spilled over into the questioning of more recent uses of coercion to deal with dissent. As Tsuyoshi Hasegawa notes, the rehabilitation of Bukharin is symptomatic of support for a more peaceful way of building socialism (see Chapter 2). Recent steps to regularize emigration procedures, ease restrictions on religious practices, and release the vast majority of prisoners of conscience all indicate serious movement away from traditional coercive methods. Although the enormous coercive machine remains intact, the Gorbachev leadership has taken a far more permissive view of protest and a more sophisticated political stance towards its management. Traditional coercive responses have been the exception rather than the rule under perestroika, and have attracted official regret and widespread condemnation, as in the case of the Tbilisi clashes of spring 1989. Generally, the regime has exhibited remarkable restraint in the face of movements such as the Baltic protests and the miners' strikes of summer 1989, which would in the past have elicited violent repression. Instead, Gorbachev has preferred political means of accommodation, something he has commended to Chinese leaders in connection with the crushing of protests in Beijing.[27]

Similar shifts have taken place in international policy. One of the major lessons drawn from critical discussion of international politics in general and Soviet foreign policy in particular is the declining utility of military force. Its use is now seen as rarely yielding gains but often exacerbating problems (for example, in Afghanistan) and a strengthening cohesion among adversaries (such as SS-20 deployment).

Complementing this shift away from coercive means is a more tentative yet equally significant move towards legal frameworks and instruments to manage conflict both at home and abroad. Gorbachev's declared aim to elevate law and create a law-based state (*pravovoe gosudarstvo*) parallels his stress on the importance of the international law and international regulatory agencies. The new level and quality of commitment to law under perestroika could still be seen as a largely declaratory one. Yet steps taken to codify and clarify domestic laws, strengthen judicial process and introduce mechanisms of checks and balances and constitutional review all point to a serious intent to create a legal culture (see Chapter 3). Moves in a similar direction on the international front include acceptance of the mandatory jurisdiction of the International Court in The Hague and of the principle that all Soviet legislation, especially that relating to civil and human rights, must be brought into line with international covenants.[28] A new commitment to the role of international law and associated organizations is reflected in the substantial increase in Soviet financial as well as political support for the United Nations.[29]

Trends in thinking about the management of domestic and international policy problems thus run along remarkably similar lines. This of course does not mean that they necessarily produce identical prescriptions in every case. General approval of pluralism, for instance, translates into greater latitude for autonomous action for groups the further they are located from Moscow. Acceptance of socialist pluralism has hardly dented the principle of democratic centralism within the party and made limited inroads into the party's leading role while it has extended radically the leeway for informal political activity. 'Freedom of choice' as a principle of 'new thinking' is understandably applied in more qualified fashion to the republics of the USSR than to the states of Eastern Europe, let alone the Third World. But however differentiated according to context, what remains remarkable is the distance travelled by 'perestroika thinking' towards greater democracy and openness within the USSR *and* in relations between the Soviet Union and the world.

Advances in thinking in both spheres have interacted to generate overall forward movement. Whereas the 'new thinking' on foreign policy issues clearly owes its ascendancy to the change in domestic climate, influence has flowed predominantly from the international to the internal sphere. This is due to the fact that new thinking was easier to formulate and deploy successfully than reform ideas on the less tractable domestic front. Success has given 'new thinking' and associated policies considerable impact on domestic developments. The withdrawal from Afghanistan and endorsement of movement towards greater autonomy in Hungary has, for instance, encouraged nationalist leaders in the Baltic to pursue national independence.[30] Although this is one example of the unintended stimulation of domestic change by foreign policy innovation, Gorbachev has on occasion deliberately sought to use the international success of 'new thinking' to boost the domestic fortunes of perestroika.[31] The need to build on improved ties with the West is invoked to promote domestic reforms (mostly in the area of civil and human rights) that flow from international undertakings or policy commitments. The notion of a Common European House performs a useful function not just in policy towards Western Europe (which Hannes Adomeit discusses in Chapter 12); it also acts as a vehicle for advancing 'European' democratic values in the domestic political arena. Efforts of this kind to reinforce the linkage between international and domestic policy thinking contribute to the general thickening of connections between international issues and domestic politics, to which we now turn.

Domestic Politics

The remarkable changes on the Soviet domestic political scene, coupled with the radical shifts in foreign policy, have exposed international issues to more probing debate, greater controversy and wider involvement. As a result, foreign and security policy has become more politicized under perestroika.

Glasnost has helped to create a freer discussion on foreign policy, though, as Marie Mendras notes, criticism came later and more hesitantly to the international than to the domestic policy field. Only since 1988 have critical discussions focused on foreign policy issues. Many such discussions have taken the form of reassessments of historical questions, such as Stalin's conduct of the war, Katyn, and the Molotov–Ribbentrop pact, the issue with the greatest domestic ramifications. Criticism has also extended to more recent episodes in Soviet foreign policy, notably the deployment of the SS-20s and the decision to intervene in Afghanistan. Glasnost has also helped to lift a corner of the heavy veil of secrecy that has traditionally hung over all security and military affairs.

Discussion of previously taboo foreign and security issues has heightened popular awareness and interest in this area. Yet, given natural preoccupation with debates surrounding domestic changes, it would be surprising if the *relative* salience of international affairs had not diminished under perestroika. Gorbachev himself has expressed concern about the relative neglect of foreign policy issues.[32] One obvious motive the President might have for urging that greater attention be paid to international issues is that his foreign policy offers a source of much-needed popularity. There is little doubt that Gorbachev has profited considerably at home from his success in reducing East–West military tensions and withdrawing Soviet troops from Afghanistan. Popular feelings also played a part in the politics of the decision. Before Gorbachev came to power, a growing majority of the population were eager to see an end to the war which was beginning to affect families throughout Soviet society. The ground-swell of complaint, amplified by glasnost, probably figured importantly in the leadership's decision, both as a reason to withdraw and as a hedge against criticism.

Soviet public opinion may well increasingly play a role of this kind in other issues that straddle the areas of domestic and foreign policy. For instance, measures to reduce defence expenditure seem to evince strong feeling and command public support. In a June 1989 poll, large majorities of respondents in major cities endorsed the 14 per cent cut announced and many wanted to see larger reductions.[33]

The political importance of such public attitudes is enhanced by the apparent tendency of many of the newly elected parliamentary deputies to share these views, not just on defence but on the entire thrust of security and foreign policy. Deputies signalled their support for the new departures in foreign policy by giving Shevardnadze a smooth passage through the reappointment process. In one poll deputies gave Shevardnadze a far higher approval rate than any other minister.[34] Whereas even two years ago the opinions of Supreme Soviet deputies might have been dismissed as politically unimportant, this is no longer the case as the new parliament looks set to play a significant role in foreign policy as in other areas (see Chapter 3). It is not simply that Shevardnadze and others have called for a more open and democratic foreign policy process; the deputies themselves have shown an ability to submit ministers to probing questions on sensitive issues, such as to Yazov on the military, and to refuse on occasion to sanction reappointment (as in the case of Kamentsev, the minister in charge of external economic relations). The parliament, and especially its committees, are likely to exercise important scrutiny and some influence over foreign and security policy. Even at this early stage, domestic political reform has begun to affect the way in which foreign policy is presented and alternatives are formulated.

Major decisions will of course continue to be made within the leadership where foreign policy changes and their domestic ramifications have stirred considerable controversy, albeit less than the radical nature of those changes might have led one to expect. This is largely because conservative leaders and elites have been preoccupied with fighting rearguard actions on domestic issues. At the same time, while critics of perestroika do not align exactly on domestic and international issues, their leaders do make a point of linking radical internal reforms with those in foreign policy. The notorious Andreeva letter, published in March 1988 as a major broadside against perestroika, attacked the whole notion of opening up the country to nefarious foreign influences. Ligachev, in his Gorkii speech in the summer of 1988, pointedly criticized both domestic moves to a socialist market and the de-ideologization of international relations, thus linking these as planks of a single political platform. Gorbachev has further tightened this policy linkage by identifying such critics with hard-line Western opponents of perestroika.[35]

A closely related aspect of the politicization of external issues under perestroika – discussed by Marie Mendras in Chapter 10 – is the extent to which power configurations within the leadership have affected foreign and security policy. Although we have little hard evidence by which to assess this, some analysts have linked hesitation and even temporary retreat in foreign and security policy with shifts in leadership alignments.[36] There does appear to be some correlation between improvements in Gorbachev's position within the leadership and vigorous pursuit of foreign and security policy initiatives, as for instance in the autumn of 1986 and 1988.

Differences on foreign and security policy within the leadership, and indeed within the public debate generally, have centred around three areas: the acceptance of universal (Western) values; the demilitarization of security; and closer economic interaction with the capitalist world. All these issue areas have attracted controversy because they question basic traditions and affect a large number of interests. In doing so they have furthered the politicization of security and foreign policy by deepening the political debates surrounding it and enlarging the constituencies concerned with international issues.

The first issue area revolves around the elevation of all-human values and interests above those of class. This fundamental innovation of perestroika thinking seems to be supported by a majority of specialists working in the international relations field. Few of these apparently believe that ideology has an important role in relations with the United States or should play a key role in Soviet foreign policy objectives.[37] However, the demotion of class goals and norms does worry many conservatives. In Chapter 10 Marie Mendras traces the public exchanges between Ligachev on the one hand and Shevardnadze and Yakovlev on the other about the official reformist declaration that peaceful coexistence is no longer to be considered a form of class struggle. It is hardly surprising that Ligachev concentrated his critical fire on this new foreign policy principle since it symbolizes and legitimizes the whole strategy of more 'open' cooperation with capitalist states, and implies a corresponding weakening of commitment to socialism throughout the world, a general acceptance of international (Western) standards and an opening of the Soviet Union to Western influence. Conservatives see the principle as intimately linked with excessively permissive attitudes towards undesirable forces at home.[38]

Although such conservative views attract very little support from specialists and probably only minority sympathy from the population, policy opinion is more evenly divided on the second area of controversy and politicization – the demilitarization of security. Even many specialists apparently find it difficult to accept the new stress on the economic rather than military nature of the Western threat which is one of the rationales for far lower levels of Soviet capabilities. As Naomi Koizumi shows in Chapter 8, opinions differ within the military establishment on the reforms in security policy Gorbachev and his civilian advisers advocate. Whereas some in the armed forces may agree that traditional Soviet policy tended towards military 'over-insurance', others feel uneasy about the notion of 'reasonable sufficiency' now central to security policy. Even key Gorbachev appointees, such as Defence Minister Yazov, tend also to use the term 'reliable' sufficiency and lay stress on more traditional concepts like equal and identical security.[39] If the military leadership generally seem to accept the principle of a more defensive military doctrine, they remain chary of civilian proposals on technical issues relating to restructuring forces in non-offensive postures. Not only do many in the military resent this as unwarranted interference in areas traditionally their professional preserve. They also tend to feel strongly that the Soviet armed forces must retain the capacity to launch counter-offensive operations.

Policy differences over these issues overlap with those over arms control and disarmament. Although Gorbachev's overall strategy here has encountered little if any direct opposition, its speed and asymmetry have aroused concern, particularly within military circles. The Soviet unilateral moratorium on nuclear testing, the unfavourable asymmetries of the INF treaty, acceptance of intrusive verification and greater transparency and the unilateral cut in conventional forces all stand out as politically controversial moves.[40]

The fact that many of the innovations in military doctrine and arms control made under perestroika have aroused controversy and scepticism among the military does not mean that the military as a whole have responded negatively. The younger and more forward-looking members of the military establishment probably appreciate the role which disarmament can play in freeing resources for technological modernization which in turn holds the key to the qualitative cutting edge of military capabilities. Still, important groups in the military elite, perhaps especially its older contingent, view with apprehension the mounting chorus of deprecation, from politicians, journalists and writers alike, of the utility of military force and the performance of the armed forces. It is in the context of what many generals see as a wider erosion of the military's traditional, almost sacred unassailability that they find the prospect of deep cuts in forces and budgets particularly worrying. The larger these cuts and the greater the economic transfers from military to civilian production, the more will security become enmeshed in domestic politics. Given the very large reductions in armed forces and expenditure scheduled for the first half of the 1990s, the next few years are likely to see a continued growth in the politicization of security policy.

Closer economic interaction with the capitalist world is the third issue area attracting controversy and acting as an avenue for the politicization of external policy change. External economic policy has long attracted heated debate in the Soviet Union – witness the sharp differences voiced in the early 1920s over the dangers of exploitation and dependency involved in the NEP policy of opening up towards the West.[41] Persistent concern with the problems of dependency inherent in taking larger Western credits is reflected in the critical stance that Gorbachev and Ryzhkov have adopted on this issue.[42] Even though most of the additional consumer goods imported under the pressure of labour unrest in summer 1989 came from socialist states, imports from the West have risen and arguments to take on larger debts to reduce popular dissatisfaction may well grow. Any moves to take on more debt are likely further to increase the criticism voiced by a wide spectrum of opinion over the dangers of expanding and intensifying economic exchange and involvement with capitalist states. Critics of joint ventures (and mooted special economic zones) question the material benefits they are likely to bring and raise the spectre of capitalist exploitation.[43]

By extension, similar arguments can be applied to other forms of interaction with the West, such as cooperation on environmental problems.

However one assesses such critical views of more openness, the issue evokes widespread controversy. And as the new foreign economic policy makes progress, so the greater penetration of the Soviet economy by foreign commercial interests will make these issues the subject of growing controversy. Progress will also politicize this area by bringing a much larger number of questions related to foreign economic policy onto the domestic political agenda. And these will be of direct interest to a far greater number of actors. For the development of joint ventures and direct, decentralized trade links will mean a dramatic extension of the range of groups with vested interests in Soviet economic relations in particular and Soviet foreign policy in general. Apart from the approximately 5,000 units (ministries, departments, local authorities, enterprises and cooperatives) involved in foreign trade activity in mid–1989, the decision to introduce by 1991 part-payment in hard currency for farmers whose production makes possible savings on food imports[44] means a further extension of the range of groups with stakes in developments in foreign economic policy.

This multiplication of constituencies with international policy concerns is likely to alter the environment for Soviet foreign policy makers. For the first time since NEP they will have to deal with a wide array of preferences and even pressures from outside the traditional range of institutions. And they will have to do this within the framework of a changing political system which imposes greater constraints and affords far greater opportunities for group lobbying activity. Powerful potential lobbyists include associations of foreign traders, economic regions (and special economic and enterprise zones if these are established in any numbers) and, most importantly, republics. Union republics have been encouraged to pursue their own economic strategies and develop autonomous external economic links. As far as future republican roles in foreign policy are concerned, Baltic developments suggest that we may see the increasing pursuit of distinctive external economic policy which in turn will affect the republics' general foreign relations with key commercial partners. All this, when added to the domestic social and political repercussions of direct foreign trade links and joint ventures, promises to make the running of Soviet foreign policy a far more complex political exercise. Opening up the Soviet Union to global economic influences will inevitably expand the role of 'low politics' in the foreign policy process. In this sense perestroika is likely to change the web of connections between domestic and foreign policy into something more akin to that found in Western states. A broader, more complex, variegated and ultimately thicker web does not of course necessarily mean a shift of Soviet foreign policy in any predetermined direction. None the less, it makes likely a more open foreign policy debate and process involving larger numbers of constituencies and participants who will bring to bear a wider range of domestic considerations and interests. Greater interdependence between East and West may thus bring closer links between domestic and foreign policy within the Soviet Union.

Notes

* This chapter draws in part on my paper 'Linkages between domestic and foreign policy in the Soviet Union', in A. Clesse and T. C. Schelling (eds), *The Western Community and the Gorbachev Challenge* (Baden Baden: Nomos, 1989), pp. 92–107.

1. Speech at dinner for Mrs Thatcher, *Pravda*, 1 April 1987: 2.

2. For example, L. Lyubimov, 'Novoe myshlenie i sovetsko-amerikanskie otnosheniya', *Mirovaya ekonomika i mezhdunarodnye otnosheniya*, 10 (1987): 3–14.

3. Alex Dallin perhaps has discussed this problem most thoroughly; see 'The Domestic sources of Soviet foreign policy' in S. Bialer (ed.), *The Domestic Context of Soviet Foreign Policy* (Boulder, CO/London: Westview Press/Croom Helm, 1981), pp. 335–408. Also see M. Schwartz, *The Foreign Policy of the USSR: Domestic Factors* (Encino: Dickenson, 1975); J. N. Rosenau, 'Towards single-country theories of foreign policy: the case of the USSR', in C.F. Hermann, C.W. Kegley and J.N. Rosenau (eds), *New Directions in the Study of Foreign Policy* (London: Allen & Unwin, 1987), pp. 53–76; and for one general treatment of these issues, J.N. Rosenua, *The Domestic Sources of Foreign Policy* (Princeton, NJ: Princeton University Press, 1965).

4. Gorbachev speech to CPSU Central Committee, *Pravda*, 19 Feb. 1988: 2.

5. Gorbachev, speech in the British Parliament, 18 Dec. 1984, appendix 8 of House of Commons, Foreign Affairs Committee, Second Report, 185–86 session, *UK–Soviet Relations*, vol. II (London: HMSO, 1986), p. 333.

6. Cf. S. Bialer, 'Soviet foreign policy: sources, perceptions, trends' in *The Domestic Context of Soviet Foreign Policy*, (fn. 3), pp. 409–41; Bialer organizes his discussion under the headings capabilities, politics and beliefs.

7. See, for instance, M. McCain, 'Allocation politics and the arms race: a Soviet constituency for arms control', in T.F. Remington (ed.), *Essays in Honour of F.C. Barghoorn* (London: Macmillan), pp. 125–30.

8. Gorbachev at meeting with members of the Trilateral Commission, see *Pravda*, 19 Jan. 1989: 2.

9. Shevardnadze report on 25 July 1988 to the Ministry of Foreign Affairs post-nineteenth Party Conference meeting, *International Affairs*, 10 (1988): 8.

10. Ryzhkov, *Izvestiya*, 8 June 1989: 2.

11. For instance, see M.S. Gorbachev, *Perestroika: New Thinking for our Country and the World* (London: Collins, 1987), p. 219.

12. Gorbachev at meeting with members of the Trilateral Commission: see *Pravda*, 19 Jan. 1989: 2.

13. The official Soviet figures given by Ryzhkov on 7 June 1989 were 77.3 billion roubles for the military and 3.9 billion roubles for space developments with military applications; see *Izvestiya*, 8 June 1989: 3. This is well below the range of CIA estimates of 120 to 137 billion roubles but not far below those of SIPRI of 100 billion roubles; see World Armament Capitals and Disarmament, *SIPRI Year Book 1989* (Oxford: Oxford University Press), pp. 150–3.

14. Ryzhkov, *Izvestiya*, 8 June 1989: 3.

15. Chazov, *Pravda*, 30 June 1988.

16. Meat consumption in urban areas in 1913 exceeded that in the USSR in 1985; see A.S. Zaichenko, 'O novom myshlenii v sovetsko-amerikanskom ekonomicheskom sotrudnichestve', *SShA. Ekonomika, Politika, Ideologiya*, 12, 1988: 16. For Gorbachev's emphasis on general decline, see *Perestroika*, (fn. 11), pp. 18–20.

17. Shevardnadze, 'Bezuslovnoe trebovanie- povernut'sya litsom k ekonomike' speech on 4 July 1987 at a meeting of the *aktiv* of the Ministry of Foreign Affairs, *Vestnik Ministerstva inostrannykh del SSSR*, 3 (1987); 4.

18. *Izvestiya*, 2 Aug. 1989: 2.

19. Joint ventures numbers in first half-year report for 1989. Tass in English, 19 July 1989, in BBC, *Summary of World Broadcasts*, SU/W0087 A/3, 28 July 1989.

20. *Izvestiya*, 2 Aug. 1989: 2.

21. Shevardnadze, 4 July 1987.

22. Speech to the Supreme Soviet, Moscow radio home service, 1 Aug. 1989, BBC, *Summary of World Broadcasts*, SU/0525, p. C/7.

23. See in particular the vigorous comments in Shevardnadze's important report to the post-19th party conference meeting of the Ministry of Foreign Affairs, *International Affairs*, 10 (1988): 25–6.

24. See, for instance, Abalkin, *Spiegel*, 6 July 1987, translated in Foreign Broadcast Information Service, *Soviet Union Daily Report*, 10 July 1987: 51.

25. See Gorbachev's speech to the UN, Soviet television, 7 Dec. 1988, BBC, *Summary of World Broadcasts* SU/0330, C1/2.

26. *Izvestiya*, 2 Aug. 1989, p. 1.

27. Ibid., p. 2.

28. For instance, see V.S. Vershchetin and P.A. Myullerson, 'Novoe myshlenie i mezhdunarodnoe pravo', *Sovetskoe gosudarstvo i pravo*, 3 (1988): 3–9.

29. For an early major statement on the UN, see M.S. Gorbachev, 'Realnost' i garantii bezopasnosti mira', *Pravda*, 17 Sept. 1987: 1–2.

30. See an interview with T. Velliste, a prominent Estonian nationalist, in *Kodumaa*, 22 March 1989, translated in BBC, *Summary of World Broadcasts*, Soviet Union 0426, pp. B1–4.

31. See, for instance, his speech to the Supreme Soviet, *Izvestiya*, 2 Aug. 1989: 2.

32. Ibid.

33. *Izvestiya*, 4 June 1989: 1. Support for the officially announced 14% cut ranged from 10% in Tbilisi to 45% in Alma Ata. Between a quarter (Alma Ata) and two-thirds (Tallin) wanted deeper cuts.

34. *Literaturnaya gazeta*, 21 June 1989: 11.

35. Gorbachev, 29 March 1989.

36. See, for instance, B. Parrott, 'Soviet national security under Gorbachev', *Problems of Communism*, XXXVII (6) (Nov.–Dec. 1988): 23.

37. Only one in fifteen of the 120 specialists (including military and diplomats as well as academics) thought that spreading the socialist system on a global scale should be the main objective of Soviet foreign policy; see A. Iu. Mel'vil' and A.I. Nikitin, 'Sovetskie eksperty o mirovoi politike', *SSha. Ekonomika, Politika, Ideologiya*, 6 (1989): 15.

38. See, for instance, Chebrikov, *Pravda*, 11 Sept. 1987.

39. For a thorough analysis of the debate on security issues, see R.L. Garthoff, 'New thinking in Soviet military doctrine', *The Washington Quarterly*, 11 (3) (Summer 1988): 131–58.

40. For one survey, see H. Gelman, *The Soviet Military Leadership and the Question of Soviet Deployment Retreats*, Rand Report R-3664-AF, Nov. 1988.

41. See L. Geron, 'Soviet foreign economic policy under NEP and Perestroika: a comparative analysis' D.Phil. thesis, Oxford 1989, pp. 78–104.

42. For instance, Gorbachev, *Pravda*, 24 Jan. 1989; and Ryzhkov in Supreme Soviet debate, Soviet television, 30 June 1989, *Foreign Broadcast Information Service, Soviet Union. Daily Report*, 89–126, p. 60.

43. For instance, see M. Antonov, 'Idti svoim putem', *Molodaya gvardiya*, 1 (1988): 197, cited in Geron, *Soviet Foreign Economic Policy*, p. 246; and ibid., passim, pp. 239–63.

44. See the *Financial Times*, 11 Aug. 1989.

2

Perestroika in Historical Perspective

Tsuyoshi Hasegawa

It is generally recognized that Gorbachev's reforms constitute a major turning-point in Soviet history. In order to assess their significance, however, it is important to place them in a longer historical perspective, for, in my opinion, the problems and challenges Gorbachev faces have historical antecedents that can be traced back into Russian history before 1917. Nevertheless, social scientists studying the ongoing changes in the Soviet Union rarely examine them in the larger historical framework. Of course, there are a number of comparisons between Gorbachev's reforms and the previous reforms during the Brezhnev and Khrushchev periods, while more historically minded social scientists venture to trace the sources of Gorbachev's reforms to the New Economic Policy (NEP) period. But rarely do they go beyond 1917 to see connections between perestroika and various reforms from above in the imperial period.[1] Conversely, historians studying the pre-revolutionary period seldom comment on the transformation that the Soviet Union is undergoing at the present moment, but merely cast scornful glances at those who concentrate on current affairs.[2] Moreover, historians dislike ahistorical generalities that disregard specific historical circumstances. If the rich texture of specific occurrences and circumstances, unrepeatable beyond a certain time and place, are what excites historians, the generalizations and theories that social scientists like to develop from 'case studies' make them wince with embarrassment. Thus, it is difficult to establish dialogue between social scientists and historians without having them go for one another's throats.

The importance of elucidating continuities and changes between pre-revolutionary Russia and Soviet history has long been recognized. In the 1950s when Russian studies were still young in the United States, two interdisciplinary symposia were dedicated to precisely this subject.[3] The subsequent development of Russia/Soviet studies in the United States has contributed to diversification and specialization, but this otherwise positive development has

ironically made it difficult to raise the broad issues that our predecessors attempted to answer in the later 1950s. It seems that the
demarcation line of 1917 is being observed by contemporary
researchers more scrupulously than it was thirty years ago. In Japan
both social scientists and historians stake out the boundary of their
research topic more narrowly than their counterparts in the West,
rarely venturing into the larger territory beyond their own narrow
confines.

In my view, Gorbachev's perestroika constitutes a momentous
event that has far-reaching significance, not only for the future but
also for interpretations of the past. Moreover, Soviet intellectuals
are beginning a search for connections between perestroika and
their history. I believe it is therefore extremely important for both
social scientists and historians to get together and pool their knowledge to interpret the meaning of the phenomena we are now witnessing in the Soviet Union.

The following is an attempt to examine the significance of perestroika in a longer historical perspective. It is necessary to state at
the outset that this is a preliminary attempt intended to generate
further discussions.

Revolution from Above

One of the most important features of Gorbachev's reforms is the
recognition that purely economic reforms would not be sufficient:
in order to change the economy, they have to be accompanied
by political and social reforms. This awareness sets Gorbachev's
programme clearly apart from other economic reforms under
Khrushchev and Brezhnev. Specifically, Gorbachev's reforms, at
least in intention, represent an attempt to reject Stalinist socialism
not only in the economic system, but also in the political and social
spheres. In the sense that they are intended to revamp the Stalinist
system completely and create something totally new, they may be
said to constitute a 'revolution' rather than 'reforms'. However,
this revolution is not being swept along by a mass rising from below,
but has to be carried out as 'reforms' from above. Paradoxically,
revolution from above, which has to recreate a new system while
the old system still continues to exist, is very much more difficult
to carry through than revolution from below, which first destroys
the old system before creating a new one on its ruins.[4]

Revolution from above has been a unique characteristic of Russi-
an/Soviet history, more so, I dare say, than revolution from below.
In fact, revolution from below was integrally connected with revol-

ution from above. Obvious examples of revolution from above are Peter the Great's reforms, Alexander II's Great Reforms and Stalin's revolution from above. Each case is a unique response to particular historical circumstances, and obviously no simple comparisons will do justice to the subtleties and peculiarities of each great event. Nevertheless, comparisons will not be worthless if they serve to highlight the nature of Gorbachev's reforms. What I am concerned with here is not necessarily the subtle colours inside each historical event, but the contours drawn with a broad brush on a large historical canvas.

Gorbachev's reforms are similar to these precedents in some respects, and different in others; there is no sense in enumerating the similarities and differences in detail. It may be useful, however, to treat Peter's reforms and the Great Reforms as one pair and Stalin's revolution and Gorbachev's reforms as another. The Great Reforms were necessary because of the impasse reached by the system created by the Petrine reforms, as Gorbachev's reforms arose from the awareness that the Stalinist system had spent its historical usefulness. The Petrine reforms and Stalin's revolution were motivated by the rulers' ambitious desire to remake the state and society according to the image they envisaged, though they did not have a precise blueprint. Certainly, Peter's Westernization and Stalin's socialism in one country were complete opposites in the orientation of their social engineering. Nevertheless, in both cases changes were imposed from above, not because the nation faced a serious crisis that threatened the very existence of the regime, but because such changes were deemed necessary by the ruler to acquire sufficient national strength to compete and survive in the international arena. The Great Reforms and Gorbachev's reforms, in contrast, arose from the acute sense of crisis threatening the regime's very existence.[5]

Peter's reforms and Stalin's revolution from above have another important similarity. Both achieved transformation of state and society by regimentation. Peter's reforms changed a backward country within a generation into one of the major powers in Europe, as Stalin's industrialization transformed a predominantly agrarian society into an industrial, military power. Peter's reforms, however, left three major negative legacies for the future. First, Peter strengthened serfdom, when this institution was disappearing in the West, thus leaving a major social and moral burden for future generations. Second, this created a profound gap between the elite who benefited from Westernization and the masses who were virtually untouched by Westernization, dividing the country into two nations which shared neither a culture, nor values, nor a language.[6] This, in turn, was responsible for profound resentment and hatred that the masses felt for the elite, while the gulf produced a gnawing sense of guilt as well as a primordial fear among the elite. The sense of guilt prompted part of the elite to seek identification with the masses, producing the impetus for the development of an intelligentsia, while the fear led the elite to recoil time and again from fundamental reforms. Third, Peter left the legacy of autocracy. It is fair to say that Peter himself was aware of the need to restrict autocratic power, as he stated that the sovereign was the subject of the state. Nevertheless, he had no choice but to strengthen autocratic power, since it was the only available vehicle for modernization.[7]

Likewise, Stalin's revolution from above left indelible scars on the Soviet state and society. The nature of the Stalinist system cannot be described here.[8] It suffices to say that the Stalinist system, characterized by a command economy, a symbiotic relationship between the state and the party, absorption of the society by the state, monopoly of ideology, use of terror and absence of the rule of law, and isolation from the outside world, had already exhausted its dynamic quality by the dictator's death. Despite various attempts at reform within the framework of the Stalinist system under Khrushchev and Brezhnev, by the latter half of Brezhnev's reign, signs of a systemic crisis were multiplying.

In tsarist Russia, by the end of the eighteenth century, the Russian elite, both in and out of power, became aware of the inherent contradictions of the framework of Peter's reforms, an awareness that caused the fateful 'parting of the ways' of the Russian educated class.[9] Fully recognizing the need to abolish serfdom, the tsars and their bureaucracy long hesitated to carry out this surgical operation, fearing that it might lead to the ultimate destruction of the state which was closely identified with autocracy. It was not until Alexander II undertook the Great Reforms that serfdom was abolished. This necessitated other reforms: of local self-government, of the judiciary and the military. These reforms created the conditions for rapid modernization in the late nineteenth and early twentieth centuries.

Like the tsarist bureaucracy, the Communist Party leadership recoiled from a systemic reform which would inevitably mean questioning the very foundations of the Stalinist system, upon which their power rested. As in the tsarist regime, which had to be pushed to the wall by defeat in the Crimean War before it embarked upon the Great Reforms, an acute sense of crisis caused by clear signs of decline of national power both on the domestic and the international scene had to be experienced widely before Gorbachev launched perestroika.

Yet there is a fundamental difference between the Great Reforms and Gorbachev's perestroika. Alexander II explained to the nobility the reasons for the emancipation of the serfs: 'It is better to begin to abolish bondage from above than to wait for the time when it will begin to abolish itself spontaneously from below.'[10] This is an indication of how dark a shadow the institution of serfdom had cast on the consciousness of the tsars and the ruling elite. This brooding obsession that reforms were competing with revolution from below continued to exist to the last day of the imperial period. Competition with revolution thus became a main theme in the subsequent important reforms in the late tsarist period. Gorbachev is essentially free from fear of revolution from below. Certainly, fear of revolution from below is not the motivation for perestroika.

One of the most important positive legacies of the Petrine reforms was the creation of a Russian elite dedicated to the welfare of the state. The Russian bureaucracy was by no means always an obscurantist body which resisted change. In fact, the major impetus for reform came from the most advanced part of the bureaucracy; in this respect, the Russian bureaucracy can be said to have inherited the positive tradition of the Petrine reforms. In the absence of other powerful groups that could become a vehicle of reform, therefore, there was no alternative but to rely on the bureaucracy to carry through the reforms. Kiselev's reforms of the state serfs, the Great Reforms, Witte's industrialization and Stolypin's reforms were all initiated and carried out by the bureaucracy. Nevertheless, the bureaucracy was dependent on the autocracy, and it identified not only the interests of its own group, but also the interests of the state, with autocracy. Thus, when it came to limiting autocratic power, it recoiled from reform. This situation created a vicious circle from which the Russian state never found an escape: reforming initiatives had to come from above, so long as the process strengthened autocratic power. In the end autocracy itself was never fundamentally reformed, and ultimately it was destroyed, as many of the best defenders of the regime had feared, by revolution.[11]

The bureaucracy created by Stalin's revolution had more difficulty in generating changes from within than was the case with the bureaucracy created by Peter. The purges annihilated huge numbers of the Soviet elite who could think critically and act beyond the official line. Those who advanced into positions of power vacated by their purged predecessors (the *vydvizhentsy*) – the generation that ruled the Soviet Union until Gorbachev came to power – were themselves beneficiaries of Stalinism, thus unlikely to carry out reforms that might undermine the system upon which their existence depended. That was why Khrushchev's de-Stalinization and economic reforms, as well as the economic innovations under Brezhnev, stopped short of systemic change.

Gorbachev's task is daunting. Like Peter the Great and Alexander II, who possessed no other instrument than the bureaucracy to implement reforms, Gorbachev has no other instrument of reform but the Communist Party. On the one hand, the Communist Party can be a formidable force of resistance, but on the other, at least theoretically, it can be transformed into the most effective and powerful instrument for reform; similarly, Peter used the new emerging service nobility as the instrument of reform and Alexander II relied on the enlightened section of the bureaucracy. This is why the most severe battle is being waged over personnel questions. Nevertheless, it remains to be seen whether the Communist Party can succeed in deposing its own dictatorial power, precisely when such power will be needed to overcome resistance to change.[12]

It is also important to remember that once Peter's reforms and the Great Reforms were carried out, they were never completely overturned. It was totally out of the question to return to the old Muscovite ways after Peter's death, and even Alexander III's deliberate counter-reform measures did not succeed in reinstituting serfdom or abolishing the *zemstvos* and the reformed legal system. The conscious strategy that Gorbachev's supporters are adopting to 'make perestroika irreversible' can be explained by the analogy with the two pre-revolutionary reforms. The question is: have Gorbachev's reforms reached the point where they become irreversible? To the extent that perestroika is still closely associated with Gorbachev himself and to the extent that most of the goals that perestroika is attempting to achieve are still in the planning stage and have not actually been implemented, one can say that they have not reached that decisive point of irreversibility. Nevertheless, it is not conceivable that the USSR could return to the Brezhnevite or Stalinist system. To that extent, Gorbachev's reforms have passed the point of no return, and with or without Gorbachev, whatever is going to happen from now on is bound to be something new.

Political Reforms

While it is clear that Gorbachev's reforms are an antithesis of Stalin's revolution from above, by comparison with the two pre-revolutionary reforms, they strive, in a sense, for far more ambitious goals. Peter's reforms, radical as they were, attempted modernization by strengthening serfdom. The Great Reforms, which had by far more comprehensive aims, none the less failed to 'crown the edifice' by limiting autocracy itself. Gorbachev's goals are more ambitious, since he is trying to combine socio-economic reforms with political reforms.

Autocracy as the ultimate source of authority and law was not abolished until 1917. There were, nevertheless, a number of attempts to restrict the autocractic power of the sovereign, notable examples of which were the Supreme Privy Council's attempt to restrict Empress Ann's power in 1730, the Legislative Assembly in 1775, Speransky's Constitutional Project, Novosil'tsev's Constitutional Charter, various appeals made by *zemstvo* activists for a constitution, Loris-Melikov's constitution, and the Fundamental Laws that instituted the Duma and the State Council, and the Progressive Bloc's demand for a responsible ministry during World War I.[13] Despite these efforts, the concept of the rule of law (*pravovoe gosudarstvo*) never took root in Russia, since in an ultimate sense the person of the autocrat, limited by no laws and no constitutional mechanism, remained the ultimate and sole source of law and legitimacy. That was why Russia was not a *Rechtsstaat*, but a state that was ruled by *proizvol* in which no personal security of rule of law was established.

If anything dented autocracy, it was revolutionary pressure. The 1905 Revolution forced Nicholas II to issue the October Manifesto, and the subsequent Fundamental Laws instituted the Duma. Although the Duma was unable to restrict the autocratic power of the sovereign, a failure that became painfully apparent at the time of *Rasputinshchina* during the war, parliamentary politics after 1906 significantly changed the nature of autocracy. Nevertheless, the conflict between the Duma and autocracy ultimately remained unresolved, and led the Duma to take the side of the revolution against autocracy.

The February Revolution brought about two forms of government. The first was a government formed by democratically elected representatives of the people regardless of class origins (*nadklassnost'*), while the second was a soviet type of government based on the class principle, according to which only the toiling masses had the right to participate in the political process to the exclusion of the privileged. Immediately after the February Revolution power was predominantly transferred to the first type of government in various localities.[14] In Petrograd itself, it was at first the district dumas that controlled the two most vital areas: police power and food supplies.[15] A violent social schism that swept through the Russian Empire in 1917, however, made it impossible for this form of government to continue, and everywhere the locus of power shifted to the soviets, as the revolutionary process intensified. The October Revolution was a logical conclusion of this process; the forcible dissolution of the Constituent Assembly by the Bolsheviks dealt a *coup de grâce* to the hope that had been awakened by the February Revolution of establishing democracy.

After the revolution, *proizvol* of a proletarian class nature rejected the concept of an objective and neutral law governing every citizen in a society. The Bolshevik theory of the dictatorship of the proletariat elevated the Communist Party as the vanguard of the proletariat, thus the ultimate source of authority and law. Trotsky presciently predicted the danger of the Leninist theory of the dictatorship of the proletariat: 'the proletariat would be replaced by a party, a party by a group of Central Committee, and ultimately a committee by a single dictator'. Here a handful of men in the Politburo at the centre and the first secretaries in *oblasti* (regions), possessing no mandate from the population, enjoy omnipotence, excluding the vast majority of the people from the political process, as in the pre-revolutionary period, but this time in the name of people they disenfranchise.

Gorbachev's political reforms thus have momentous significance. For the first time in the history of Russia and the Soviet Union (with the exception of a brief period during the Russian Revolution and the election to the Constituent Assembly), people will be given the opportunity to participate in the democratic process. For the first time, a clearly delineated division of power between the legislature, the executive and the judiciary is envisaged. Soviets are, it is envisaged, to be given real power rather than being rubber-stamp organizations, and the hitherto omniscient and omnipresent party is to recede into the background, and become subject to the law, not above it. After elections by the deputies to the Supreme Soviet, the General Secretary of the Communist Party will become the Chairman of this highest legislative body, and official head of state who can serve for a maximum of two terms or ten years.

Along with constitutionalism, there is another important principle that Gorbachev is seeking to implement: real local self-government. In this respect, it is important to recall that for the first time in Soviet history local soviets will be given the right to collect taxation for local needs. This is a right that the *zemstvos* sought from the tsarist government in vain, a factor that fatally hindered the autonomous development of local self-government.[16]

It is doubtful that these goals will be accomplished without difficulties. In fact, the practical and psychological obstacles to implementing these reforms will be enormous.[17] If they are implemented, however, it will be a truly remarkable feat not only in the evolution of the Soviet political system, but also in the history of Russia. The first democratically elected soviet will fulfil the centuries-old dreams of a constitutional system: this was not accomplished by the zemskii sobors in the seventeenth century, the Legislative Assembly in 1775, the four Dumas in 1906–17, or the Constituent Assembly in 1918.

State and Civil Society

In my view there are two reasons why all attempts to limit autocracy in the pre-revolutionary period ended in failure. First, there emerged within established Russian society no groups or estates strong enough to limit the power of autocracy. In Marc Raeff's words, 'Russia never became a *Staendestaat*, and the imperial government prevented the creation of a dynamic and flexible *Rechtsstaat*.'[18] Second, from the end of the eighteenth century on, autocracy lived in fear of revolution from below, from the masses that were placed outside established society.

Russian society was fragmented and atomized under Muscovy. Peter's reforms facilitated this process of fragmentation. A large bulk of the population, the peasantry, became the property of individual serf owners through the introduction of the poll tax, and were thus placed outside society. Cities and burghers were politically and economically insignificant; dependent on the tsar's favours, they could hardly be expected to play as assertive a role as the third estate did in the West. The only group that could possibly challenge autocratic power was the nobility.

Peter's reforms, however, fragmented the nobility as well. The service obligation and requirement of education that Peter imposed on the nobility disrupted the nobles' traditional ties with families and localities. Individual nobles' fortunes ultimately depended on the tsar's favours. Thus, the nobility became divided between those who advocated special status on the basis of service merits and those who claimed special status on the grounds of birthright, a division that prevented the nobility from forming a cohesive *esprit de corps*.[19] Moreover, the Russian nobility was divided into the service nobility whose mainstay was government service in the bureaucracy, and the landed nobility. As Raeff argues, the emancipation of the nobility from state service in 1762 actually meant that, due to the qualitative and quantitative development of the service nobility, the state no longer needed the service of the landed nobility. This explains why the Charter to the Nobility in 1785 did not actually establish the security and inviolability of the nobility from the encroachment of autocratic power, since the other half of the nobility, which was more important and powerful, continued to depend on the tsar; in fact, under Paul this charter was flagrantly violated with no concerted protest from the nobility. Their tragic division and lack of cohesion were responsible for the failure to limit autocratic power. Attempts to establish the security of the nobility as a corporate group by limiting the absolute power of autocracy were always aborted by powerful opposition from within the group itself. This led to the situation on which Speransky commented as follows:

> I should like someone to point out the difference between the dependence of the peasants on the landlords and the dependence of the nobles on the sovereign; I should like someone to discover whether in fact the sovereign does not have the same right over the landlords as the landlords have over the peasants. Thus, instead of all the splendid divisions of a free Russian people into the very free classes of nobility, merchants and the rest, I find in Russia two classes: the slaves of the sovereign and the slaves of the landowners. The first are called free only in relation to the second, but there are no truly free persons in Russia, except beggars and philosophers.[20]

Nevertheless, fragile though it might be, a civil society, *obshchestvo*, that existed independently, separate from the state, came into being at the end of the eighteenth and beginning of the nineteenth centuries in private salons, associations and organizations. The tragedy of Russian history is that the state never made peace with the civil society, always persecuting and antagonizing it. Thus, Novikov and Radishchev were arrested and exiled; the Decembrists, whose ideas were mostly moderate (with the possible exception of Pestel's), were driven to revolt against the state; Chaadaev, who cannot be called a political radical by any stretch of the imagination, was placed under house arrest; and the Petrashevtsy were arrested and executed. Nevertheless, the civil society grew in size and power, as professionalization which was the inevitable consequence of modernization proceeded even under the repressive reign of

Nicholas I, and later with accelerated pace, as a consequence of the Great Reforms and industrialization in the latter half of the nineteenth century. By the time Vasilii Maklakov published a famous book in which he contrasted the state (*gosudarstvo*) and the society (*obshchestvo*), the civil society had become unmistakably more powerful, and important enough to compete with the state. As the state intransigently refused to acknowledge the existence of the civil society, however, the latter became radicalized to the extent that it, too, stood in opposition to the state in the end.

The February Revolution that put an end to autocracy combined revolt by the masses against established society with revolt by the civil society against the state.[21] Nevertheless, what the society stood for, which was best expressed in the liberal demands, must be distinguished from what radical revolutionaries advocated. The liberals demanded a rule of law to which 'all shall be subordinated, and first and foremost the representatives of state power',[22] parliamentary democracy, civil liberties and local self-government. As William Rosenberg, argues, the most distinctive character of the kadets, the best example of the Russian liberals, lay in its *nadklassnost'*, 'the commitment to the welfare of Russian society as a whole rather than to the advancement of any particular social class or socioeconomic interest'.[23] In the brutal period of the revolution and the civil war, in which the unbridgeable gulf between the *verkhi* and *nizy* was clearly revealed, *nadklassnost'*, which the Russian liberals advocated, had to be subordinated to *verkhi* class interests. Ultimately, the liberals' desire to legitimate the civil society as a viable, independent realm, free from intervention by the state, was crushed by the sweeping revolt of the masses against society.[24] A civil society has no place in the dictatorship of the proletariat, in which the Leviathan state, as the embodiment of interests of the proletarian class, devours all elements of society.[25] Unlike the liberal notion of the state as a neutral arbiter between the differing interests of various groups in society, the Marxist state is an instrument by which one social class exercises control over the others in the vicious struggle that is governed by the brutal principle of *kto kogo*. This notion of the state is in direct opposition to the Russian liberals' notion of *nadklassnost'*. There can be no pluralistic interests in society, since the interests of the proletarian class are single and united. As long as the Communist Party is the vanguard of the proletariat, the party is inevitably equated with the state.

Admittedly, a civil society did not completely disappear in the Soviet period. During the NEP period, in fact, a civil society functioned side by side with the dictatorship of the Communist Party.[26]

This resulted, first, from the nature of the mixed economy, and second, from the relative weakness of the Communist Party. Nevertheless, despite the attempt by perestroika supporters to find the source of inspiration in the NEP, this period was regarded as a transition and a temporary retreat. Even Bukharin, a most ardent advocate of the continuation of the NEP and a 'most untotalitarian Bolshevik',[27] did not have a comprehensive political theory legitimizing a civil society in relation to the dictatorship of the proletariat. It is also important to note that during the NEP period precisely because of the relative strength of the civil society, an authoritarian tendency dominated the Communist Party, annihilating the plurality of opinions within itself. Sheila Fitzpatrick warns us that the image of NEP tolerance is exaggerated.[28] When revolution from above was made 'suddenly, without warning' in 1929, it was inevitable that the party should fill the vacuum created by the destruction of the civil society; and there was no reason why such a party should allow pluralism in society unless it was made to.

Gorbachev's reforms are an attempt to create a civil society that exists free from the state and to change the nature of the state from being an arbitrary organ that absorbs the entire realm between itself and the people to a neutral organ that arbitrates various conflicting interests of society. The concept of civil society has not been accepted in the Soviet Union.[29] Ambartsumov is perhaps one of the first Soviet thinkers to uphold the need to create a civil society in the Soviet Union, seeing this as a major purpose of the political reforms. According to Ambartsumov, 'socialist civil society' is a realm in which different social interests can express themselves, clash with one another, and finally resolve themselves into a definite unity. He defines the political sphere as part of this realm. In Ambartsumov's view, in a socialist society it is important to defend not only the general interests of classes, but also the private interests of citizens. In fact, it is essential to restore the concept of 'citizen' in its primary sense in a socialist society. A citizen in the true meaning of the word is endowed with a sense of responsibility to society; this self-regulating force is much more effective in creating cohesion in society than the sense of duty imposed by the state. An authoritarian state imposes prior prohibitions on all kinds of citizens' activities, 'just in case'. A democratic society encourages the initiatives of citizens from below. This is the meaning of the transition that the current political reforms envisage: a transition from a society in which everything that is not permitted is forbidden to a society in which everything that is not forbidden is permitted. Allowing different interests to express themselves freely would not lead to political chaos, but rather to ensuring the dynamic inner development of society. A democratic society that allows free expression of different interests can contain within itself an inherent internal force for unity, thus possessing the ability to deal with crises within its own inner mechanism. An authoritarian society, which lacks such an independent self-regulating civil society, has to impose solutions from above, externally.[30]

Gorbachev's political reforms, which aim to establish such a civil society, can be regarded, therefore, as a momentous event not only in Soviet history, but also in the longer perspective of Russian history. Ambartsumov recognized this historical significance. In his opinion, pre-revolutionary reforms failed because in Russia there existed no 'bourgeois democracy' such as existed in the West, and because instead Russia was characterized by absolute state power, prevalent and stagnant bureaucracy, absence of legal consciousness or respect for personal inviolability, absence of rights among the masses and their familiarity with rule by authoritarian methods. In his opinion, the Russian Revolution attempted to put an end to these historical characteristics, but Soviet isolation and the mentality of being encircled by enemies prevented the Soviet Union from developing democracy fully.[31]

Gorbachev's reforms can, in a way, be seen as vindication of the liberal ideas that the ill-fated Russian liberals had expounded in the late nineteenth and early twentieth centuries. Squeezed between intransigent autocracy and radical revolutionaries, the liberals had no possibility of success in the increasingly polarized society. Nevertheless, their call for a just society, though silenced by the brutalities of the era, has finally been resurrected from the grave.

Fear of Revolution and Sources of Instability

Another important reason why reforms to limit autocracy failed stems from the fear that once autocratic principles were compromised, the deluge of revolution would sweep away the entire edifice of the state. This fear basically came from two factors. First, the ruling elite was aware of the gulf that separated it from the bulk of the masses. Second, the ruling elite also knew that part of its own class had crossed to the other side of the barricade, seeking an alliance with the people in their revolt against the state. In other words, they knew that what Crane Brinton calls 'transfer of allegiance' had already taken place. To them compromise seemed to breed greater radicalism – the Great Reforms had given rise to the Narodniki revolutionary movement and the Tsar Liberator had been hunted by terrorists. On the day Alexander II finally signed a manifesto granting the concession of Loris-Melikov's constitution, he was assassinated. Such experience reinforced the siege mentality of those who defended autocracy. In the end, however, autocracy itself revealed its inner contradictions during the process of modernization, and this constituted an important reason for the Revolution.

The period between the Great Reforms and the Russian Revolution was a crucial period of dynamic change including industrialization, agrarian reform and the institution of parliamentarism. But these changes themselves bred new problems that contributed to instability. Two processes of polarization – polarization within the educated class between the bureaucracy and the intelligentsia and polarization between *verkhi* and *nizy* – were not eliminated, but, rather, intensified.[32] World War I revealed the organic weaknesses of the Russian state and society, and the accumulated contradictions could only be settled by the explosion of the February Revolution.[33]

Since its inception the communist dictatorship has ruled the people with an iron fist, primarily because of its awareness that it lacked legitimacy. Nevertheless, the communist dictatorship is fundamentally different from tsarist autocracy. The Revolution basically eliminated the gulf between the elite and the masses by actually annihilating the upper echelons of society. After the elimination of the Bolshevik intelligentsia during the purge, Soviet power was assumed by those who rose from the ranks of the masses; these people, though they acquired the privileges available only to the *nomenklatura*, were not haunted by the sense of doom that had gripped the Russian elite in the pre-revolutionary period. First, the *nomenklatura* shares the same social background with the people over whom they rule. Second, as the people of privilege, they do not possess their own superior culture. As a consequence, they do not have the consciousness that their existence is based on the oppression of the masses. Finally, the existence of the *nomenklatura* has the ideological justification that it represents the interests of the masses.

This is not to say that Soviet government is free from sources of instability. There obviously exist sources of instability that, in my view, are liable to threaten the existence of the Soviet state itself, but they are different in nature from the almost fateful gulf that had separated the elite from the masses in the pre-revolutionary days. In carrying out his reforms, therefore, Gorbachev has to be concerned with sources of instability that might derail his reforms, but unlike the reforming tsars and bureaucrats, he is, in my opinion, free from a fear of revolution from below.

There seem to exist three basic sources of instability in the Soviet Union. First, there is the problem of the aspirations of the masses of the working class. The Revolution eliminated the barrier between the two nations by removing the top layers of society, but this did not mean that the masses were integrated into the political process. Under the dictatorship of the Communist Party, the masses became controlled by the state, but they were effectively excluded from the political process as they had been in the pre-revolutionary period. Since the process of economic perestroika is surely going to impose hardships on the masses, and when one takes into consideration the inherent conservatism and xenophobia of the Russian working class as well as their total lack of political experience, it is an open question how the masses will react to perestroika.[34] Trotsky once said that the ruling class had not taught the masses good manners, and these words can still be applied to the Soviet situation. Ambartsumov argues that *stikhiya* (spontaneity) is a source of creativity, not something to be feared, but until the masses become reasonably integrated into the political process, I would argue that *stikhiya* is a source of instability, if not of revolution.[35]

Nevertheless, this unrest is not likely to assume the dimensions of the cataclysm that swept through Russia in 1917, since there is no such gulf between the people and the communist *nomenklatura* as had existed between the masses and the privileged in the pre-revolutionary period. Moreover, as Lenin correctly pointed out, a revolution is impossible without a revolutionary ideology, and such a revolutionary ideology can be injected into the masses only from outside by the revolutionary intelligentsia. The intelligentsia who support perestroika are, if anything, the antithesis of the revolutionary intelligentsia of the pre-revolutionary days. They reject violence as a means of change, and they seek evolutionary change rather than a Utopian, eschatological vision characteristic of the pre-revolutionary radical intelligentsia. Therefore, any popular unrest will be more likely, if anything, to be connected with conservatives and serve as a force to resist further changes by perestroika.

The second and third sources of instability are the problem of nationalities within the Soviet Union and the problem of Eastern Europe: problems that the Soviet Union as a multinational empire has inherited from the Russian Empire. Since former European imperialist powers were forced to abandon their colonies, the Soviet Empire remains the last on earth to retain colonies within and outside itself. Accumulated grievances and contradictions, suppressed only by repression and force, are bound to burst open under glasnost and *demokratizatsiya*. The trouble in Nagorno-Karabakh and the Baltic republics were not isolated events. Gorbachev will be confronted with further nationality problems, to which there can be no perfect solution.

The third source of instability is Eastern Europe. Economic collapse and/or political upheavals in Eastern Europe are probably the most pressing dangers for Gorbachev. Furthermore, instability in Eastern Europe is closely connected with nationality questions within the Soviet Union. In the long run Gorbachev might be prepared to accept the 'Finlandization' of Eastern Europe, but if confronted with political upheaval in this region, he will not be able to abandon the Brezhnev doctrine completely.

The roots of these problems go back further than 1917. The Soviet power, which exploited the weaknesses inherent in the tsarist regime, is confronted with the same weaknesses as far as the nationality question is concerned.

Intelligentsia

Gorbachev's reforms are said to represent the emancipation of the Soviet intelligentsia, and the most spectacular changes under perestroika are undoubtedly taking place in the realm of intellectual activities. What, then, is the implication of the emancipation of the intelligentsia in a longer historical perspective?

Westernization, the elite's relation to the state, and the existence of serfdom contributed to the emergence of a Russian intelligentsia with unique characteristics. Peter I imposed Westernized education on reluctant nobles as a prerequisite to entering the ranks of the nobility. In a few generations the Russian elite was Westernized; absorbing Western technology, manners and knowledge, the Russian educated class established connections with the intellectual communities of the West. Peter the Great left another important imprint on the make-up of the Russian educated class by imposing compulsory state service on the nobility. This service to the state gradually inculcated among the nobility a broader sense of dedication to the nation and to the welfare of their fellow men. The emancipation of the Russian nobility from state service in 1762, however, ironically contributed to a sense of alienation of which a part of the nobility were acutely aware by the end of the eighteenth century. This sense of alienation was doubly reinforced by the social conditions of serfdom. The Russian educated class became painfully aware of the gulf that separated them from the masses of the peasants chained to the brutality of serfdom and to the forces of darkness and ignorance. Awareness that their knowledge and privilege were built on the evil of serfdom suffered by the oppressed masses, and haunted by a sense of alienation both from the state and from the people, they felt an inner urge to dedicate their knowledge to the welfare of the people and to serve as their moral guide and a teacher.[36] This explains the basically humanistic approach that characterized the Russian intellectual tradition in the pre-revolutionary period.

Intellectually, Westernization confronted the Russian educated class with the problem of its own identity. The resulting enquiries produced brilliant and unique achievements in thought and literature which had boomerang effects on Western culture itself. At the basis of the brilliance of Russian culture, there existed, though often grossly underestimated, Russian Orthodox tradition.[37]

As for the uniqueness of the Russian intellectual tradition, I feel that far too much attention has been devoted to its political aspects at the expense of other hitherto neglected but equally significant dimensions, particularly philosophical-religious aspects; further, that in the political aspects of the Russian intellectual tradition, far too much emphasis has been placed on the revolutionary intelligentsia, which constituted only a tiny fraction of the much wider and more diverse groups. As for Russian political thought, we have been too fascinated by one strand; that is, revolutionary political thought than runs from Pestel', Herzen, Chernyshevsky and the *Narodniki*, to the Russian Marxists and finally the Bolsheviks. They generally preferred a social rather than a political solution to the miseries of Russia, and adopted an eschatological view that a just society could be established only after the entire edifice of the tsarist regime was completely destroyed.[38] The Soviet regime is a direct legacy of this thinking, and the seventy-year history of the Soviet Union has clearly proved the hollowness of such ideas. There existed, however, another strand of political thinking, including, for example, Speransky, Tyutchev, Chicherin, Turgenev and the Russian liberals. They preferred evolutionary to revolutionary change and advocated political reform rather than social revolution.[39] Now that Soviet society faces the challenge of political reform and evolutionary change, it is interesting to note that the Soviet intelligentsia are beginning to turn their attention to these forgotten thinkers.

The Russian Revolution succeeded in eliminating the fateful gulf between the elite and the masses. The schizophrenia that Russia had suffered owing to the existence of 'two nations' was cured by physically eliminating the top layers of society. But this surgical operation was carried out at tremendous cost. By annihilating the class that had been the bearer of culture, the Revolution put an end to the brilliant humanistic Russian intellectual tradition, although many of its most exquisite blossoms must be counted as *les fleurs du mal*. The disappearance of this cultural class not only shattered continuity with the past, but the superior culture produced by the privileged who were physically annihilated came to haunt those in power in the proletarian state: this explains why they fought with such vengeance the ghost of the culture whose bearers had been long eliminated.

The Soviet intelligentsia, defined as one of the pillars of Soviet power together with the working class and the toiling peasants, have nothing in common with the pre-revolutionary intelligentsia. They are a product of mass education mostly of a technical nature, a group indispensable to an industrial society.[40] They have neither the same high level of educational background nor the same inner urge to serve the people as the pre-revolutionary intelligentsia. Certainly, they are alienated from the state to the extent that every citizen in the Soviet Union is alienated from it. They are alienated from the workers, and engineers bitterly complain they get the thin end of the wedge in the workers' paradise.

None the less, two observations must be made on the Soviet intelligentsia. First, there is an impact of professionalization: as Soviet society had matured, there has emerged a group of highly skilled professionals. They exert considerable influence in the intricate workings of this complex society. Despite diversity in the professions, these highly educated, increasingly confident people are developing an *esprit de corps* as the emerging Soviet intelligentsia. Just as we might say that a civil society, however feeble, came into being at the beginning of the nineteenth century, this emergent intelligentsia might be said to form an embryo civil society, one that exists separate from the state and functions independent of it.[41]

Second, although the pre-revolutionary intellectual tradition was brutally cut off by the Revolution, the Soviet regime could not completely eradicate it. In fact, despite the brutal suppression of the past, it has been transmitted secretly, in whispers and underground, so to speak, by a thinking minority. The intelligentsia in the true sense and the brilliant humanistic tradition have thus survived.

There was a paradox in Soviet society. The more empty and barren the official ideology became, the more passionately the intelligentsia in Soviet society tried to search for connections with the destroyed world, like a man who has lost his memory trying to seek his identity by seeking his past. Paradoxically, nowhere in the world have knowledge and culture in their true sense more significance than in the Soviet Union. Under the façade of meaningless official ideology, the Soviet intelligentsia read, thought and discussed in private.

Thus perestroika is the emancipation of the Soviet intelligentsia in two important, mutually connected ways. First, it acknowledges the place of the emerging professional class in society. Second, the Soviet intelligentsia, freed from the shackles of the official ideology, can now freely search for the lost thread from the past and establish their own identity. It should be emphasized that the intellectual movement under perestroika goes in two directions: towards the outside, seeking integration with the world civilization; and backwards, seeking its own identity with the past.[42] Unfettered and able to acquire its lost intellectual tradition, the Soviet intelligentsia could make an enormous contribution to world civilization, just as the pre-revolutionary Russian intelligentsia in many ways led world civilization.

The End of Ideology

If we look for analogy in Russian history, we may compare the crisis of socialism in the Soviet Union with the crisis of the Muscovite state in the seventeenth century. This may at first glance seem outlandish; after all, the Soviet Union is an industrialized superpower vastly different from the traditional, insignificant Muscovite state. Nevertheless, the Muscovite state, which was a self-contained world governed by Orthodoxy, just as the Soviet Union is a self-contained world governed by Marxism-Leninism, experienced an acute ideological crisis in the latter half of the seventeenth century, not unlike the one that faces the Soviet Union. The first and foremost characteristic of Muscovy was the symbiosis between church and state. As Raeff states:

> In Muscovy religion served both as a cultural underpinning of the regime and as a principle in terms of which Russia was able to define itself as a nation. Specifically, the Tsar and his subjects defined themselves as members of the Russian Orthodox Church, whose teachings functioned

as what we would nowadays call an ideology. It should come as no surprise, then, that any challenge to or conflict involving the rituals and teachings of the church had profound repercussions on the political and cultural life of the nation and struck at the very roots of Muscovite national identity and spiritual unity.[43]

It does not require a leap of the imagination to notice that if one replaces 'religion' with 'Marxism-Leninism' and 'the Russian Orthodox Church' with 'the CPSU', this statement is almost applicable to the Soviet Union.

Challenges to the unity of the traditional world came mainly from three directions. First, the religious schism destroyed Muscovite religious and cultural unity. Second, social and political strife that was expressed in violent uprisings of peasants, townsmen and *strel'tsy*, weakened the social and political cohesion of Muscovy. Third, there was growing Western influence, which undermined the traditional Muscovite ideology. Particularly after Muscovy acquired Kiev, powerful intellectual forces from the Ukraine, both ecclesiastical and secular, came to dominate in Muscovy. Feofan Prokopovich and Stefan Yavorsky, who provided intellectual force for Peter's reforms, are two notable examples.[44]

Just as the self-contained Muscovite world crumbled, with confidence shaken in its ideology and its religious and cultural unity disintegrating, the Soviet Union is suffering from a marked lack of confidence in ideology and witnessing the disintegration of its ideological and cultural identity as the leading socialist nation. Confidence in the superiority of socialism – the confidence that communists have held tenaciously throughout Soviet history – has been badly shaken, while capitalism and socialism are no longer perceived as two systems at differing stages of historical development with an inevitable progression from the former to the latter. Even worse is the sober recognition that socialism, as we know it, is destined to be left hopelessly behind capitalism and may eventually become extinct.

Second, perestroika may represent the end of the road of Marxism-Leninism as we know it.[45] The principal ideas that underlie perestroika are in contradiction with Marxism-Leninism. First of all, the economic reform is nothing other than an admission of the bankruptcy of Marxism which had aspired to achieve both economic efficiency and social justice.[46] The Soviet leaders, whether reformers or conservatives, are faced with the dilemma of either choosing economic efficiency at the expense of socialist principles (such as full employment, egalitarian pay-scales, subsidized prices for essential goods and services, and so on) or upholding socialist principles at the risk of suffering further economic decline. The reformers are those who have chosen to wager, as did Stolypin, on 'the sober and the strong', but the conservatives, appalled by the erosion of what they consider to be the essence of socialism, have none the less no economic remedy to offer.[47] Moreover, the political reform is based on a philosophy alien to Marxism-Leninism and counter to the idea of the dictatorship of the proletariat; further, it elevates bourgeois concepts like the rule of law and the separation of powers as positive normative values that transcend their class contents. The new thinking, which places all human values above class struggle, represents the third component that is in contradiction with Marxism-Leninism.[48]

It is important to emphasize that one impetus for the erosion of the official ideology has come from the West – and I include Japan here – just as Westernization contributed to the disintegration of the cultural and religious cohesion of Muscovy. Even a casual reader of the literature of perestroika must be struck by the degree to which Western ideas and Western technology influence the thinking of the reformers – whether in economic reforms, management, political reforms or foreign policy.[49]

What impact the end of ideology might have on the future development of the Soviet Union is an open question. Egor Ligachev, the champion of the conservative opposition to perestroika, delivered an important speech in Gorky at the beginning of August 1988 in which he attacked those who tried to establish a market mechanism in a socialist economy and to abandon the principle of class struggle in foreign policy.[50] Ligachev was later stripped of his post as second secretary, and put in charge of agricultural policy. Yet, in January 1989, another conservative leader, Viktor Chebrikov, delivered a speech in which he denounced informal political groups and upheld the principle of the hegemonic power of the Communist Party. Is it possible that a great schism is taking place in the Soviet Union, comparable to that in the seventeenth century? If so, what will be its impact on the future development of the Soviet Union? Will the reforms succeed in creating a new ideology to replace the old? What will happen if the old believers, though unable to provide an alternative, use the tremendous means at their disposal to resist the reforms? Will the Soviet Empire survive even if ideological unity, which, together with actual coercion, has constituted one of the main means of containing the build-up of contradictions and grievances, is destroyed? No one knows the answers yet.

There is the famous *anekdot* going around Moscow: 'Socialism is a long and painful stage between capitalism and capitalism.'

Though amusing, it does not convey the essence of perestroika, which is above all an attempt to redefine socialism.[51] Soviet thinkers are beginning to redefine socialism, drawing not only on such Marxist sources as the young Marx, Gramsci and Bukharin, but also on non-Marxist sources as well. Whatever the outcome of this redefinition may be, the thrust of the argument that is being unfolded in the Soviet Union seems to indicate that its basic direction is to recapture the humanism that was once inherent in socialism, but was lost in Bolshevism.[52]

New Thinking and the Approach to Violence[53]

Marxism contributed to the political theory of war. Contrary to the Western liberal tradition, which stressed consensus as the basis of political community, Marxism saw the basis of social relations in the conflict between classes. Behind the façade of apparent social harmony there is violence in the form of exploitation perpetrated by one class over another. Social progress is only achieved when the exploited turn on their exploiters and overthrow them. The metaphor of war was used to describe this struggle. At the same time, real war between nations was regarded not as a serious breakdown in international relations but as an extension of class struggle. In other words, Marxism saw in peace an element of war, and in war nothing extraordinary.

The Marxist approach becomes dangerous when it ceases to be a useful antidote to the prevailing bourgeois political philosophies and is turned into the sole official ideology. As Pipes has noted, Lenin turned Clausewitz on his head and advocated war as the continuation of politics by other means.[54] Indeed, Lenin was probably the first politician to militarize domestic politics. An examination of Lenin's writings during the revolutionary days of 1917 shows his striking use of imagery of war. The civil war was not merely imposed by outside forces hostile to the Bolshevik regime; it was a logical consequence of Lenin's strategy.

The metaphor of war was transformed into real war in the Soviet Union. The distinction between war fought between nations and war waged in society was obliterated, and the methods used only in wars between states were indiscriminately applied within the society. The civil war mentality encouraged the communist habit of settling differences by military means. Even at the end of the civil war, the mentality of *kto-kogo* did not disappear; rather, it was reinforced by the isolation of the communist regime in a sea of imperialist nations. Domestically as well, the communist regime was surrounded by essentially hostile class enemies such as Nepmen and the kulaks. It is no accident, to borrow a Soviet phrase, that at precisely the time of economic liberalization, during the NEP period, the internal freedom of the Communist Party was stifled. It was characteristic of Lenin to make a primarily military reference. In criticizing the opposition faction within the Communist Party, Lenin exclaimed that it was better to 'discuss with rifles'. Furthermore, in his major report on the NEP at the Tenth Party Congress in 1921, Lenin stated:

> Discipline must be more conscious and is a hundred times more necessary, because when a whole army retreats . . . it does not see where it will stop; it sees only retreat. Then sometimes a few panic voices are enough to start everyone running. Then the danger is immense. When such a retreat is being carried out with a real army, machine-guns are brought out and, when the orderly retreat becomes disorderly, the command is given: 'Fire'. And quite right. . . . At such a moment it is indispensable to punish strictly, secretly, unsparingly the slightest breach of discipline.[55]

It is well known that this argument directly led to Point Seven of the Resolution of Party Unity, which was to give Stalin his most effective weapon against his opponents.

I suspect that the mentality of militarization advocated by Lenin was enthusiastically endorsed by the young communist cadres who had won the civil war and who saw in the NEP only a retreat. Against this prevailing current, the attempt by Bukharin and his supporters to reconstruct a theory of the socialist state on the basis of social peace and reconciliation had no chance of gaining acceptance.[56] Bukharin's rehabilitation is therefore significant, not only because his economic ideas provide the reformers with a source of inspiration, but also because his political philosophy can give them a new political foundation.

The application of military methods to domestic politics was further accelerated by Stalin's revolution from above. Collectivization was an 'offensive against the kulaks'. The military factor in industrialization was unmistakable, as we see in Stalin's famous speech in 1931: 'We are fifty or a hundred years behind the advanced countries. We must make good this distance in ten years. Either we do so, or we shall go under.'[57] Julian Cooper's study makes it clear that the first priority of the industrialization drive between 1929 and 1941 was the military, at the cost of diverting necessary resources from other sectors, even heavy industry.[58] The slogan during the industrialization drive was 'There is no fortress that the Bolsheviks cannot take'. As Bialer has stated, military images were firmly entrenched even in the language.[59]

The militarization of society relentlessly pursued by Lenin and Stalin not only prepared the country for a possible war; it was also used to fan a class warfare in a society in which no enemies exist. Its logical conclusion was the Great Purges and the madness of the Gulag Archipelago.

Ironically, however, Marxism-Leninism has not been applied in Soviet foreign policy as clearly and relentlessly as it was in the society itself. Four factors have contributed to the diminishing role of ideology and its eventual disappearance as an operating principle in Soviet foreign policy. First, the Soviet Union had to survive in a world of nation states, and ideological purity had to be sacrificed for the sake of the survival of the state. When the Soviet regime chose peace, and consequently the survival of the state at the expense of revolutionary war at Brest-Litovsk in 1918, it subjugated ideology to the dictates of the national interest. Henceforth, ideology ceased to be the guide of policy; instead, it became a tool for the justification of policy.

Second, after World War II different roads to socialism emerged. Yugoslavia split from the Soviet Union. More importantly, the Sino-Soviet split had a profound influence on the devaluation of Marxist-Leninist ideology. The Soviet Union could no longer claim to be the sole fatherland of socialism to which all communists in other countries had to swear blind obedience. The mystique that formerly surrounded the Moscow-led communist movement was once and for all destroyed.

Third, the Soviet model of industrialization, which had once captured the imagination of intellectuals in the underdeveloped nations seeking modernization, ceased to be an attractive alternative to capitalism.

Fourth, the invention of nuclear weapons fundamentally altered the Marxist-Leninist approach to war. As nuclear weapons became integrated into Soviet foreign-military policy, the leadership had to face basic contradictions between the fundamental postulates of Marxism-Leninism and the implications of the operational system of foreign-military policy which included nuclear weapons. The first Marxist-Leninist dogma to be thrown out of the window was the inevitability of war. This raised difficult questions on the other postulate of the historical inevitability of the transition from capitalism to socialism. Khrushchev, denying the inevitability of war, nevertheless clung to the belief that a nuclear war could be won and that the Soviet Union had to seek military superiority as a guarantee of peace. In the latter half of the 1970s, Brezhnev rejected the pursuit of superiority and the belief that a nuclear war could be won.[60]

Nevertheless, neither Khrushchev nor Brezhnev brought the implication of the doctrinal change to its logical conclusion. Both Khrushchev and Brezhnev stood for the position that the world is basically divided between the two fundamentally hostile social systems of capitalism and socialism, and that capitalism is always ready to attack and destroy socialism. As long as the Soviet leadership took this position, it had no choice but to rely on military means to protect itself.

The new thinking that has emerged under Gorbachev represents a new approach to international relations. The concept of mutual security central to the new thinking presupposes that one side's national security depends on the understanding and good intentions of the other. It takes the position that nuclear weapons threaten socialism and capitalism alike, and to that extent the fate of both systems are bound together by the danger of mutual extinction. Neither side can remove this danger unilaterally by military-technical means alone; unilateral attempts are bound to increase the danger. Staking one's security on the understanding and intention of the other side is not a matter of choice, but of necessity.[61] In his speech at the seventieth anniversary of the October Revolution, Gorbachev clearly formulated the revised approach to imperialism: in this new stage of world interdependence, the most dangerous aspects of imperialism can be suppressed, and imperialism can exist without militarism.[62] In the nuclear age, all human values are said to take precedence over class struggle. As for the last vestige of the Marxist-Leninist approach to war – Clausewitz's axiom that war is an extension of politics by other means – Gorbachev dismissed it as obsolete: 'Clausewitz's classical formula has become completely obsolete. It belongs to libraries. To place all human, moral ethical norms at the foundation of international politics and to humanize inter-state relations has for the first time in history become a vital requirement.'[63] The Marxist-Leninist approach to war has thus been completely dismembered.

The gradual erosion of the Marxist-Leninist approach to war has gone hand in hand with the erosion of the theory of the dictatorship of the proletariat. Peaceful coexistence in international politics is integrally connected with the recognition that peaceful coexistence between diverse groups must be achieved in domestic politics as well. This means that Soviet political philosophy has finally made a transition from the conflict model to the consensus model. The implication of this transition is enormous, not only for foreign policy but also for domestic policy.

Conclusion

Perestroika is a major turning-point not only in Soviet history, but also in a longer historical perspective that goes back far beyond 1917. In fact, the problems that perestroika faces and the challenges that it offers can be understood only when examined in a longer historical framework. Although it has many similarities with previous examples of revolution from above, particularly with the Great Reforms, it is the first attempt to combine social transformation with political reforms, to limit autocratic power from above, and to create a civil society. It holds promises and dangers – promises in an intellectual movement that is reaching out to restore connections with world civilization, while looking back into the past for its identity, and dangers in the ideological schism that might lead to political instability and disintegration. Finally, changes in Soviet foreign policy are integrally connected with the transformation within the Soviet Union. We do not know where the Soviet Union under perestroika is headed, but we are certain that whatever its final destination might be, it has already opened up a new page in Russian/Soviet history.

Notes

1. Seweryn Bialer dismisses such comparisons as not helpful since they 'tell us little about the substance and relative significance of the reforms begun by Gorbachev'. Seweryn Bialer, 'Gorbachev's program of change: sources, significance, prospects', in S. Bialer and M. Mandelbaum (eds), *Gorbachev's Russia and American Foreign Policy* (Boulder and London: Westview Press, 1987), p. 251. I submit that the opposite is true.

2. Exceptions are: F. Frederick Starr, 'The changing nature of change in the USSR', in Bialer and Mandelbaum, *Gorbachev's Russia*, (fn. 1), pp. 3–35; Wada Haruki, *Watashino mita perestroika* [*Perestroika I Saw*] (Tokyo: Iwanami Shinsho, 1987). When I say social scientists and historians here, I have in mind specialists outside the Soviet Union. Some in the Soviet Union are beginning to see the significance of Gorbachev's reforms in a longer historical perspective that goes beyond the Soviet period. For instance, see E. Ambartsumov, 'O putyakh sovershenstvovaniya politicheskoi sistemy sotsializma', in Yu. N. Afanas'ev (ed.), *Inogo ne dano: perestroika, glasnost', sotsializm: sud'by perestroika, vglyadyvayas' v proshloe, vozvrashchenie k budushchemu* (Moscow: Progress, 1988), p. 81.

3. See Ernest J. Simmons (ed.), *Continuity and Change in Russian and Soviet Thought* (New York: Russel and Russel, 1955). Topics dealt with in this symposium are: (1) Realism and Utopia in Russian Economic Thought; (2) Authoritarianism

and Democracy; (3) Collectivism and Individualism; (4) Rationality and Non-rationality, and (5) Literature, State and Society. The second symposium was organized in 1958; papers were published in Cyril E. Black (ed.), *The Transformation of Russian Society: Aspects of Social Change since 1861* (Cambridge, Mass: Harvard University Press, 1960).

4. Bialer, 'Gorbachev's program of change', (fn. 1), pp. 272–3.

5. Quoted in Bialer, 'Gorbachev's program of change', (fn. 1), p. 297.

6. See two brilliant books: Vladimir Weidle, *Russia, Absent and Present* (New York: Vintage Books, 1961); Marc Raeff, *Understanding Imperial Russia: State and Society in the Old Regime*, translated by Arthur Goldhammer, foreword by John Keep (New York: Columbia University Press, 1984).

7. For the influence of Peter the Great's reforms and his subsequent image in Russian and Soviet history, see Nicholas V. Riasanovsky, *The Image of Peter the Great in Russian History and Thought* (New York and Oxford: Oxford University Press, 1985).

8. For the nature of the Stalinist system, see Seweryn Bialer, *Stalin's Successors* (Cambridge: Cambridge University Press, 1980), pp. 7–61; Robert C. Tucker (ed.), *Stalinism: Essays in Historical Interpretation* (New York: Norton, 1977); a monumental work by Tanisuchi Yuzuru, *Sutarin seijitaisei no seiritsu* [Formation of the Stalinist Political System], 4 vols (Tokyo: Iwanami Shoten, 1970–86).

9. See Nicholas V. Riasanovsky, *A Parting of Ways: Government and Educated Public in Russia 1801–1855* (Oxford: Oxford University Press, 1976); Marc Raeff, *Origins of the Russian Intelligentsia: The Eighteenth Century Nobility* (New York: Harcourt, Brace & World, 1966).

10. Quoted in Michael T. Florinsky's *Russia: A History and an Interpretation* (New York: Macmillan, 1963), vol. 2, p. 883.

11. See Raeff, *Understanding Imperial Russia*, (fn. 6).

12. See Bialer, 'Gorbachev's program of change', (fn. 1), pp. 255–6.

13. See Marc Raeff, *Plans for Political Reform in Imperial Russia, 1730–1905* (Englewood Cliffs, NJ: Prentice-Hall, 1966).

14. See V. I. Startsev, *Revolyutsiya i vlast'* (Moscow: Mysl', 1978), pp. 11–46; W. G. Rosenberg, 'Les Libéraux russes et le changement du pouvoir en mars, 1917', *Cahiers du monde russe et soviétique*, 9 (1968): 46–57.

15. My ongoing research on crime and social aspects of revolutionary Petrograd in 1917–18 indicates this. See Tsuyoshi Hasegawa, 'Hanzai, keisatsu, samosudo: roshia kakumei ka petorogurado no shakaishi eno ichishiron' [Crime, Police, and *Samosudy* in Petrograd during the Russian Revolution], *Suravu Kenkyu*, 34 (1987): 27–55.

16. The importance of local self-government for democratization is recognized by Ambartsumov, 'O putyakh sovershenstvovaniya politicheskoi sistemy sotsializma', (fn. 2), pp. 82–3.

17. For detailed discussions on these obstacles, see Seweryn Bialer's unpublished manuscript on the nineteenth party conference.

18. Raeff, *Plans for Political Reform in Imperial Russia*, (fn. 13), p. 38.

19. Ibid., p. 17.

20. Quoted in Hugh Seton-Watson, *The Russian Empire, 1801–1917* (Oxford: Clarendon Press, 1967), p. 103.

21. See Tsuyoshi Hasegawa, *The February Revolution: Petrograd 1917* (Seattle: University of Washington Press, 1967), p. 103.

22. F. Rodichev, quoted in W. G. Rosenberg, *Liberals in Russian Revolution* (Princeton, NJ: Princeton University Press, 1974), p. 15.

23. Ibid., p. 13.

24. This process is best described by Rosenberg (ibid.).

25. This is not an aberration of Marxism. Marx himself rejects the notion of civil society in the dictatorship of the proletariat. See his *Contribution to the Critique of Hegel's Philosophy of Right: Introduction*, in Robert C. Tucker, *The Marx-Engels Reader*, second edition (New York: Norton, 1978), pp. 64–5.

26. Stephen F. Cohen, *Bukharin and the Bolshevik Revolution: A Political Biography, 1888–1938* (New York: Random House, 1973), pp. 270–6.

27. Ibid., p. 208.

28. Sheila Fitzpatrick, 'Sources of change in Soviet history: state, society, and entrepreneurial tradition', in Bialer and Mandelbaum, *Gorbachev's Russia*, (fn. 1), pp. 41–2.

29. In fact, until recently this concept has been alien to even the most advanced section of the Soviet intelligentsia. At one conference held in 1987 in Sapporo, one Soviet economist, responding to a participant's comment that there was no civil society in the Soviet Union, angrily stated that Soviet society was a *civilized* society.

30. Ambartsumov, 'O putyakh sovershenstvovaniya politicheskoi sistemy sotsializma', (fn. 2), pp. 83–7.

31. Ibid., p. 81.

32. See Leopold Haimson, 'The problem of social stability in urban Russia, 1905–1917', *Slavic Review*, 23 (4) (1964): 619–42; 24 (1) (1965): 1–22. This article is an important contribution to the American historiography of modern Russia. Generally speaking, the predominant interpretation prior to this article was similar to that of the Russian liberals, who took the position (1) that Russia was moving towards the establishment of a pluralistic society and of democratic parliamentary political system before World War I; (2) that this trend was obstructed by tsarist intransigence and revolutionary extremism; and (3) that had World War I not intervened, the Russian Revolution could have been avoided. After the appearance of Haimson's article, the predominant trend of American historiography has been social history that emphasizes the unbridgeable gap between *verkhi* and *nizy* and the inevitability of the Russian Revolution. See an insightful essay by Ronald Gregory Suny, 'Toward a social history of the October Revolution', *American Historical Review*, 88 (1983): 31–52. It is interesting to note that under perestroika Soviet historians have rediscovered the significance of the Russian liberals. In my private conversations with Soviet intelligentsia, the most radical element takes a position similar to the liberal interpretation.

33. See Hasegawa, *The February Revolution: Petrograd 1917*, (fn. 21). The relationship between autocracy and the liberals during World War I was complex and cannot be reduced to a simplified schema that contrasts the obsolete and obscurantist autocracy with the progressive and democratic liberals. See a valuable study of the relationship between the two with regard to the food supply question during World War I – Matsusato Kimitaka, 'Daiichiji taisenki Roshia ni okeru shokuryojigyo: soryokusen no seijishi' [The Food Supply Question in Russia during World War I: A Political History under Total War], Master's thesis, Tokyo University, 1987; see also Raymond Pearson, *The Russian Moderates and the Crisis of Tsarism, 1914–1917* (New York: Barnes & Noble, 1977).

34. It is, however, wrong to state simply that the masses are inherently opposed

to perestroika. For the complexities of social groups and their respective attitude towards perestroika, see T. Zaslavskaya, 'O strategii sotsial'nogo upravleniya perestroiki', in Afanas'ev, *Inogo ne dano*, (fn. 2), pp. 9–50. Sporadic labour unrests are reported, for instance, among automobile workers in Moscow, bus workers in Moldavia, and Moscow air controllers. See John Burns, 'Soviet air controllers try to shame authorities', *International Herald Tribune*, 24 Feb. 1989.

35. Ambartsumov, 'O putyakh sovershenstvovaniya politicheskoi sistemy sotsializma', (fn. 2), pp. 87–8.

36. See Raeff, *Origins of the Russian Intelligentsia*, (fn 9); Martin Malia, 'What is the Intelligentsia?', in Richard Pipes (ed.), *The Russian Intelligentsia* (New York: Columbia University Press, 1961), pp. 1–18.

37. See Sir Isaiah Berlin, *Russian Thinkers* (New York: Viking Press, 1978); Donald W. Treadgold, *The West in Russia and China* (Cambridge: Cambridge University Press, 1983), vol. 1, *Russia, 1472–1917*); James H. Billington, *Icon and Axe: An Interpretive History of Russian Culture* (New York: Knopf, 1966).

38. See an essay written by Sir Isaiah Berlin, Introduction to Franco Venturi, *Roots of Revolution: A History of the Populist and Socialist Movements in Nineteenth Century Russia* (New York: Knopf, 1960), pp. vii–xxx.

39. See Leonard Schapiro's brilliant lectures published in *Rationalism and Nationalism in Russian Nineteenth Century Political Thought* (New Haven, CT: Yale University Press, 1967).

40. Richard Pipes, 'The historical evolution of the Russian intelligentsia', in R. Pipes (ed.), *The Russian Intelligentsia*, (fn. 36), p. 51.

41. See Bialer, 'Gorbachev's program of change', (fn. 1), pp. 237–9.

42. It should be noted that two strands of intellectuals – one in the tradition of the West and the other that of the Slavophiles – are appearing on the Soviet intellectual scene and often engage in bitter debates. The most extreme example of the latter group is Pamyat with a strong anti-Semitic inclination. Nevertheless, it is impossible to divide Soviet intellectuals schematically into two groups. The best example who combines both elements, reaching out to join world civilization, while looking into the past to restore the last ties with the Russian intellectual tradition, is Dimitrii Likhachev.

43. Raeff, *Understanding Imperial Russia*, (fn. 6), pp. 2–3.

44. Ibid., pp. 14–33.

45. James Scanlan argues that perestroika is an attempt to return to original Marxism, and is carried out within the confines of Marxism. James Scanlan, 'Ideology and reform', in P. Juviler and H. Kimura (eds), *Gorbachev's Reforms* (New York: Aldine de Gruyter, 1988), pp. 49–62. On this crucial point in an otherwise insightful essay, I disagree.

46. See James Scanlan's paper presented at the symposium of the Slavic Research Centre and my comment, 'Soren ni okeru peresutoroika no shakaitekiseijiteki sokumen' [Social and Political Aspects of *Perestroika* in the Soviet Union], in Slavic Research Centre, Hokkaido University, *Gorubachofu kaikauno hamon: soren naigai no takakuteki bunseki* [Impact of Gorbachev's Reforms], *Slavic Research Conference Report*, No. 24 (Sapporo: Slavic Research Centre, 1988), pp. 1–11.

47. Ironically, the most radical economic reformers in the Soviet Union sound like American conservative economists such as Milton Friedman. This paradox is well illustrated in Hakamada Shigeki, *Soren: gokai, o toku 25 no shiten* [The Soviet Union: 25 Viewpoints to Avoid Misunderstanding] (Tokyo: Chuo Koronsha, 1987).

48. This important problem is treated separately in the next section. Suffice it to say here that the abandonment of class struggle in foreign policy inflicts a heavy blow to the international communist movement of which the Soviet Union has claimed to be the head.

49. Now that one of the alumni of the exchange programme between the United States and the Soviet Union sits in the Politburo, we realize how short-sighted were the criticisms levelled by such people as Richard Pipes against exchange programmes.

50. *Pravda*, 5 August 1988.

51. Bialer, 'Gorbachev's program of change', (fn. 1), p. 270.

52. Immediately after the Bolshevik assumption of power, Yulii Martov wrote:

> It is not only because of my deep conviction that to impose socialism on an economically and culturally backward country is a senseless Utopia, but also because of my organic inability to reconcile myself to that Arakcheevian conception of socialism and Pugachevian understanding of the class struggle which are a natural product of that very attempt to plant a European ideal in Asian soil. The outcome is such a bouquet that one can hardly carry it. To me socialism always meant not the negation of personal liberty, and individuality, but, on the contrary, their highest realization.

Izrael Getzler, *Martov: A Political Biography of a Russian Social Democrat* (Cambridge: Cambridge University Press, 1967), pp. 171–2. The redefinition of socialism will inevitably lead to reconciliation with this kind of criticism of Bolshevism. In this sense, the fear expressed by Nina Andreeva that perestroika is essentially a rejection of Bolshevism is justified.

53. This section is a revised version of part of my article, 'The military factor in Soviet foreign policy', in Kinya Niiseki (ed.), *The Soviet Union in Transition* (Boulder, Co: Westview Press; London: Avebery, 1987), pp. 147–66. The part I have taken here is from pp. 152–6.

54. Richard Pipes, 'Soviet global strategy', *US–Soviet Relations in the Era of Détente* (Boulder, Co: Westview Press, 1981), p. 175.

55. Quoted in E. H. Carr, *The Bolshevik Revolution*, vol. 1 (London: Macmillan, 1960), pp. 199, 211.

56. Regarding Bukharin's attempts to reconstruct a new theory, see Cohen, *Bukharin and the Bolshevik Revolution*, (fn. 26).

57. Alec Nove, *An Economic History of the USSR* (London: Allen Lane, 1969), p. 188.

58. Julian Cooper, 'Defence production and the Soviet economy, 1929–41', *CREES Discussion Paper*, 3 (1976).

59. Seweryn Bialer, *Stalin's Successors: Leadership, Stability, and Change in the Soviet Union* (Cambridge: Cambridge University Press, 1980), p. 22.

60. This part of the argument is taken from my article, (fn. 45), 'Gorbachev, the new thinking of Soviet foreign security policy and the military'.

61. For a discussion on world peace and the class analysis, see Stephen Shenfield, *The Nuclear Predicament: Explorations in Soviet Ideology* (London, New York, Andover: The Royal Institute of International Affairs/Routledge & Kegan Paul, 1987), *Chatham House Papers*, 37: 40–7.

62. 'Oktyabr' i perestroika: revolyutsiya prodolzhaetsya', *Izvestiya*, 3 Nov. 1987:

5; for an English translation of this speech, see Mikhail Gorbachev, *October and Perestroika: The Revolution Continues* (Moscow: Novosti, 1987).

63. M. S. Gorbachev, *Perestroika i novoe myshlenie dlya nashei strany i dlya vsego mira* (Moscow, 1987), p. 141 (transl. as *Perestroika: New Thinking for Our Country and the World*) (New York: Harper & Row, 1987).

3

Perestroika and the Political System*

Archie Brown

A new Soviet political system is being created from day to day. At the moment the new sits uneasily alongside the old, and the old is not giving way without a fight. The changes call into question much that has been taken for granted throughout most of Soviet history and it has become more difficult than ever before to predict what the system will look like a decade from now. But even those who, as recently as 1987, were arguing – wrongly – that nothing of consequence had changed in the Soviet Union must now recognize that dramatic and fundamentally important change is taking place.[1]

Political reform is, of course, proceeding far faster and more successfully than economic reform. So long as material shortages get worse rather than better and there is no improvement in the standard of living of the average Soviet citizen, the successful continuation of political reform cannot be taken for granted. But many Western commentators, once they belatedly accepted that Gorbachev was serious about radical reform, have underestimated his staying power and the prospects for perestroika moving forward. It has been argued that the opposition of the party and state apparatus represents an insurmountable obstacle and sometimes too readily assumed that conservative forces will necessarily be the main beneficiaries of popular grievances and disappointed expectations.[2]

The combination of freedom to criticize and lack of economic progress is undoubtedly an important factor in the Soviet political equation, but so far, while it has reduced Gorbachev's *popularity* at home as compared with the early days of his leadership in 1985, it has not undermined his *power*.[3] On the contrary, Gorbachev has skilfully used both the old and new institutions (on the one hand, the powers of the party General Secretaryship and, on the other, the outcome of the elections to the Congress of People's Deputies and the first meeting of that Congress) to reduce the numerical weight and political influence of conservative communists in the highest echelons of the party and state apparatus.

The energetic part being played by radically reformist journalists, social scientists and writers has helped to create a political climate in which it is far from easy for conservative party and state bureaucrats to turn present domestic economic and social problems to their own advantage. There are many differences between the contemporary period of Soviet history and Khrushchev's time of attempted reform. One, of course, is the greater political insight and subtlety of Gorbachev, but no less important is the far greater sophistication of the political analyses appearing in the era of glasnost in many (though not all) Soviet journals and newspapers and some radio and television programmes. There has been a dramatic increase in the circulation of the most liberal and forward-looking weeklies and monthlies, and the enhanced political education of their readers is now a factor to be reckoned with.[4]

New ways of thinking and speaking about Soviet politics as well as new ways of behaving have emerged in Gorbachev's USSR, especially since 1987. As recently as late 1986, while emphasizing the significance of the political developments already under way, I could characterize the change (itself an important one) in the postwar Soviet Union as movement 'from quasi-totalitarianism to authoritarianism to the beginnings of a more enlightened authoritarian regime'.[5] In the last two-and-a-half years, the Soviet system has developed beyond that. It is now indeed a more enlightened authoritarian regime and one, furthermore, which already contains some significant elements of political pluralism and of democratization.

In this chapter, after first putting the changes in context, I focus on two aspects of political development which are, however, interconnected: conceptual change and institutional change. Some attention is paid also to the resistance which is manifesting itself both to the new thinking and to the institutional developments. The resistance takes many forms, and although (or perhaps because) the Gorbachev era has thus far been one of unprecedented progress on the part of Soviet political reformers, there is still an intense political struggle taking place. On the one hand, new actors have emerged on the political stage who have adopted positions more radical than that of Gorbachev. On the other hand, Gorbachev remains significantly more of a political reformer than a majority of the Central Committee of the party, even after his spectacular success in late April 1989 in engineering the removal of more veteran members of the Central Committee than had ever before left that body in between the quinquennial Party Congresses.[6]

Models of Socialism

So far as *political* change is concerned, what is happening now in the Soviet Union is the most comprehensive reform effort since the Bolshevik Revolution, not excluding Lenin's New Economic Policy (NEP) launched in 1921. One of the most important elements of that change is in the realm of language and ideas. Given the explicit role accorded to theory and ideology in communist states, and the vast resources which traditionally in the Soviet Union have been devoted to bolstering the position of official political doctrine, here, even more than elsewhere, 'conceptual change must be understood politically, and political change conceptually'.[7]

Some of the new ideas which are now being proclaimed in the Soviet Union had their cautious origins in Brezhnev's time, but as one of the most innovative thinkers then and now, Evgeny Ambartsumov, has put it, in those days – so far as the social sciences at least were concerned – 'creative search and bold scientific endeavour were reprehensible and even risky'.[8] As Ambartsumov notes:

> The tone was set by hallelujah-singers who eulogized the status quo, by dogmatists and scholastics who studied speculative, far-fetched, unrepresentative categories and properties and not real processes. Given the atmosphere of ostentation and social apologetics, this was an intellectually fruitless, but paying occupation. This is why many young and some mature scientists took the line of least resistance, adjusting themselves to the situation. Even if they dared to pose a burning question, they tended to mask it with verbosity, seeking safety behind platitudes and commonplace statements.[9]

In contrast with Brezhnev's time, when it was firmly held that while there could be different *roads* to socialism, there were not different *models* of it (socialism was what was to be found in the Soviet Union and in other orthodox communist states at any given time), there is now a cautious espousal by the top party leadership and a more wholehearted embracing by many party intellectuals of the idea that different models of socialism can and do exist and a much greater willingness to learn from the experience of others.[10]

There has been close scrutiny of what has been happening in communist countries as diverse as China, Hungary, Poland, East Germany, Czechoslovakia and Yugoslavia. Different Soviet leaders draw upon different models. Thus, aspects of the Hungarian and Chinese economic reforms, especially in agriculture, appeal to those of more radical reformist orientation, while Egor Ligachev, the overlord of Soviet agriculture within the Central Committee

Secretariat, has preferred to look to the hitherto more conservative communist states of East Germany and Czechoslovakia to justify his faith in the essentials of the state and collective farm structure.

Of course, attention is being paid to the negative as well as the positive aspects of the experience of other communist countries. In the case of China, with which the Soviet Union has re-established inter-party as well as inter-state relations following Gorbachev's visit in May 1989 (itself an important event but overshadowed by the collapse in the authority of the Chinese leadership which was, coincidentally, taking place), it has for some time been agreed by social scientists in the Soviet Union and China with knowledge of the other country that Deng Xiaoping's China was ahead of the Soviet Union in terms of the radicalism of its economic reform but that the Soviet Union was well ahead of China in political reform and in relative freedom of expression.[11]

The mass student protests of May and early June and the eventual brutal military suppression of peaceful and popular demonstrations in Beijing were interpreted in very different ways by different opinion groupings within the Soviet Communist Party. For some, it was confirmation of the dangers of allowing spontaneous political movements to get out of hand and of the need for an early restoration of firmer 'discipline' within the Soviet Union itself. For reformers, however, it was one more justification of the correctness of creating political institutions (the freest Soviet elections in seventy years and the nearest thing to a parliament the Soviet Union has ever had) which provide a mechanism for a higher degree than hitherto of accountability on the part of political office-holders and a forum for criticism and debate. The present period of remarkable ferment and innovation in a significant part of the communist world (notably, in Hungary, Czechoslovakia, Poland, East Germany, Romania and Bulgaria as well as the Soviet Union and China) is one in which events in one country can have a dramatic impact on another, and not always in predictable ways.

It is not only, however, what is happening in other communist states that is now influencing the top Soviet leadership. The sources of learning have been extended to include certain institutions to be found in the political systems of 'bourgeois democratic' countries and not merely, as in the past, technical or managerial features of their economic systems. Both Mikhail Gorbachev and Vadim Medvedev, a Politburo member and Secretary of the Central Committee with responsibility for ideology, have stressed the necessity of learning from the non-socialist world as well as from other socialist countries.[12] Medvedev appeared to call for a reinterpretation of the achievements of European social democracy, of which there have been numerous other signs in Soviet publications (and on Soviet television), including sympathetic discussion of Sweden and other Scandinavian countries.[13] Indeed, on the reform wing of the Soviet Communist Party the long-standing barrier between communism, on the one hand, and social democracy or democratic socialism, on the other, is crumbling. In a dramatic break with the past, it is not uncommon now to hear prominent Soviet party intellectuals and some of the more enlightened officials say that they regard Sweden not only as an example of socialism but as the best model currently on view.

At the inaugural meeting of the Congress of People's Deputies, held at the end of May and beginning of June 1989, the prominent Soviet writer Chingiz Aitmatov went further. Instead of making an idol of socialism as 'the holy of holies of our theoretical doctrine', and instead of laying down the law on what did and what did not constitute socialism, it was necessary, he said, to reach an understanding whereby it was judged by its fruits – that is, by its contribution to people's creativity and prosperity. Aitmatov suggested that the Soviet Union could learn from other countries for whom the Soviet example had performed the service of demonstrating how *not* to go about constructing socialism.

> I have in mind the flourishing law-governed societies of Sweden, Austria, Finland, Norway, the Netherlands, Spain and finally, Canada across the ocean. About Switzerland I don't even speak – it's a model. The working person in those countries earns on average four to five times more than our workers. The social protection and the level of welfare of those societies are something we can only dream about. This is real and, if you like, worker trade union socialism, although these countries do not call themselves socialist, but are none the worse for that.[14]

The comparisons that important Soviet reformers now make not only with Western countries but also with the Soviet past are remarkable. Aleksandr Yakovlev, Gorbachev's closest ally in the Politburo, said in response to the questions of a Soviet television journalist on 27 May 1989, 'For the first time in the history of our country we have a platform of conscience, a platform of morality.'[15] When he was asked whether the Congress of People's Deputies could be compared with parliaments abroad, Yakovlev did not argue for the superiority of the new Soviet legislature, though until very recently Soviet officials routinely suggested that even the unreformed Supreme Soviet was vastly more democratic than Western parliaments. Instead, he emphasized the comparative underdevelopment of Soviet parliamentary theory and practice:

Parliaments in other countries have existed for decades and they have entirely different traditions. They have written many volumes about procedural matters there. We do not have that. Of course, we must learn professionalism in the economy and politics; above all we must learn democratic professionalism. We must learn democracy, tolerance of others' opinions and thoughts. That's not easy. I believe that the work of the Soviet parliament will demonstrate where we are right and where we are wrong; what we must continue and what must be corrected.[16]

New Concepts

As James Farr has noted in a recent essay, 'Where there are different concepts, there are different beliefs, and so different actions and practices', even though political practice is only partly constituted by concepts.[17] But while acting politically 'for strategic and partisan purposes', people do so 'in and through language' and 'language is an arena of political action'. Accordingly, 'political change and conceptual change must be understood as one complex and interrelated process'.[18]

In the Soviet context, three new concepts in particular deserve special emphasis, for they help to open up space for new political activity and provide a theoretical underpinning for some of the concrete reforms that the more radical interpreters of perestroika are attempting to implement. It is worth noting that within a period of eighteen months – between the summer of 1987 and the end of 1988 – all three received the endorsement of Gorbachev.

The first of these concepts is that of 'socialist pluralism', and its adoption represents a radical break with past Soviet doctrine. It is of interest that whereas many reformist concepts are to be encountered first in the writings of scholarly specialists and only later in the speeches of party leaders, in this instance it was Gorbachev who took the bold step of embracing the concept of 'pluralism' in public before anyone else had done so.[19] Indeed, the notion of pluralism had been the subject of so many attacks by Soviet leaders and ideologists after it was adopted by 'Prague Spring' intellectuals in the late 1960s and by 'Eurocommunists' in the 1970s that it would have been difficult for anyone other than the top leader to break the taboo on endorsing it.

But Gorbachev took the lead on this because he was persuaded that to continue to attack 'pluralism' was to play into the hands of those in the Soviet Union who wished to stifle debate and innovative thought and to assist the enemies, rather than the proponents, of perestroika. Only one year separated Gorbachev's first use of the term 'socialist pluralism', in the limited context of opening up the columns of Soviet newspapers to a wider range of writers in order that 'the whole of socialist pluralism, so to speak, is present',[20] to his employment of the concept in a broader sense, and the endorsement of that use in a most authoritative party forum, the nineteenth conference of the Soviet Communist Party in the summer of 1988.[21]

Thus what had seemed to some to be no more than a throwaway remark when first used by Gorbachev in conversation with Soviet writers in July 1987 had a year later been elevated into new party doctrine, the traditional 'monist' theory of the Soviet state and oft-repeated claim of the 'monolithic unity' of the party and the people notwithstanding. Gorbachev's adoption of the concept of 'socialist pluralism' and the positive reference made to a 'socialist pluralism of opinions' in the resolution on glasnost adopted by the party conference represented a considerable boost for the more radical Soviet political reformers. These endorsements provided a legitimacy previously lacking for political debate and diversity of opinion on political and social issues in Soviet publications, even though the fact that 'pluralism' was qualified by the adjective 'socialist' indicated that there were still limits on what was deemed fit to print.

Whereas in Poland and Hungary, following fierce struggles, the top party leaderships now speak approvingly of 'political pluralism' (though there remains room for argument concerning its scope in practice), Gorbachev and even the reform wing of the Soviet leadership continued to make a distinction between 'socialist pluralism' – desirable – and 'political pluralism' – still suspect because of its free-for-all connotations and implication that under such a banner the 'leading role' of the Communist Party might cease to be guaranteed. In practice, a 'socialist pluralism of opinion' made ample room for publications by Roy Medvedev, previously regarded as a dissident but now a member of the new Supreme Soviet and also readmitted to the Communist Party, but had not up to the summer of 1989 accommodated Alexsandr Solzhenitsyn, who made increasingly clear after the publication of his works in Russia ceased in the mid-1960s that his rejection of the Soviet system was a root-and-branch one that embraced Lenin and Leninism as well as Stalin and Stalinism. Even in Solzhenitsyn's case, however, some important recent movement has taken place. TASS, the Soviet news service, reported on 6 June 1989 that the publishing house Sovetskaya Rossiya would be bringing out Solzhenitsyn's *Cancer Ward*, written in the Soviet Union but never published there, as well as *One Day in the Life of Ivan Denisovich* and

Matryona's Home. In July *Novyi Mir* published Solzhenitsyn's Nobel lecture and announced that in subsequent issues chapters from his *Gulag Archipelago* would appear. More remarkably, the publishing house Sovetskii Pisatel declared that it would publish the *Gulag* in full.[22]

The boundaries of 'socialist pluralism' are quite evidently not fixed. On the one hand, many Soviet commentators now use the term 'pluralism' positively – and with reference to political, cultural and intellectual life – in the mass media, without finding it necessary to qualify it either with 'socialist' or 'political'. On the other, all this is being accompanied by a debate on, and constant redefinition of, socialism itself. If that process continues, the shackles imposed by the word 'socialist' may be far removed from the constraints it implied in the Soviet past.[23]

The second concept adopted in recent times which is of great importance for the advancement of the cause of political and legal reform is that of the *pravovoe gosudarstvo*, or the state based upon the rule of law. Although there is nothing new about an emphasis on 'socialist legality', the idea of the *pravovoe gosudarstvo* goes beyond that. The 'socialist legality' introduced under Khrushchev meant an end to the excesses and extremes of arbitrariness of Stalin's time, but lawyers and the legal system remained firmly subordinated to the party leadership. The aim of the serious proponents of the *pravovoe gosudarstvo* is a system in which all institutions and individuals are subordinate to the law as administered by impartial and independent courts. What is more, while it is generally assumed in Soviet writings that a 'socialist legality' has prevailed in the Soviet Union throughout the post-Stalin era, the state based upon the rule of law is seen as a goal to which Soviet society should aspire, rather than as one that has already been attained.

The idea of the law-governed state is part of a much more profound analysis of arbitrary rule and the abuse of power than took place in Khrushchev's time. It reflects a consciousness of the extent to which powerful individuals and institutions have been able to bend the law to their own purposes, as well as a concern with the inadequacy of the rights of advocates and of the independence of judges in cases where the interests and views of well-connected officials are involved. A prominent Soviet scholar of notably reformist disposition, Mikhail Piskotin, who was from 1978 until 1987 chief editor of the major legal journal *Sovetskoe gosudarstvo i pravo*, and who now edits the journal of the new Soviet legislature, *Narodnii Deputat*, has written in the newspaper *Sovetskaya kul'tura* that it is still 'far from possible to regard our state as fully based on the rule of law', adding that the attainment of the *pravovoe gosudarstvo* depends on reform of the political system.[24]

The concept of the state based upon the rule of law has not only been embraced by Gorbachev but was also included in the resolution on legal reform adopted by the nineteenth party conference in early July 1988.[25] It leaves open many questions, including, not least, the issue of whether in practice courts will have any independence *vis-à-vis* the very highest party and state authorities, as distinct from the ability to check abuses of power at local levels. As with other innovative concepts which have been accepted by the Soviet leadership, different leaders and theorists can interpret the idea of the law-governed state in different ways. But adoption of the concept marks a considerable step forward in the advancement of the *role* of law – even if there does not yet exist in practice a fully fledged *rule* of law – in Soviet society.

The third concept that is quite new in the Soviet context is that of 'checks and balances'. Its adoption is a remarkable departure from previous patterns of Soviet thought and it, too, is part of the breakthrough in thinking about the Soviet political system which took place in 1987 and 1988. In the past, the notion of checks and balances, in so far as it was referred to at all, was viewed as part of the deceptive screen behind which the ruling class exercised untrammelled power in bourgeois states. But the more serious study in recent years by Soviet scholars of foreign political systems, as well as the contemplation of some of the horrendous results of unchecked power within the Soviet Union (especially in the Stalin period), have led to a re-evaluation of the theory and practice of checks and balances. The idea that the concept might have something to offer reformers of the Soviet political system was first broached in print in Moscow in July 1987,[26] and was adopted by Gorbachev at the end of November 1988 when he concluded a discussion in the Supreme Soviet of the proposed Committee for Supervision of the Constitution by commenting, 'Thus, one may say comrades, that our own socialist system of "checks and balances" is taking shape in this country, designed to protect society against any violation of socialist legality at the highest state level.'[27] For the leader of the Soviet Communist Party and head of the Soviet state to accept the need for checks and balances, albeit *socialist* checks and balances, is a significant illustration of the 'new thinking' which has emerged on Soviet political institutions and not only on foreign policy, to which that term is normally applied.

The Process of Institutional Change

The most important point about the reform of the political system is that it is not an event but a *process* and, in all probability, a *long-term* process if the reform wing of the Communist Party continues to prevail, as it has increasingly done since Gorbachev became General Secretary (and especially since 1987). Democratization could even be speeded up significantly if the pressures from public opinion which began to manifest themselves politically in 1989 continue, but without getting out of hand. Gorbachev himself has emphasized that the reforms adopted by the old Supreme Soviet at the end of November 1988 represent only the first phase of reform of the political system. It is impossible to say where they will end, for Soviet reformers themselves do not know. There was much less serious thinking about reform of the political system than about reform of the economy (inadequate though that was) prior to perestroika, and ideas on institutional change are being elaborated all the time. It is entirely possible that reform of the Soviet political system will go very much further than it has gone already if the balance of influence continues to shift in favour of 'new thinkers' as it has over the past few years.

The institutional change that has already taken place is far from inconsequential. On the one hand, some major existing institutions are functioning in a significantly different way from before. This is true of the Communist Party as a whole and of some of its constituent elements. On the other hand, a number of essentially new political institutions have been created. Thus, for example, Soviet elections in 1989 were so different from what were called 'elections' in the Soviet Union in the past that they have little in common except the name. Similarly, the new Supreme Soviet has already shown itself to be a much more serious legislature than the body that carried that name previously, and it has been elected by a novel (and already important) institution, the Congress of People's Deputies. There is a new-style presidency, and there is to be a Committee for Supervision of the Constitution. Though it is not possible to provide here an exhaustive survey of the changes in Soviet political institutions, three aspects in particular of this process merit closer examination: electoral reform, the evolving legislature, and the changing structure and role of the party.

Elections
As early as 1987, by way of 'experiment', Soviet voters were offered a choice of candidates in elections to local soviets in approximately

5 per cent of the constituencies.[28] But the big breakthrough in the Soviet electoral system came with the elections to the new Congress of People's Deputies in late March 1989. Of the 2,250 members of the Congress, 1,500 are drawn from territorial constituencies, with 750 seats distributed among the various parts of the country on the basis of population density and 750 divided equally among the national-territorial units from union republics to autonomous regions (thus giving disproportionate representation to the smaller nationalities, since tiny Estonia and the enormous Russian republic return the same number of deputies on this 'nationality slate'). Approximately three-quarters of the territorial elections to the congress were competitive ones,[29] but even running in a single-candidate district was no guarantee against defeat, as a number of party officials discovered to their dismay when they failed to secure 50 per cent support from those who voted.

A negative vote could be cast by crossing out the names of the candidate or candidates a voter wished to reject. Moreover, all voters had to pass through the voting booth, even if they wished to support the prospective deputy in a single-candidate election. This was an important change from previous Soviet electoral practice, whereby voters were not obliged to enter the voting booth at all. The 1989 all-union elections were, in fact, the first in Soviet history to combine universal adult suffrage with secrecy of the ballot and the competitive principle in at least a majority of seats.

The electoral process varied widely from one part of the country to another and had many imperfections. The party apparatus was, for example, much more successful in Soviet Central Asia than in the major European cities in getting its favoured candidates elected. But elsewhere the attempt of party officials to foist themselves or their nominees on the electorate provoked, in many cases, an effective backlash. Thus, with the entire Moscow party apparatus opposed to the election of the maverick populist Boris Yel'tsin and putting its resources behind his factory manager opponent, Yel'tsin won a landslide victory with approximately 90 per cent of the votes in a constituency comprising the entire city of Moscow. In fact, the three major Soviet cities – Moscow, Leningrad and Kiev – all returned deputies who were chosen by the electorate in defiance of their city party bureaucracies. In Moscow, they included not only Roy Medvedev but also the radically reformist director of the Moscow Historical-Archival Institute, Yuri Afanas'ev, who was elected in a working-class district near Moscow where the overt hostility to him of the local party machine evidently counted in his favour with the electorate. In Moscow, Leningrad and Kiev there was an easily detectable 'anti-apparatus' vote, of which the most highly placed victim was Yuri Solov'ev, the first secretary of the Leningrad regional party organization and a candidate member of the Politburo.

Not surprisingly, the election results (even though they included a comfortable majority of successful candidates who could be relied on to go along with the top party leadership at the Congress of People's Deputies) sent shock waves of alarm and anger through the party apparatus. At a Central Committee plenary session held in late April 1989, many of the regional party secretaries who spoke blamed shortages, the mass media, insufficient party unity, and the central party leadership for their lack of electoral success. The first secretary of the Krasnodar regional party committee, Ivan Polozkov, said it was getting harder to answer people's questions as to why there was no butter, children's shoes, prams or bicycles for sale. He added sarcastically: 'They listen, but they do not understand very well. And as for the absence of soap, they do not wish even to listen.'[30] Aleksandr Mel'nikov, a former Central Committee department head and now a regional party secretary, complained that ordinary people had been led astray by 'a massive onslaught from the mass media'.[31]

The defeated Leningrad party chief, Yuri Solov'ev, noted that 'not one of the six leaders of the party and soviet in Leningrad and its region assembled the necessary number of votes'.[32] This, as he pointed out, was not unique to Leningrad, and the only pattern he detected in such votes against the local official establishments was that they had been cast in 'major industrial, scientific and cultural centres'.[33] That was hardly an encouraging postmortem for the Central Committee.

The 750 deputies who were chosen by public organizations – ranging in size and political weight from the Communist Party itself to the Soviet Culture Foundation and the Soviet Peace Foundation, and including such important bodies as the Academy of Sciences, the Komsomol, and the creative unions (writers, artists and so on) – produced a still clearer majority of people who could be relied upon not to rock the boat too much.[34]

At the same time, though, these organizations provided a minority of deputies who were among the most radical people to attend the inaugural session of the Congress of People's Deputies. This was especially true of the Academy of Sciences, whose Presidium initially produced a list of only twenty-three candidates, out of which the membership was to choose twenty representatives – and left off the list some of the country's most talented and politically outspoken scientists and scholars, including Academician Andrei Sakharov, who had been nominated by some sixty scientific institutes. In response, the Academy voters struck out fifteen of the names presented to them, giving the required 50 per cent support to only eight of the candidates. These results necessitated a second round of voting, this time for a list that included the names of some of the Soviet Union's most prominent reformers (the Presidium had learned its lesson). In the end, practically every deputy elected from the Academy was close to the liberal or radical reformist end of the Soviet political spectrum. In the second round, Sakharov was elected comfortably and one of the boldest of economic reformers, Nikolai Shmelev, topped the poll.[35]

The move from elections without choice, in which the social composition as well as the political conformity of the deputies could be determined in advance, to competitive elections and opportunities for citizens to nominate candidates from below (though still within the framework of a one-party system) had a number of consequences probably unintended by the top party leadership. One was that in certain republics, especially the Baltic ones, only those candidates – whether party or non-party – who were prepared to take a strongly national line and defend the interests of the titular nationality of their republic could rely upon being elected. Another was the radical shift in the occupational and class composition of the Congress of People's Deputies as compared with that of its predecessor, the unreformed Supreme Soviet 'elected' in 1984. The proportion of industrial and farm workers, for example, went down from 49.5 to 23.1 per cent. The representation of employees with higher education and of intellectuals went up. Heads of higher educational institutions, who were entirely unrepresented in the 1984 Supreme Soviet, made up 4.1 per cent (eighty-three deputies) of the 1989 Congress of People's Deputies. The representation of senior KGB officials went down between 1984 and 1989 from 1.1 per cent to 0.5 per cent, while entirely new categories of occupation to be represented in the list of deputies included those of scientific workers (sixty-one deputies: 3 per cent), journalists (twenty-eight deputies: 1.4 per cent), advocates (two deputies: 0.1 per cent) and clergymen (five deputies: 0.2 per cent).[36]

In practice, these changes meant a strengthened representation of highly articulate deputies; not surprisingly, though, the decline in worker representation was strongly attacked by opponents of reform. The growing importance of initiative from below, as opposed to control from above, also led to a sharp fall in the proportion of women deputies as compared with the old Supreme

Soviet. This may be a backhanded tribute to the vastly greater significance of the new legislature, given the generally weak position of women in Soviet political life; there has for many years been an inverse relationship between the power of an institution in the Soviet political system and the percentage of women to be found in that body.

Taking the elections as a whole, they must be seen as a remarkable landmark in the process of the democratization of the Soviet political system. The fact that they were still held within the framework of a one-party system did not, as many Soviet citizens feared, mean that there was nothing to choose between one candidate and another in terms of their policies and principles. The political reality that the Soviet Communist Party itself (a 20 million-strong body comprising approximately 10 per cent of adult citizens) is a coalition of very diverse viewpoints and interests became clearer than ever. In a number of the major cities, there was a lively clash of opinions in the course of the election campaign. This was notwithstanding the fact that 85.3 per cent of candidates nominated and 87.6 per cent of those actually elected to the Congress of People's Deputies were party members.[37] Short of a 'counter-revolutionary' reversal of the entire process of perestroika, it is difficult to see any return to the sham elections of the past. In view of the evident dissatisfaction of many of the electorates presented with only a single candidate in the 1989 elections, it is much more likely that movement will be in the direction of electoral choice in *all* constituencies.

One issue that remained only partly resolved in 1989 was whether party first secretaries who were defeated in the elections for the Congress of People's Deputies should resign their party office (or be forced to resign by their party committee). In July Gorbachev went to Leningrad to preside over the removal from the Leningrad regional party secretaryship of Solov'ev, and there have been signs that he regards this as the most appropriate response to a party leader's electorate defeat. The line taken by the top party leadership as a whole has been that a case-by-case approach to this question should be adopted by the various party committees concerned. It would have been even more difficult for first secretaries at the republican, regional, city and district level to keep their party posts if they were defeated in elections to soviets at those levels (as distinct from the all-union Congress of People's Deputies). This is no doubt one reason (though the need to improve the electoral law is given as the main one) why the Central Committee decided to postpone local elections from late 1989 to the spring of 1990, though when that decision was contested in some republics, leeway for inter-republican variation on the electoral timetable was granted.

Given that the breakthrough towards heterodox voting has already been made, and given the decline in the authority of the party apparatus that was acknowledged both at the April 1989 plenary session of the Central Committee and at the Congress of People's Deputies, defeat for many local party bosses in the elections for local soviets became a real possibility. As a consequence many party secretaries decided not even to stand in the local elections, thus opening up for the first time the possibility of a division rather than fusion of power at the local level. Hitherto the soviets at all levels have been poor relations to the dominant party organization, but it cannot be taken for granted that this will be the case in the future.

This electoral dilemma should be seen in a broader context. A revitalized and politicized Soviet society – no longer 'the most silent majority in the world'[38] – poses entirely new challenges to the party. This has been recognized by Gorbachev. In his closing address to the First Congress of People's Deputies in June 1989, he contended that Soviet society still needed a vanguard party, but added that if it is going to be such a vanguard, then 'the party must reconstruct itself faster than society'.[39]

The New Legislature

Just one of the many unique features of the First Congress of People's Deputies was that no one (not even Gorbachev) knew how long it was going to last. As originally conceived, it appeared that the main task of the 2,250 deputies was to elect the inner body, the bicameral 542-member Supreme Soviet. It is the Supreme Soviet that is to be the more or less permanently functioning part of parliament, meeting for more than half of the year, unlike the old Supreme Soviet, which met for only a few days annually. But the First Congress of People's Deputies itself was in session for far longer than was the pattern with the unreformed Supreme Soviet; it began its deliberations on 25 May, and ended them on 9 June 1989. If the elections that brought the deputies to the Palace of Congresses in Moscow were a milestone on the road to a form of democracy in the Soviet Union, the Congress itself broke new frontiers in public freedom of speech. And it was quite a public. What made the impassioned debate and the breaking of one taboo after another of far greater political consequence than would otherwise have been the case was the live broadcasting on Soviet television and radio of the Congress proceedings. The speeches were heard by an estimated audience of between 90 and 100 million people.[40] Some of the addresses, if they had been distributed even in ninety or 100 copies six years ago, would undoubtedly have earned their authors a spell in a labour camp.

The atmosphere at the First Congress of People's Deputies was characterized by one Soviet commentator, Vitaly Tretyakov, as 'glasnost galore'. Even more important, the Congress had, in Tretyakov's words, 'reduced to a minimum the distance between the canonized glasnost and freedom of speech'.[41] And this was, said the same author, a 'selfless glasnost' because 'as is very well known, the legal and political guarantees of any glasnost are pretty weak in our country still'.[42]

One speaker Tretyakov probably had in mind was Yuri Vlasov, a writer and former champion weightlifter who devoted most of his speech (carried, like the others, live on Soviet television and radio) to an attack on the KGB. Vlasov described that organization as 'not a service, but a real underground empire' that was 'subordinate only to the apparatus' and not 'under the control of the people'. He called for the KGB to be moved out of its Dzerzhinsky Square headquarters in central Moscow to 'a modest building in the suburbs' and insisted that it must be held accountable for its activities to the new Supreme Soviet.[43] Vlasov's speech, *Izvestiya* noted, was greeted with 'prolonged applause'.[44]

One of the most important outcomes of the First Congress of People's Deputies and of the initial sessions of the new Supreme Soviet was the setting up of a whole series of commissions (both permanent and *ad hoc*) and committees, which include a new permanent committee of the Supreme Soviet on defence and state security.[45] There are already signs that at least a minority of deputies on that committee and in the Supreme Soviet as a whole are prepared to ask awkward questions and to demand that steps be taken towards making the defence establishment and the state security organs answerable to the legislature. Previously, the military and the KGB were politically accountable only to the party leadership, but if the Congress of People's Deputies and the Supreme Soviet continue as they have begun, these bodies may be subjected to a more detailed scrutiny than that to which they have become accustomed.

The Committee on Defence and State Security is just one of fifteen committees set up by the Supreme Soviet as a whole. In addition, each of the two chambers of the Supreme Soviet (the Soviet of the Union and the Soviet of Nationalities) has set up standing commissions of its own. Thus, for example, the Soviet of

Nationalities established a commission on national policy and inter-ethnic relations within the Soviet Union.[46] The Congress of People's Deputies, in response to pressure from many of the deputies who addressed it, also set up commissions of its own to investigate particularly sensitive issues. These included a commission 'to investigate the circumstances connected with events in Tbilisi on 9 April 1989'[47] (the killing and wounding of a number of Georgian demonstrators by soldiers, an event that outraged public opinion in Georgia and became a major bone of contention at the Congress, with deputies from the Baltic republics and Moscow giving support to their Georgian colleagues), and a commission to make a 'political and legal appraisal of the Soviet–German non-aggression pact of 1939'.[48] The latter commission was formed after deputies from the three Baltic republics had insistently brought up the issue of a secret protocol to the Molotov–Ribbentrop Pact sanctioning the forcible incorporation of Estonia, Latvia and Lithuania into the Soviet Union.

It is noteworthy that the composition of the various commissions was the subject of discussion both in front of the cameras and behind the scenes, and that enough deputies of independent mind and, in some cases, of radically libertarian views were included to give the commissions authority in the eyes of the aggrieved parties. Aleksandr Yakovlev (himself very much on the 'new-thinking' wing of the Politburo) was named chairman of the twenty-six-member commission on the Soviet–German pact. The Baltic republics themselves were strongly represented on the commission, which included also such liberal or radical non-Balts as the historian, Yuri Afanas'ev; the Armenian sociologist Lyudmila Arutyunyan; and the editor of *Ogonek*, Vitaly Korotich. Among the other members were the writer Chingiz Aitmatov; the director of the Institute of the USA and Canada, Georgy Arbatov; and the head of the International Department of the party Central Committee, Valentin Falin.[49]

A particularly important body created by the Congress of People's Deputies towards the end of its deliberations was the Constitutional Commission chaired by Gorbachev. It has been decided that the Soviet Union needs a substantially rewritten constitution to replace the current one, which was adopted in 1977 under Brezhnev, and the main task of the Constitutional Commission is to draft that new fundamental law.[50] The plan is to produce quite quickly some amendments to the existing constitution and then, some time after the Twenty-eighth Party Congress, to undertake the writing of a completely new constitution to replace the 1977

Brezhnev one. This provides opportunities to develop further the reform of the Soviet political system and to institutionalize and solidify some of the changes for the better – such as the great strides towards freedom of expression – that have already manifested themselves, but which are still excessively dependent on the enlightened intervention or benign non-intervention of Gorbachev and the reform wing of the party leadership.

Although *radical* reformers do not – and that is hardly surprising – constitute a majority of members, the Constitutional Commission includes enough people who both fit that description and possess intellectual weight for them to exercise a more than proportionate influence on the elaboration of a new constitution. The most remarkable name on the list, in the context of recent Soviet history, was that of the late Andrei Sakharov. Such bold reformers as Oleg Bogomolov, Gavril Popov and Tat'yana Zaslavskaya are also members of the commission, as is the radicalized and unpredictable Boris Yel'tsin. Two members likely to be important are Fedor Burlatsky and Georgy Shakhnazarov. Both of them have long records as significant within-system reformers whose whole lives have, in a sense, been a preparation for the opportunities open to them in the era of perestroika. Burlatsky – now a member of the Supreme Soviet as well as political commentator for the Writers' Union newspaper, *Literaturnaya gazeta* – has never been short of ideas for political reform, and Shakhnazarov – one of Gorbachev's full-time aides and, therefore, especially well-placed to make an impact on the content of the new constitution – has, like Burlatsky, been in the forefront of 'new thinking' on both foreign and domestic policy.

The tone of the Congress of People's Deputies was set on the first day, shortly after Gorbachev was proposed as chairman of the Supreme Soviet (the new and more powerful state presidency). One of the very first speakers to be called to the rostrum by Gorbachev was Sakharov, who protested against the fact that only Gorbachev was being nominated for the presidency and argued for the necessity of a competitive election. Sakharov said that he did 'not see anyone else who could lead our country', but he stressed that his support for Gorbachev was 'of a conditional nature'.[51] Though many conservative voices were heard as well at the Congress of People's Deputies, and the speeches embraced a very wide spectrum of political opinion, the radicals from Moscow (who were soon being dubbed the 'Moscow group' or even the 'Moscow faction'), the Baltic republics and elsewhere were given a greater share of time to speak than their minority representation within the total body of deputies strictly merited. This was partly a tribute to their determination and articulateness, but it could not have happened without Gorbachev's guidance and support and his uphill struggle to create a spirit of tolerance in an atmosphere that was often highly charged.

In the event, Gorbachev did have a challenger in the election for the presidency – a self-proposed, previously unknown but nevertheless impressive 46-year-old engineer/designer from the Leningrad region, Aleksandr Obolensky. A non-party member, Obolensky attacked the privileges attached to the *nomenklatura*, which, he said, corrupted its beneficiaries by giving them a material interest in the maintenance of the existing system and also provided a convenient level for controlling them.[52] Obolensky, who, like Sakharov, was concerned to establish a precedent of competition for all high political offices, was able to make his case at length, but in a vote as to whether his name should appear on the ballot, a majority of deputies – 1,415 – voted against, though a very sizable minority – 689 (there were 33 abstentions) – voted in favour. In the secret ballot for or against Gorbachev which followed, the general secretary was supported for the presidency by 95.6 per cent of those who voted, with 87 votes cast against him.[53]

One of the most controversial, as well as important, parts of the work of the Congress of People's Deputies was its election of the Supreme Soviet. After the election had taken place, Yuri Afanas'ev made a combative speech in which he accused the deputies of having chosen an inner body that was no better than the Supreme Soviet of Stalin's and Brezhnev's time.[54] That was a considerable exaggeration. Many of the republics and regions put forward no more candidates than was their entitlement for the Soviet of the Union and the Soviet of Nationalities, and so the conservative majority in the Congress of People's Deputies had no choice but to endorse them. This ensured that a significant minority of outspoken critics – from, for example, the Baltic republics, Georgia and Armenia – made their way into the Supreme Soviet. The cause of the dissatisfaction of Afanas'ev and that of other radicals was the fate of the Moscow slate of candidates. Endorsing the principle of competitive elections, the Moscow group of deputies put up fifty-five candidates for its allotted twenty-nine places in the Soviet of the Union and twelve candidates for eleven places in the Soviet of Nationalities. This gave the regional party secretaries and their like-minded colleagues who formed a majority in the Congress an opportunity to take their revenge on the most outspoken Moscow intellectuals and cross out the names of Popov, Stankevich, Zaslavskaya and others from the list. Even so, Roy Medvedev and Fedor Burlatsky were among the twenty-nine from Moscow who made their way into the Soviet of the Union.

The cause of greatest outrage was Boris Yel'tsin's finishing in the twelfth place in the election for the Soviet of Nationalities, so that he became the *only* Moscow nominee for that body to fail to be elected, notwithstanding the fact that he had been supported in the elections to the Congress of People's Deputies by more Muscovites than anyone else. For Gorbachev and the reformers within the leadership, this was an embarrassment, even though Yel'tsin has become one of their critics (while saving his harshest remarks for Egor Ligachev). When another elected deputy resigned to make way for Yel'tsin, Gorbachev lost little time in guiding the congress to accept that proposal.[55] Yel'tsin is already a thorn in the flesh of the leadership from within the Supreme Soviet, but he would be of even more danger to them – and, in particular, to the authority of the new legislature – if he were excluded from that body, given the level of popular support he commands. It may well be that helping to make the Supreme Soviet a critic of the executive and holding ministers and party leaders to account will be the most useful function Yel'tsin can perform. Every parliament needs its Yel'tsins, whereas it is highly unlikely that he could lead the Communist Party or head the Soviet state with the imagination and skill of a Gorbachev.

Intra-party Change

The Communist Party is undergoing significant change as a result of the reform of its internal structure, the personnel changes that have reduced the decision-making power of conservative communists, and the creation of new state institutions. In particular, the introduction of competitive elections and the formation of a new legislative assembly have helped to bring to life dormant political forces within the Soviet Union and compelled the party to become more responsive to that society as a whole, if it is to retain authority and, perhaps, even its power.

In a memorandum to the Politburo dated 24 August 1988 (but published in a new Soviet journal only in 1989),[56] Gorbachev put forward concrete proposals for the restructuring of the Central Committee apparatus. By authorizing its subsequent publication, he revealed publicly for the first time the precise size of that body immediately prior to its reorganization, which was implemented in October. 'Today', Gorbachev wrote in the memorandum, 'the apparatus of the Central Committee numbers 1,940 responsible

workers and 1,275 technical staff.'[57] Western estimates of the
number of officials working in the Central Committee apparatus
have generally varied between 1,000 and 1,500, whereas the actual
figure was close to 2,000, excluding support staff. By the beginning
of 1989, the numbers were closer to what Western observers had
imagined they were before. Gorbachev was aiming at a 50 per cent
cut in the size of the central apparatus, and by the end of 1988
approximately 40 per cent of Central Committee officials had
moved either into retirement or to other posts.

The most important feature of this party restructuring was the
reduction of the number of Central Committee departments from
twenty to nine[58] and the creation of six new Central Committee
commissions, the latter giving senior party members outside the
apparatus a greater opportunity to exercise influence on policy. The
commissions, approved at the Central Committee plenary session at
the end of September 1988, concern party construction and cadres
policy (chaired by Georgy Razumovsky), ideology (headed by
Vadim Medvedev), social and economic policy (chaired by Nikolai
Slyun'kov), agriculture (headed by Egor Ligachev), international
policy (chaired by Aleksandr Yakovlev) and legal policy (chaired
initially by Viktor Chebrikov).[59] Three of the six commission chairmen – Razumovsky, Yakovlev and Medvedev – were close to Gorbachev (especially the first two) and could be regarded as serious
reformers. Ligachev and Chebrikov were on the more conservative
wing of the Politburo, while Slyun'kov stood somewhere in
between. Taken in conjunction with the leadership changes at the
same September plenum of the Central Committee – the retirement
of Andrei Gromyko and Mikhail Solomentsev from full membership of the Politburo, and the removal of three candidate members
(Vladimir Dolgikh, Petr Demichev and Anatoly Dobrynin, of
whom the first two were far from enthusiastic about the Soviet
Union's dramatic turn towards reform), the creation of the new
commissions represented a considerable strengthening of Gorbachev's personal position and of the commitment to perestroika within
the leadership.[60]

It involved, however, some short-term compromises on Gorbachev's part. The price he paid for moving Chebrikov out of the
chairmanship of the KGB was, in effect, to promote him, for
Chebrikov became a secretary of the Central Committee alongside
the full membership of the Politburo he already enjoyed. Moreover,
his twenty-two years in a senior position in the KGB did not make
him the most obvious person to head a commission with responsibility for advancing the cause of the state based on the rule of law.

Similarly, by cutting back on Ligachev's supervisory responsibilities within the Secretariat – which had previously included agriculture, but also much more – and confining him to agriculture, Gorbachev forced Ligachev to concentrate his attention on an area crucial to the success of reform, and one that might have benefited from being in the hands of someone less suspicious of marketization. Given, however, Gorbachev's knowledge and personal interest in agriculture and his degree of commitment to the introduction of a leasehold system granting greater autonomy to groups of farmers (including family groups), Ligachev's new post gave him fewer possibilities to apply a brake to the process of reform than he had previously enjoyed.

Gorbachev's skill and determination in using both his authority and power to the full to advance the cause of reform were shown again in April 1989 when the first Central Committee plenum after the elections for the Congress of People's Deputies took place. While many of the current members of the Central Committee took the opportunity to voice their discontent about the new insecurity of their positions generated by the elections and the changed political climate, the plenum accepted the resignation of seventy-four full members of the Central Committee, twenty-four candidate members and twelve members of the Central Auditing Commission.[61] At the same time, it promoted twenty-four candidate members of the Central Committee to full membership. Taking into account both the resignations and the promotions, the number of voting Central Committee members was reduced from 303 to 251.[62]

This was an unprecedented degree of turnover to occur between party congresses. Since it is only at these congresses, normally held every five years, that regular elections for the Central Committee take place, Gorbachev's chances of achieving a Central Committee more atuned to the spirit of the time (that of 1989 rather than 1986, when the present Central Committee was elected) seemed slim. But by *persuading* those Central Committee members who had lost the jobs that justified their membership in that body in the first place (a fact that itself made them a disgruntled and potentially dangerous group within the Central Committee) that they should resign in April rather than wait to be removed at the next regular elections (at the end of the Twenty-eighth Party Congress), he was able at a stroke to reduce substantially the conservative deadweight within that important party institution.[63]

As general secretary, Gorbachev has played a major role in the radicalization of the political reform agenda, but at every stage he has had to carry his Politburo colleagues with him. He began as the most radical member of the Politburo he inherited and, quite apart from the extent to which some of his own views have developed, could not have proposed to that body in 1985 some of the things he advocated in 1987, 1988 and 1989. With the emergence of glasnost, competitive elections and a legislature in which radicals have been given a forum for public protest, Gorbachev and the progress of perestroika now have liberal as well as conservative critics. While in some ways this makes life even tougher for the Soviet leader, on balance it is to his political advantage. He can play the role of a centrist, albeit one clearly leaning to the liberal side of centre, while taking on board more of the policies of the liberal critics than of their conservative counterparts. The conservatives, in any event, suffer from their lack of a viable alternative policy or programme. There are those who would wish to turn the clock back only fifteen years and others who would be happier turning it back forty years, but none of them has a vision remotely relevant to the twenty-first century. Gorbachev, in contrast, has in his mind's eye a Soviet Union that in the year 2000 will be far more democratic and markedly more efficient economically than ever before. His daunting task is getting from here to there, for the problems of the transition period are horrendously difficult.

The Challenge Ahead

The transition to a political system that is qualitatively different from the one that has prevailed in the Soviet Union for so long is well under way. It has made remarkable progress within the space of four years. However, the transition from a centrally administered command economy to one in which market forces play a major role has brought the Soviet Union still closer to economic crisis than did the unreformed economic system that Gorbachev inherited. Though some mistakes in economic strategy have been made, the present alarming situation is in no small measure due, as Philip Hanson shows in Chapter 5, to the intrinsic difficulties of moving from one type of economic system to another without serious dislocation. The problems of the Soviet leadership have been exacerbated by the drop in the country's foreign earnings as a result of the fall in oil prices, as well as by expensive man-made and natural disasters, including the Chernobyl nuclear accident in 1986 and the Armenian earthquake in 1988.

Money incomes have risen much faster than the supply of goods, so that the shortages of foodstuffs and consumer goods were worse in 1989 than they were in 1985. A major contribution to a dangerously high budget deficit has been made by the cutbacks introduced early in the Gorbachev era in the manufacture of vodka, sales of which in the past have enabled the Soviet state to come much closer to balancing the budget.

Whereas a halfway house of political reform has had mainly beneficial results – raising levels of political consciousness, introducing political accountability, opening up new opportunities for meaningful popular participation in the political process, and pushing back the limits on freedom of expression and debate – a halfway house of economic reform has made things worse. The old economic institutions have lost some of their powers and much of their authority, but the intermediate institutions of a market-oriented system – such as commercial banks and wholesale trading operations – do not yet exist.

The observer of the Soviet scene can quickly move from optimism to pessimism simply by focusing on the economy rather than the polity. Yet there is ultimately, of course, a strong interlinkage between political and economic reform. Some organizations, such as certain departments of the party Central Committee and many of the ministries, are simultaneously important political and economic institutions. They have, moreover, become an arena of recent change. In the reorganization of the Central Committee apparatus which took place in October 1988, the largest single category of department to be abolished was that of the branch economic departments. In the process of bringing the total number of departments down from twenty to nine, such departments as those responsible for heavy industry and energy, machine-building, chemical industry, military industry, and light industry and consumer goods were abolished completely.[64] The sole branch economic department existing today at the Central Committee level is the Agriculture Department. The only other economic department of any description, the Social and Economic Department, has more general overseeing responsibilities.[65] So long as there were numerous Central Committee branch economic departments, whose structure corresponded broadly to that of Gosplan (the State Planning Committee), the leadership's protestations that it wished to withdraw the party from detailed economic tutelage rang hollow. The abolition of departments whose *raison d'être* was to supervise economic ministries and to intervene in economic decision-making is evidence of a new degree of seriousness of that intent.

In June 1989, Nikolai Ryzhkov, after being nominated by Gorbachev to continue in office as chairman of the Council of Ministers and being confirmed in that post by the Congress of People's Deputies, introduced the most drastic restructuring of the ministerial system to have been undertaken in the era of perestroika. He announced a reduction in the number of branch industrial ministries from fifty to thirty-two and, in answer to a deputy of the Supreme Soviet's question about what this would mean in terms of reduction in the size of the administrative apparatus, Ryzhkov said that ministerial staffs should be cut by at least 30 per cent.[66] Moreover, the personnel changes among the ministers themselves were dramatic. As Ryzhkov put it to the Supreme Soviet: 'I want to inform you that, of the government which was formed in 1984 and numbered 100 people without counting the chairmen of the union republican council of ministers . . . only ten people remain in the composition which is being proposed today.'[67] More than half of the members of the Council of Ministers holding office at the beginning of June 1989 were relieved of their offices, and there was a considerable infusion of new blood. The changes were even greater than Ryzhkov intended, for in a remarkable flexing of its new political muscle, the Supreme Soviet rejected a number of his nominees.

A potentially important appointment was that of one of the Soviet Union's leading academic economists, Leonid Abalkin, hitherto the director of the Institute of Economics of the Academy of Sciences, to head a new state commission for economic reform with the rank of deputy chairman of the Council of Ministers. One of the difficulties with the introduction of Soviet economic reform has been the lack of an overseer of the reforms with a conceptual grasp of what is required and responsibility for avoiding contradictions and ambiguities. The task is greater than Gorbachev or Ryzhkov – with their multifarious other duties – are able to perform, and the appointment of Abalkin and the creation of the new state commission constitute grounds for hope that the strategy for economic reform will acquire greater coherence.

How long the Soviet population will give credence to a leadership that does not produce concrete economic results remains a moot point. The relevance of political reform in this context is that it provides institutional forums for pressure, criticism and debate, and enough freedom of information and expression to make it hard for conservative communists to sustain the argument that the problem could be solved by returning to the status quo ante. Gorbachev's consolidation of his power at the top of the party and state hierarchy, together with the process of institutional change, have probably secured for the reformers in the Soviet leadership several more years in which to make some improvements in living standards to accompany and reinforce political progress. There are many people, both in the Soviet Union and the West, who would regard that view as too optimistic, and hold that instant improvement is required if a counter-reformation is to be avoided.[68] Since instant enhancement of living standards is impossible, that is a counsel of despair. It underestimates the primacy of politics in the Soviet system (even though developments in the 1980s have been described as 'the revenge of the base on the superstructure') and the new institutions and political climate that would make a Kremlin coup of the kind that overthrew Nikita Khrushchev in October 1964 much more difficult to implement.

Clearly, of course, there exist powerful people who feel that their institutional and individual interests have been undermined. As the April plenum of the Central Committee made clear, such people are to be found in the party apparatus. It is quite evident that they must also exist in the ministerial apparatus, as well as in the military and the KGB, though opinion in these bodies is divided. That there is considerable diversity of view even within the army emerged from the line taken by different military candidates in the 1989 elections for the Congress of People's Deputies.

The ethnic unrest in the contemporary Soviet Union cannot go unmentioned. An unintended consequence of perestroika but, at a more profound level, a product of decades of pre-perestroika insensitivity to national feelings and aspirations, ethnic unrest continues, along with the critical economic situation (which in the summer of 1989 provoked miners' strikes in Siberia and the Ukraine), to be the main danger to the further progress of reform and one of the potential justifications that might be offered for intervention by a potential 'national saviour' offering to restore 'order'. In reality, strong-arm tactics would, of course, be a disaster. The present path, characterized by the Soviet leadership's increasing responsiveness to national grievances and its apparent determination to move towards a fully fledged federalism, offers the best hope of dealing with an almost intractable 'national question'. Even a genuine federalism, however, would by no means solve all the problems, for some of the most bitter conflicts are not between the centre and periphery but between one neighbouring republic and another (above all, the dispute between Armenians and Azeris over Nagorno-Karabakh) or between the titular nationality of a republic and a minority ethnic group within its boundaries (as the case of the Uzbek assault on the Meskhetians in the summer of 1989 and the tensions and sporadic violence between the Georgians and the Abkhaz people starkly illustrate). It is clear that there is a legitimate role for the army or police in protecting one national group from another – especially the minority from the majority in a number of areas – but that any attempt to 'solve' the national question by means of coercion would be doomed to failure.

A combination of severe economic and nationality problems, together with a reduction in the budget of the military and – as must follow if political reform continues – of the KGB, could provoke individuals in those organizations to take action against the reformist leadership. It may be worth noting the high public profile that has been sought by General Boris Gromov, the former commander of the Soviet armed forces in Afghanistan. Gromov vigorously defended the Soviet military and its role in Afghanistan in his speech at the nineteenth party conference in 1988,[69] and later ostentatiously announced that he would be the last Soviet soldier to leave Afghanistan. He was subsequently duly filmed crossing the border. Having been elected to the Congress of People's Deputies, he withdrew his candidacy for the Supreme Soviet, since election to that body would have forced him to relinquish his military command, and he deemed it 'inexpedient' to leave his post as commander of the Kiev Military District.[70]

However, the traditionally rather effective Soviet political control over the military has acquired new bases of support. A combination of economic hardship and the release of far more information than hitherto about the size of the military burden on the Soviet economy has, according to public opinion polls, led a majority of Soviet citizens to support reductions in military expenditure equal to, or even greater than, the 14 per cent announced by Gorbachev at the First Congress of People's Deputies.[71] Although the publication of such poll results may be unwelcome to the military, they both reveal and reinforce popular support for the Gorbachev leadership's 'new thinking' on foreign and defence policy. Public opinion constraints may not totally rule out an intervention at some point against democratization and the new thinking by an alliance of conservative communists and the military (as has happened in China), but it is not the most probable outcome of the political struggle in the Soviet Union. With the balance of power and influence in the higher echelons of the party moving in favour of the reformers, and with the development of electoral and legislative checks on the holders of executive power, it has become much more difficult to put this entire process into reverse.

The communist world as a whole is in a period of unprecedented volatility. The Chinese gerontocracy took fright in 1989 at the very prospect of political dialogue with its own citizenry, a dialogue which is already an encouraging reality in the Soviet Union. Hungary and Poland have already carried political change significantly beyond the stage reached by the Dubcek leadership in Czechoslovakia in 1968, which was at that time sufficient to provoke Soviet military intervention. (The point is rapidly approaching when it will no longer be meaningful to regard Hungary and Poland as communist systems and the changes which began in Czechoslovakia in November 1989 are also likely to be far-reaching.) But the most important change – for better or worse – in terms of its global impact is that occurring in the Soviet Union. The politics and economics of the transition period are imposing almost intolerable burdens on and challenges to Gorbachev and committed Soviet reformers. In the political sphere, these reformers have already changed more than even the optimists predicted four years ago, and the sceptics, who doubted the seriousness of their intentions, have been confounded. If the Soviet reformers succeed, it will be as great a victory in peace as the Soviet Union almost half a century ago attained in war. And unlike the latter victory – with its postwar imposition of a Stalinist order on Eastern Europe – it will be possible to welcome it in retrospect as much as the Soviet contribution to the defeat of Nazism was welcomed at the time.

Notes

* In its earliest version, this chapter was presented as a paper to the European–Japanese symposium on *perestroika* at Chatham House in December 1988. It was published as a much fuller article in *World Policy Journal*, 6 (3) (Summer 1989), with whose permission the present abbreviated but updated version appears.

1. I have, from the outset of Mikhail Gorbachev's general secretaryship, suggested that he was a reformer by disposition and that he would be an agent of significant change. See, for example, my articles 'Gorbachev: new man in the Kremlin', *Problems of Communism*, 34 (3) (May–June 1985); and 'Can Gorbachev make a difference?' *Detente*, 3 (May 1985). By 1987, change – especially in the political climate and reform agenda – was proceeding faster than *anyone* had foretold, though it has gone still further in the two years since the June Central Committee plenum of that year. Yet in 1987 there was still a blinkered inability on the part of many observers to understand what was happening in the Soviet Union. A review article of mine on Soviet politics, 'Change and challenge', published in the *Times Literary Supplement* (27 March 1987) that should, with the benefit of hindsight, have been criticized for its excess of caution, was vehemently attacked for its excessive optimism in a series of readers' letters published between 15 May and 10 July. One of the letter-writers (and by no means the most virulent), Françoise Thom, was the co-author with Alain Besançon of a rather extreme contribution to a symposium entitled 'What's Happening in Moscow?' published in *The National Interest*, 8 (Summer 1987). The symposium embraced a wide spectrum of views, including my own, but in their almost total misunderstanding of Soviet developments, Besançon and Thom

were in a class apart. Gorbachev's policy, these authors tell us, 'consists of an all-out attack on civil society' (p. 27) and the Soviet Union remains 'a uniform, atomized and voiceless society' (p. 27). Such a view could scarcely survive the reading of even a single chapter of Alec Nove's highly illuminating recent book, *Glasnost in Action: Cultural Renaissance in Russia* (London: Unwin Hyman, 1989).

2. In the above-mentioned symposium in *The National Interest*, Peter Reddaway did not make the mistake of thinking that Soviet change was merely cosmetic, but he was pessimistic about the prospects for Gorbachev and glasnost:

> If Gorbachev is trying to square the circle by embarking on the democratization of the Soviet system, as he shows every sign of doing, then, in my view, he is unlikely to remain in power for many more years. Sooner or later, the *nomenklatura* will surely remove him. And in that case glasnost would be bound to suffer in the inevitable conservative reaction. (1987: 76)

3. I have discussed Gorbachev's consolidation of his power at some length in my contribution to A. Brown (ed.), *Political Leadership in the Soviet Union* (London: Macmillan, 1989). See also S. Bialer (ed.), *Politics, Society and Nationality Inside Gorbachev's Russia* (Boulder, CO: Westview Press, 1989), especially Bialer's final chapter; the symposium, 'Gorbachev and Gorbachevism' in *The Journal of Communist Studies*, 4 (4) (Dec. 1988), especially the contributions of R. J. Hill, A. Pravda and S. White; and P. Cockburn, 'Gorbachev and Soviet conservatism', *World Policy Journal*, 6 (1) (Winter 1988–9).

4. The most spectacular example of this trend is the weekly *Ogonek* which, since Vitaly Korotich became its editor in 1986, has increased its circulation from a few hundred thousand to almost 3½ million. The monthly journal *Znamya*, now under the editorial direction of Georgy Baklanov and Vladimir Lakshin, had a circulation of 980,000 copies in 1989 as compared with 175,000 in 1985; and *Novyi Mir* in 1989 had a print-run of 1,573,000 copies monthly as compared with approximately 496,000 as recently as late 1987. Its announcement that it would serialize George Orwell's *Nineteen Eighty-Four* in 1989 – which it has, indeed, now published – was one stimulus to the substantial rise in the number of subscriptions taken out for that year.

5. A. Brown, 'Soviet political developments and prospects', *World Policy Journal*, 4 (1) (Winter 1986–7).

6. *Pravda*, 26 April 1989: 1.

7. T. Ball, J. Farr and R. L. Hanson (eds), *Political Innovation and Conceptual Change* (Cambridge: Cambridge University Press, 1989), p. x.

8. Foreword by E. A. Ambartsumov to A. N. Yakovlev et al., *Soviet Society: Philosophy and Development* (Moscow: Progress, 1988), p. 6.

9. Ibid., p. 7.

10. See, for instance, V. Medvedev in *Pravda*, 5 Oct. 1988: 4; Georgy Shakhnazarov, *Pravda*, 26 Sept. 1988: 6; the press conference given by O. Bogomolov, reported in BBC, *Summary of World Broadcasts*, SU/D0381 C2/3–C2/4, 10 Feb. 1989; and E. A. Ambartsumov in A. N. Yakovlev et al., *Soviet Society*, (fn. 8), p. 9.

11. On a study visit to China in September 1988, I encountered widespread support among Chinese social scientists, including those with expert knowledge of the Soviet Union, for the political reform process under way and for the great expansion in cultural freedom and of glasnost in the mass media of the Soviet Union. One of their main hopes was that the re-establishment of harmonious relations with

the Soviet Union would be a stimulus to political reform in China. Gorbachev was held in enormously high esteem and there was a yearning (and, as later events were to show, with good reason) for a 'Chinese Gorbachev'.

12. See *Pravda*, 8 Dec. 1988: 1–2; *Pravda*, 5 Oct. 1988: 4; and BBC, *Summary of World Broadcasts*, SU/0526 C/1, 4 Aug. 1989.

13. V. Medvedev (fn. 10). For a variety of interesting views on the contemporary meaning of socialism, including some that do away with the distinction between socialism of a 'Marxist-Leninist' type and 'democratic socialism', see the symposium on the concept of socialism in *Voprosy filosofii*, 11 (Nov. 1988).

14. *Izvestiya*, 4 June 1989: 2. The director of the Institute of Economics of the World Socialist System, O. Bogomolov, has been quoted in answer to a question about what he hoped the Soviet Union would look like in twenty years from now, as replying, 'Sweden . . . Sweden or perhaps Austria'. See R. Parker, 'Assessing perestroika', *World Policy Journal*, 6 (2) (Spring 1989): 294.

15. BBC, *Summary of World Broadcasts*, SU/0473 C/1, 3 June 1989.

16. Ibid.

17. J. Farr, 'Understanding conceptual change politically', in T. Ball, J. Farr and R. L. Hanson, *Political Innovation and Conceptual Change*, (fn. 7), p. 29.

18. Ibid., pp. 30 and 32.

19. On Gorbachev's expanding use of the notion of 'socialist pluralism', see also A. Brown, 'The Soviet leadership and the struggle for political reform', *The Harriman Institute Forum*, 1 (4) (April 1988).

20. *Pravda*, 15 July 1987: 2.

21. *Pravda*, 5 July 1988: 3.

22. BBC, *Summary of World Broadcasts*, SU/0480 i, 12 June 1989; and SU/0526 B/3–4, 4 Aug. 1989.

23. For Soviet discussion of 'socialist pluralism', see 'Sotsialisticheskii plyuralizm' (the proceedings of a round table), *Sotsiologicheskie issledovaniya*, 5 (Sept.–Oct. 1988); N. N. Deev and N. F. Sharafetdinov, 'Sotsialisticheskii plyuralizm v politike' *Sovetskoe gosudarstvo i pravo*, 4 (April 1989).

24. *Sovetskaya kul'tura*, 14 July 1988: 3.

25. *Pravda*, 5 July 1988.

26. S. E. Deytsev and I. G. Shablinsky, 'Rol' politicheskikh institutov v uskorenii sotsial'no-ekonomicheskogo razvitiya', *Sovetskoe gosudarstvo i pravo*, 17 (July 1987): 120.

27. *Pravda*, 30 Nov. 1988: 2.

28. For an interesting account of these elections and of some of the surrounding discussion, see J. Hahn, 'An Experiment in Competition: The 1987 Election to the Local Soviet', *Slavic Review*, 47 (2) (Fall 1988).

29. See G. Barabashev and V. Vasil'ev, 'Etapy reformy', *Pravda*, 7 May 1989: 3.

30. *Pravda*, 27 April 1989: 5.

31. Ibid., p. 6.

32. Ibid., p. 4.

33. Ibid.

34. For a list of public organizations designated to elect deputies, their quota of representatives, and the number of candidates who competed to represent each organization in the elections to the Congress of People's Deputies (and for a useful discussion of the elections themselves), see D. Mann, 'Elections to the Congress of

People's Deputies nearly over', *Radio Liberty Report on the USSR*, 1 (15) (14 April 1989).

35. *Izvestiya*, 21 April 1989: 3.
36. *Izvestiya*, 6 May 1989: 7.
37. Ibid.
38. The phrase is that of Alexander Kabakov. In context, it reads:

For decades we have been the most silent majority in the world. Really interesting points were discussed only in kitchens, with the closest friends, in the compartments of trains, and with unknown people who do not know your name and address and, therefore, are safe. Today we are probably the most vocal nation. Everything left unsaid accumulated over a long time, and it is impossible to talk about all points at the same time.'

See *Moscow News*, 24 (11 June 1989): 14.

39. *Pravda*, 10 June 1989: 14.
40. Telephone polls of respondents in major Soviet cities suggested that, in fact, the overwhelming majority of these urban dwellers were watching or listening to the Congress proceedings all or most of the time, whether at home or at work. Thus, for example, a poll conducted on 29 May found 81% of Muscovites following the proceedings constantly or almost constantly, a figure that had dropped only to 78% by early June. The other cities included in these polls were Leningrad, Kiev, Tallin, Tbilisi, and Alma-Ata; other questions put to the respondents brought out wide differences in the reaction of the inhabitants to some of the major issues discussed at the Congress. See *Izvestiya*, 31 May 1989: 7, and *Izvestiya*, 4 June 1989: 1.
41. V. Tretyakov, 'Congress of People's Deputies: whose hopes will it justify?', *Moscow News*, 24 (11 June 1989): 7.
42. Ibid.
43. *Izvestiya*, 2 June 1989: 4–5.
44. Ibid., p. 5.
45. *Izvestiya*, 8 June 1989: 1.
46. Ibid.
47. *Pravda*, 1 June 1989: 1.
48. *Pravda*, 3 June 1989: 6.
49. Ibid.
50. For a list of members of the Constitutional Commission, see *Pravda*, 10 June 1989: 6.
51. *Izvestiya*, 26 May 1989: 4.
52. *Izvestiya*, 27 May 1989: 4.
53. Ibid.
54. *Izvestiya*, 29 May 1989: 1.
55. Soviet television, 29 May 1989, as reported in BBC, *Summary of World Broadcasts*, SU/0475 C/3–C/6, 6 June 1989.
56. *Izvestiya TsK KPSS*, 1 (Jan. 1989): 81–6.
57. Ibid., p. 65.
58. For a list of the new departments and their heads, see ibid., p. 66.
59. *Kommunist*, 15 (Oct. 1988): 4.
60. For a full list of the leadership personnel changes made at the 30 September plenary session of the Central Committee, see ibid., p. 3.

61. *Izvestiya TsK KPSS*, 1 (5) (May 1989): 45–6.

62. Ibid., p. 47.

63. Fedoseev's valedictory speech damned 'socialist pluralism' with faint praise and called for the ideological unity of the party. See *Pravda*, 27 April 1989: 4. Those who departed included such former members of the top leadership team as Gromyko, Nikolai Tikhonov, Dolgikh, and Boris Ponomarov, as well as Petr Fedoseev – the man who, in his capacity as vice-president of the Academy of Sciences with special responsibility for the social sciences, bore a good deal of personal responsibility for the sorry state of those disciplines in Brezhnev's time.

64. *Izvestiya TsK KPSS*, 1 (Jan. 1989): 8.

65. Ibid.

66. Soviet television, speech of 10 June 1989, as reported in BBC, *Summary of World Broadcasts*, SU/0483 C/2–6/7, 15 June 1989.

67. Ibid.

68. The Soviet researcher Viktor Belkin, speaking in mid-June 1989, said that 'the economic situation is worse than we can ever have imagined', adding, 'Sometimes I wonder if we can survive until the autumn'. Even the newly appointed deputy chairman of the Council of Ministers in charge of economic reform, Leonid Abalkin, gave the Soviet economy only another one-and-a-half to two years to show some signs of improvement if society is not to be 'destabilized' and if 'a rightward swing' of unpredictable form is to be avoided. The leading specialist on agriculture in the Soviet Union, Vladimir Tikhonov, has said that he expects famine 'in the very near future' if peasant farmers are not soon given full control over the land, and Boris Yel'tsin has warned that a 'revolutionary situation' will develop in the Soviet Union unless living standards are raised rapidly. These dire warnings from prominent figures in Soviet life appear in a Reuters' report published in the *Guardian* (London), 17 June 1989, p. 4.

69. *XIX Vsesoyuznaya konferentsiya kommunisticheskoi partii Sovetskogo Soyuza, 28 Iyunya – 1 Iyulya 1988 goda: Stenograficheskiy otchet*, vol. 2 (Moscow: Politizdat, 1988), pp. 23–7.

70. BBC, *Summary of World Broadcasts*, SU/0470 C/7, 31 May 1989.

71. A telephone poll (by a random sample of telephone numbers) of between 250 and 300 people in each one of six cities (Moscow, Leningrad, Kiev, Tallin, Tbilisi and Alma-Ata) was conducted during the Congress of People's Deputies. See *Izvestiya*, 4 June 1989: 1.

4

Perestroika, Glasnost and Society

Nobuo Shimotomai

The year 1988 saw the start of the 'second stage, or critical stage of perestroika' (M.S. Gorbachev). Most specialists and observers of the USSR would agree, even if not fully, that a new stage of reform is in progress in the Soviet Union, particularly since the nineteenth party conference (June–July), and that perestroika has shifted from the previous stage (March 1985 to 1987), when the main objectives were the reshuffle of the Brezhnev leadership and ideological innovation, to the stage of implementation.[1] In other words, the implementation of 'radical reform' has begun, and Soviet leaders and watchers alike recognize the difficulties of the systemic changes being attempted.

First, the reform is a long historical process and it will not be completed within this century. In other words, the leadership has realized that 'the gravity and depths of the deformation and stagnation of the past' was greater than they had anticipated.[2] Second, breakthrough cannot be achieved within the existing 'system'; that is without changes in the political system and allocation of power as well as in the basic notion of 'socialism' or the fundamental principles of the Soviet state and the Communist Party (hereafter, the party).[3] Third, this is characterized as the 'second revolution', the 'social revolution' or 'revolution from above'; that is, the policy process is dynamic, sometimes impulsive and difficult to forecast, as is the case with all 'revolutions'. Fourth, the gap is widening between rising expectations, both at home and abroad, and the limited resources which Gorbachev's leadership can employ. Also, resistance to reform is not confined to the 'bureaucracy' or *nomenklatura* but is found among the masses. These general remarks on the present situation of perestroika may serve as the starting-point for further analysis.

Perestroika: From the First Stage to the New Stage

In the first stage of perestroika, Gorbachev's main aims were to reshuffle personnel and change the ideology on which the old regime was based.

Before embarking on a fuller discussion of these changes, something should be said about the nature of the Gorbachev regime at the time of his accession to power. Although by the end of 1984 Gorbachev's public statements had shown him to be a reformist, when he won the leadership by a narrow margin in March 1985, his supporters included conservatives and lukewarm reformists, as was disclosed by Ligachev at the nineteenth party conference.[4]

Gorbachev's main aim in 1985 was to get rid of old Brezhnevite politicians like Tikhonov as well as his rivals for the general secretaryship, Grishin and Romanov. He was lucky in that the leadership of the 'generation of 1937' – the generation born between 1905 and 1915 and educated as technical intellectuals (*vydvizhentsy*) when Stalin inaugurated his campaign for super-industrialization – had grown old and there was a serious need for younger people in the leadership. He was also fortunate in that the subsequent generation, born between 1915 and 1925, had largely been wiped out in World War II. The new team formed by the autumn of 1985 comprised Ligachev (the party), Ryzhkov (Council of Ministers), Shevardnadze (Foreign Affairs) and Chebrikov (KGB) – all quite young and eager to change the status quo. These appointments were followed by those of Boris Yel'tsin (Moscow City) and Zaikov (defence industry).

The highlight of this period of change was the twenty-seventh party congress in February–March 1986. The new Secretariat included people like Dobrynin, Medvedev, Biryukova, Yakovlev and Razumovsky who seemed more pro-Gorbachev and would in fact constitute the core of the new leadership which emerged in the 1988 reform. Subsequent personnel changes were characterized by the retirement of the entire Brezhnev generation, such as Kunaev, the gradual decline of Andropov's team, and the rise of the new Gorbachev generation. Special attention should be paid to the January and June Central Committee plenums, when reformists like Yakovlev and technocrats like Nikonov and Slyun'kov were elevated to full Politburo membership and law specialists were appointed, such as Luk'yanov as secretary, apparently in charge of political reform. But it goes without saying that a change of generation alone does not necessarily signify a systemic change.

What was more important was innovation in the ideology and

principles on which Soviet society is based. To be exact, some ideological innovation began in 1982–3 when the Brezhnev–Suslov team died or retired and Andropov inaugurated a cautious but clear approach to reform, or rather the 'perfection' of the Soviet economy and society. The neo-Stalinist historian Trapeznikov, head of the Science and Education Department of the Central Committee, was replaced by the reform-minded Medvedev. Even Chernenko was eager to consult public opinion, and academic journals began open discussions, though not in a systematic way and with occasional setbacks.[5] By the end of 1984, Gorbachev had turned out to be an innovative ideological leader, taking up the reformists' discussion of 'contradictions within socialism' and the new thinking in foreign policy.

This tendency was strengthened after 1985, when Gorbachev appointed Yakovlev as head of the Propaganda Department and Abel Aganbegyan as chief economic adviser. In 1986 the conservative editor of *Kommunist*, Kosolapov, was replaced by the enlightened philosopher Frolov, organizer of the 'globalist' school – a new breed of specialists in international affairs. After the Chernobyl disaster, the Soviet mass media, including TV and films, began to talk about the 'contradiction' or dark side of Soviet society. Novelists and social scientists educated in the de-Stalinization period, like Aitmatov, Zalygin and Burlatsky, became bolder, and their comments on the subject were heard at the highest level.

The highlight of this period was the January 1987 Central Committee plenum at which Gorbachev set the agenda of limited political reform and ideological innovation. Periodicals like *Ogonek* and *Moscow News* became the avant-garde of glasnost and challenged established taboos. Though less dynamic, some national papers like *Izvestiya*, *Sovetskaya kul'tura* or *Literaturnaya gazeta* were nevertheless transformed. Reformists began to organize public seminars where historians discussed forbidden issues like the significance of the New Economic Policy (NEP) and its spiritual leader Bukharin, as well as the role of Trotsky and other oppositionists in Soviet history. Gorbachev criticized the 'blank spaces' in Soviet historiography. Even informal groups and political clubs were organized, or, to be precise, their existence was acknowledged in the mass media.[6]

These changes in the ideological apparatus were prerequisites for the reform of the economy and polity: they heralded the radical reform programme which was adopted at the June 1987 plenum.[7] Some radical economists like Shmelev or Popov, along with anti-Stalinist historians like Danilov, Ambartsumov or Afanas'ev, openly criticized the 'system' which was instituted during the Stalin-ist regime and has basically survived, though modified, to this day.

Most important – but also difficult – was the implementation of the economic reform programme; the constant difficulties it had to cope with came to the fore. These difficulties intensified after the autumn of 1987. It seems likely that there was collusion between ideological conservatives and some reluctant party leaders. Con-servative reaction made itself felt even before the January plenum, which was postponed three times.

Just after August 1987, when the 'fundamental reorganization' programmes were adopted, pressure from conservative elements was manifested in the form of forceful speeches by several Politburo members attacking the 'new thinking' and anti-Stalinism. The decline of Yel'tsin, the boldest champion of change, marked the peak of this conservative tide, though conservatives like Aliev were also removed from the leadership. Contrary to expectation, Bukh-arin was not rehabilitated at the seventieth anniversary of the revol-ution. The 'dual power' of conservative elements with the reformist leadership lasted for almost a year. The nineteenth party confer-ence, and especially the September 1988 Central Committee plenum, may be regarded as signalling the decline of the conserva-tives: Andrei Gromyko, Solomentsev and other conservatives retired; Ligachev, Chebrikov and Vorotnikov were assigned to less important jobs. Newly appointed ideology chief Medvedev was elevated to full membership of the Politburo and this surely streng-thened reformist tendencies. His speeches clearly contradicted those of Ligachev, appearing similar to those of the radical reformists.[8]

However, the crucial issue is that economic reform is always accompanied by resistance from the forces of conservatism and inertia. This implies the need for political reforms to guarantee the irreversibility of the economic reforms. The role of glasnost and impact of new ideas are twofold in this context: to deepen the level of reformist thinking among the elite and the masses, and to reduce the influence of the conservatives among the *apparatchiks* and masses. It follows that the level of glasnost and reformist thinking are indicators both of the extent of systemic changes and of the degree of resistance to them. Tracing the process of glasnost casts light on the problem of perestroika and the leadership's commit-ment to changes as well as the reaction of the masses and bureaucracy.

Glasnost: Institutional Aspects

Gorbachev's most important and successful policy area so far has been that of glasnost, the level of which was raised in 1988 in particular. In the early stages of the reforms, Gorbachev appointed such reformists as Yakovlev and Frolov to ideologically important posts. Yakovlev eventually became secretary in 1986 and a Politburo member in June 1987. Frolov was appointed as an aide to Gorbachev in 1987, as was Bikkenin, new editor-in-chief of *Kommunist*. The *Kommunist* editorial board includes such active reformists as Latsis, Arab-Ogly and Dedkov. Their articles generally indicate progressive and reformist tendencies. In 1988 Bukharin's testament of Lenin was published and this heralded his rehabilitation by the party.[9] Non-communist Western writers such as S. Cohen, J. K. Galbraith and A. Nove were also invited to contribute.[10]

In 1987 pro-reform journalists occupied the editorship of *Ogonek* (Korotich), *Moscow News* (Yakovlev) and, to a lesser extent, *Argumenty i fakty*.[11] Several academic journals whose importance should not be neglected also took an innovative line. Before 1985, only *EKO, Problems of Philosophy, Soviet State and Law, MEiMO* and *Working Class and the Contemporary World* could be regarded as fairly progressive. In 1988, 'the second breath of perestroika' gave new impetus for change. *Problems of Economics* welcomed Popov as chief editor; the first issue under his editorship included a symposium on Bukharin's critical re-evaluation of the First Five Year Plan when the 'administrative command-structure' emerged, plus an essay on Kornai. Even the traditional *Problems of History* appointed the respected Japanologist Iskenderov, and new contributors include the dissident historian Roy Medvedev and others. But other historical journals like *History of the USSR* and *Problems of the History of the CPSU* seem less dynamic.[12]

A significant shift is occurring in the international journals. New *MEiMO* editor Diligensky was the first person to come out in favour of 'peaceful coexistence' and 'all-human values' rather than 'class struggle', an issue disputed by Shevardnadze, Yakovlev and the conservative Ligachev later in August.[13] *Vestnik MID* also advocates the new diplomacy, while *International Affairs* abandoned its dogmatic policy after Pyadyshev was appointed chief editor in spring 1988. *New Times* is also changing under Ignatenko's editorship and journals like *20th Century and Peace* (Soviet Committee for the Defence of Peace) could almost be taken for dissident publications. Even *Sputnik* published an article on the role of Stalin which embarrassed the GDR authorities.[14]

The forerunners of perestroika were the 'thick' journals, the role of which is reminiscent of the social criticisms of the nineteenth-century *'publicists'*. *Novyi Mir* recovered its liberal tradition of the 1960s under Zalygin's editorship. A non-communist writer, he is an active supporter of the ecology movement. Another journal, *Znamya*, which is connected to the military establishment, has also changed under Baklanov and actively criticized Stalin and his system. The Kirgiz writer Aitmatov has also been appointed as the editor of *Foreign Literature*. Though not so authoritative, *Science and Life* and *Knowledge is Power* also publish important articles.

However, ideological discrepancies are widening between the liberals and the Russian nationalists, who are represented by such journals as *Nash Sovremennik, Molodaya Gvardiya*. These 'rural writers' in European Russia had been associated with nationalist tendency ever since the 1960s, and were critical of Stalin's collectivization campaign and kolkhoz agriculture. In 1988, Glazunov, a famous painter, was a strong advocate of this tendency, though he denied his relation with Pamyat, a Russian nationalist group. These writers are particularly critical of *Ogonek* and *Znamya*.[15]

Role of Intellectuals as 'Input' for Perestroika

Glasnost naturally aroused enthusiasm among intellectuals, who were the first supporters of the reformist leadership. It is noteworthy that the Soviet Academy of Sciences took on the new role of providing input for policy when Gorbachev selected 'Institutniki' as advisers or officials.

The coalition between party reformists and the academy is now firmly entrenched. Two Politburo members, Yakovlev and Medvedev, are former directors of social science institutes, while two other 'Institutniki', Frolov and Shakhnazarov, were appointed aides to the General Secretary, a role no less important for policy formation than ordinary Politburo membership. Economists such as Aganbegyan, Bogomolov, Abalkin or Zaslavskaya are often regarded as personal advisers to Gorbachev. Academician Moiseev had proposed the establishment of a kind of group of wise men under the new chairman of the Supreme Soviet.[16]

This party-Academy coalition is more visible in practical policy areas. The agricultural policy on rent was made by the joint decision of Gosagroprom, the agricultural administration agency and the Agricultural Academy. On the nationality question, which is now one of the vital issues for perestroika, the Academy set up an inter-organizational committee under Academician Bromley (Director of the Ethnography Institute). The Council on Science and Technology was also instituted under Frolov's leadership.[17] A scientific research committee on peace and security was organized from the Academy and other institutes in the 1980s and civilian experts like Kokoshin and Arbatov play an important role in policy formation as a counterbalance to the military.

Although economic ministries have long had research institutes, such bodies are new to other spheres. For example, the Ministry of Foreign Affairs has established a scientific Coordination Centre for the collection and analysis of information. It reports directly to Shevardnadze.[18] A unique organization is the National Committee for Economic Cooperation on Asia-Pacific Affairs (SOVNA-PECC), chaired by Academician Primakov. It comprises members of the Academy – World Economics and International Relations Institute (IMEMO) and the USA and Canada Institute (ISKAN) – the Ministry of Foreign Affairs (MID), trade organizations and Far Eastern local authorities for Asia-Pacific and Siberian development.

It can be seen that the role of innovative social scientists and specialists is important and is reflected in the structure of the Soviet Academy. New leadership priorities have been reflected in the formation of new institutions. First, the World Economy and International Relations Institute of the Academy has been separated from the Economics Department, and Primakov has been appointed Academic Secretary.[19] Established departments took on a more progressive line. In the Philosophy-Law Department, party reformists like Smirnov and Frolov were elected as Academicians, and Shakhnazarov and Bikkenin along with the sociologist Osipov as corresponding members of the Academy in December 1987. But the History Department proved conservative and was reluctant to elect progressive historians.

Second, newly organized Academy and other institutions reflect new policy priorities. The Institute of Europe was set up with Zhurkin (previously ISKAN deputy director) as director. The Social Science (Party) Academy has organized the Institute for the Exchange of Experience of Socialist Construction (Popov as director).[20] Academician Zaslavskaya was appointed director of the Centre for the Study of Public Opinion on Socio-Economic Problems. MID is setting up a new foreign policy public opinion centre.[21] The Institute of Law and the State (IGPAN) has set up the long-awaited Centre for the Study of Politics, as Gorbachev has put political reform on the agenda, a breakthrough because political science has not been fully rehabilitated in academic circles. Its head, Piskotin, is known as a progressive political scientist.[22] Another sensitive discipline, sociology, is also gaining in status under Zaslavskaya, and the new director of the Institute of Sociology, Yadov, has replaced the more orthodox Ivanov. This new breed surely provides input for policy innovation.

'Socialist Pluralism': What Is the Limit?

One of the greatest successes of perestroika is glasnost. From late 1986, and particularly after the January 1987 plenum of the Central Committee, the ban on discussing such issues as Stalinism or political reform was lifted. This naturally raised the question of the theoretical problems of pluralism (discussed by Archie Brown in the last chapter), particularly after Gorbachev and his associates used the term 'socialist pluralism', a concept long associated with bourgeois political science and revisionism.[23]

Despite this reformist usage, the October 1987 Central Committee plenum adopted the term 'pluralism of opinions'. Naturally, conservatives and reformists disputed the real meaning of 'socialist pluralism'. Though not very explicitly, Soviet scholars seem to distinguish three levels of pluralism: opinions, interests and political structure.[24] In the first place, Soviet scholars see 'pluralism of opinions' as a guarantee for freedom of speech, even for dissidents. Kosolapov, the conservative former editor of *Kommunist*, defines it in terms of 'pluralism of Weltanschauung (or world-view)', while others like Bestuzhev-Lada interpret it to imply tolerance of dissidents.[25] The second level of pluralism relates to pluralism of interests, recognizing the socio-economic diversity of Soviet society. It is characterized as 'social and sociological pluralism' or pluralism of behaviour, structure, organization (Rakitsky). Zaslavskaya gave an excellent account of Soviet social strata and their attitude towards perestroika in her article in the volume *Inogo ne dano*.[26]

The third and most complicated area is 'political pluralism', which for obvious reasons Soviet scholars were unable to discuss except to criticize. But they are now approaching this topic through the terms 'monistic pluralism' (Guriev) or 'six different models of political systems under socialism' (Kurashvili). Although there has been no formal discussion of multi-party systems, academic discussion suggests a trend in this direction.[27] The ideologue in chief, Medvedev, in his interview with leadership admitted the existence

of pluralism of interests, saying that a 'proper political mechanism'
should reflect opinions, interests and social structures.[28]

The Legacy of the Stalinist System

This evolution, or rather revolution, from the monistic view is best
exemplified in attitudes towards the past, including the Stalinist
period. This tendency became particularly marked after April 1988,
when *Pravda* criticized a hardline article by a certain Andreeva in
Sovetskaya Rossiya.[29] A new wave of anti-Stalinism had begun.

First came the lifting of the ban on dissidents' works. Two of the
three most famous dissidents of the 1970s, Andrei Sakharov and
Roy Medvedev, have been writing or publishing their works in the
Soviet Union since 1988. Intellectuals have made public statements
sympathetic to another dissident, Solzhenitsyn.[30]

Roy Medvedev is active in informal circles as well as writing for
academic and news journals. Lesser-known dissidents like
Antonov-Ovseenko, Bogoraz and Shafarevich, and liberal scholars
who were forced into dissidence in the 1970s like Gefter, now
write for official journals like *Science and Life* and *Moscow News*.
Samizdat works by Beck, Pasternak, Mandel'shtam, Grossman and
Roy Medvedev are being published.

Second, Western 'anti-Soviet' documents, possession of which
used to constitute a crime under the anti-Soviet clause of the criminal code, are now also allowed. The term 'totalitarianism' is no
longer taboo in the Soviet press. Orwell, Conquest, London and
Koestler are being published.[31] Emigré writers such as Platonov
and Voinovich have also benefited from glasnost, though obviously
less crucially.

These measures symbolize the relaxation of intellectual control,
by which the authorities are preparing for the information revolution which is inevitable in this age of technology. None the less,
the authorities are still occasionally embarrassed by new, samizdat
publications like *Glasnost*.

'Blank Spaces' in History

Glasnost is also paving the way for a re-examination of the past,
especially the 1920s and 1930s, the period of the abolition of the
NEP and the consolidation of the Stalinist system which still sur-
vives in essence, though with some modifications, to this day. Ever
since the breakthrough by Ambartsumov (an economic historian
and Bogomolov's deputy at the Institute of Economy of the World

Socialist System) whose article characterizing Stalinism as war communism was printed in *Moscow News* on the sixty-ninth anniversary of the Revolution, history has been a topic of fierce dispute between progressives and conservatives.[32] The progressives include such historians as Afanas'ev, Volobuev, Danilov, Plimak, Samsonov and Lel'chuk, who are critical of the Stalinist model of socialism and favour the NEP. They are particularly critical of collectivization and the coercive political system which resulted from it.

Social scientists such as Burlatsky, Bovin and Butenko, and writers like Rybakov, Shatrov and Mozhaev were active in the campaign to bringing these issues into public debate. The neo-Stalinist legacy weighed very heavily on history, because the late Trapeznikov, historian of agrarian policy, was kept in the party education department under the Brezhnev regime.

Unfortunately for the progressives, the seventieth anniversary of the revolution was on the agenda in 1987 and the conservatives and the 'masses' did not want to commemorate it in a negative way. Against this background came the political struggle which culminated in the Yel'tsin affair and coincided with some resurgence of conservatism. Gorbachev's speech on 2 November was eclectic and full of compromise, defending Stalin's collectivization and industrialization, though, for the first time, authoritatively criticizing the Stalinist system as an 'administrative command system'. Bukharin was not rehabilitated, though his criticism of Trotsky was positively evaluated.[33]

However, the General Secretary's speech was not the final word. At the beginning of 1988 another fierce battle took place over Shatrov's controversial play *Dal'she . . . Dal'she . . . Dal'she* ('Further . . . Further . . . Further').[34] Meanwhile, the Institute of History of the Academy of Sciences had renewed its staff and the cautious progressives won. The journal *Problems of History* changed its policy so that even dissident historians could contribute.[35] A further blow was dealt to the conservatives by the 'Andreeva affair'. Young historians were now bolder and the university students studied without texts or examinations in 1988.[36] Smirnov, director of the Institute of Marxism-Leninism, also collaborated with the progressive historians in the 1988 discussions.[37]

Party Rehabilitation

The problem of 'blank spaces' is closely related to the question of the rehabilitation of party leaders eliminated by the Stalinist purges. From his accession to power, Gorbachev quietly continued with the rehabilitation of party officials, a process which had been suspended under Brezhnev. Some Trotskyists had been rehabilitated by the middle of 1987.[38] In August 1987, such non-communist economists as Sukhanov, Kondratiev and Chayanov were also rehabilitated. In his seventieth anniversary speech Gorbachev announced that a Politburo commission had been appointed to consider rehabilitation. Its chairman was reported to be Solomentsev, who was replaced by Yakovlev after his retirement from the Politburo.[39]

The most important political problem was the rehabilitation of right-wing oppositionists, such as Bukharin, Rykov and Tomsky, as well as of the leftist Trotsky. Because Bukharin symbolized the alternative to the Stalinist model of socialism, the question of his rehabilitation was a barometer of the relative strengths of conservatives and reformists in the leadership.[40] Gorbachev succeeded in rehabilitating Bukharin at the party level in June 1988, almost one-and-a-half years after his name and photograph appeared in the Soviet media.[41] Trotsky, Zinoviev and Kamenev were only rehabilitated at the public level; their names and activities were described objectively, and it is possible that they may be rehabilitated at the party level.[42]

Less known but important in this context is the rehabilitation of Ryutin, an active right-wing oppositionist who was purged after distributing pamphlets advocating the removal of Stalin from the post of General Secretary in 1932. This may pave the way for the rehabilitation of other opponents to Stalin, such as Trotsky. Then the military historian Volkogonov, who is against the 'new thinking' on military affairs, has given a fairly objective account of the role of Trotsky.[43]

The Policy Implications of Anti-Stalinism

The new waves of anti-Stalinism must surely be related to the new policy for agriculture. Based on the system of contract and lease, this is a *de facto* reversal of the kolkhoz system. It was Tikhonov, supporter of the NEP model cooperative agriculture, who first mentioned in public the more than 10 million victims of the collectivization campaign.[44]

From the summer of 1988, the Soviet media became more outspoken, talking about such taboo subjects as the famine of 1932 and the Kuban affair when Kaganovich deported the inhabitants of sixteen villages of the north Caucasus.[45] The article in *Pravda* of the progressive historian Danilov on the results of collectivization was followed by an astonishing TV programme, 'Khleb' (Bread), based on the Alekseev story about collectivization and famine in the Volga area.[46] A memoir also disclosed that Stalin's wife had committed suicide at that time.[47]

Second, history is being re-examined in the context of political reform. The role of the political police is being discussed. Stalin's extra-judicial machine was condemned and its decisions were annulled.[48] The terrorist activities of the NKVD in Belorussia have been reported, while the KGB chairman claimed that more than 20,000 'chekhists' had been victimized under Stalin's rule.[49] The role of Yezhov and Stalin in the death of Bukharin was also disclosed in *Kommunist*.[50]

Third, debates on the origins of World War II have direct implications both for nationality problems and the question of Soviet foreign relations before and after the war; the infamous Katyn massacre has a direct bearing on Soviet–Polish relations, while the Nazi–Stalin pact is related to the present status of the Baltic republics. The People's Front movements in these republics were inspired by this campaign of historical re-examination.[51] On the other hand, discussion in the Soviet magazine *Sputnik* of Stalin's role in the rise of Hitler was strongly criticized by the East German authorities.[52]

The discussion also implied that the Stalinist system had something in common with Hitler's regime. A new estimate of the victims of World War II, some 40 million instead of the official figure of 20 million, shows the horror of that system and the need for its legacy to be changed.[53]

The moves described above are related to a more profound criticism of the Stalinist system. Butenko has levelled almost the same criticism against the Soviet system as did Trotsky, that proletarian power had been usurped by bureaucrats.[54] Plimak and Volobuev have taken up Trotsky's thesis that Stalin had caused a Thermidor-style degeneration of the Revolution.[55] Burlatsky has described the Stalinist system as 'state socialism', but others do not hesitate to call it 'barracks socialism', 'totalitarianism' or 'Oriental despotism'.[56] These harsh criticisms of Stalinism are a logical stepping-stone towards a more profound transformation of the 'system'.

Glasnost and Political Reform

Apart from the political reforms (discussed by Archie Brown in Chapter 3), an important aspect of glasnost is the level of debate on the political system in the Soviet Union. Taboos on public discussion of government and society are being removed, a radical departure from the Bolshevik tradition which has neglected the problem of power and bureaucracy in the real world, looking forward to the 'withering away of the state' and 'the end of politics'; there are obvious reasons why the Stalinist legacy has prohibited the public from talking about politics. In Soviet political culture, politics has been reduced to tactics and never given full consideration.[57]

In this perspective, Soviet leaders no longer attribute their defects to personal error or accidental misfortune. They have become aware of a systemic problem resulting from the 'deformation of socialism'. This can only be corrected by a systemic change in the political structure, although the level of the required change may be disputed.[58]

It is true that in earlier periods there was some discussion of the political system and even some attempts at reform, but these tended to be partial and ineffective. Examples are the 'All-People's State' discussion at the end of the 1940s, and, particularly, Khrushchev's reforms in which the role of the party was countered by increasing the role of the 'state'.[59] Also the discussion of 'developed socialism' in the latter half of the 1960s implied a democratization of Soviet society, but this was cunningly mutilated by the conservative leadership, who simply declared that developed socialism had been achieved; no further measure for democratization was taken. Political scientists who had advocated democratization were demoted.[60]

Open, public discussion of politics – not academic discussion which began in 1983 when Piskotin became editor of *Soviet State and Law* – began in the second half of 1986, when Vasil'ev wrote in the elections to soviets in which multiple candidates could stand.[61] The opening up of political debate became particularly marked after the January plenum of the Central Committee, where Gorbachev discussed political reform for the first time. The political system and its reform became the subject of political debate. The sociologist Shubkin analysed and criticized Soviet bureaucracy for the first time in its history.[62] Young political scientists then related the phenomenon to the character of the political system, rejecting the socio-cultural explanation given by Shubkin.[63] Most significantly, this characterization of Soviet bureaucracy was adopted by Gorbachev when he criticized the 'administrative command structure' instituted in the Stalin period.[64]

State and Political Change

In 1988 the public debate on the Soviet political system became even more sophisticated on account of the nineteenth party conference scheduled for 28 June, at which party and political reform were on the agenda. This was accompanied by public debate on the state, law and party, a debate unprecedented in Soviet history. Political scientists succeeded in setting up the Centre for Political Research under the Academy's Institute of State and Law before the June conference.[65]

The February plenum inaugurated discussion on the 'socialist law-based state' (*pravovoe gosudarstvo*).[66] In 1987 specialists followed this up with discussion of the famous revolutionary slogan of 'all power to the soviets'. The debate focused on the reform of Soviet institutions for the exercise of power prescribed by the constitution. Some radical scientists like Aibazhan favoured the resurrection of the 1917-style soviets. Reformists began to call for the reorganization of the soviets on parliamentary lines: the representative function would then be differentiated from the executive. This would mean 'separation of powers', a negation of the Leninist conception of power. Barabashev, Shemeret and Vasiliev maintained that the soviet should be recognized as a kind of parliament. It was Kurashvili, a radical supporter of reform since 1983, who openly discussed such topics as the 'separation of powers'. Burlatsky followed the same line of argument when he advocated a 'Soviet presidential' system. In the 1970s this type of argument was put forward by the dissident historian Roy Medvedev.[67] It is now argued that 'parliamentarism' and 'separation of powers' are valuable developments in human history.[68]

The 'socialist law-based state' may be interpreted as *Rechtsstaat* rather than 'rule of law' where the central idea is that even the party and other law-abiding institutions should be governed by law. The Soviet conception of law is also changing: whereas previously Soviet citizens could only do what was prescribed by law, now they can do anything that is not legally prohibited.

Discussion of the party in the Soviet political system has been somewhat ambiguous with no open discussion of the multi-party system. Within the party, some have argued for multiple candidates for the office of General Secretary. But there has been no open support for factional activity within the party. On the whole, discussion has centred on the minority's or dissidents' role in the party, though this is in itself a great advance on the past.[69]

Emerging Civil Society

The iconoclastic nature of these criticisms of the Soviet political system is only understandable when set against the changes in Soviet politics which go beyond the level of administrative reform.

It was no accident that Soviet theorists began to discuss 'civil society' and mass participation in the political process.

Particular attention should be given to the role of 'informals' and other new institutions which are emerging in the Soviet political arena. From 1987, journals and other media began to discuss the 'informal groups' or civil initiatives, functioning outside the control of the 'party's leading role'. Proponents of these movements are critical of the monopoly over social life held by the 'quasi-public institutions'.[70]

These organizations themselves are not new; various groups emerged after the death of Stalin and some have a history of over twenty or twenty-five years. However, perestroika and glasnost allowed these groups to come into the open. Now there are more than 40,000 informal groups and associations.[71] Some are apolitical but others are becoming increasingly politicized and most call for alternative party status. These political clubs became a notable phenomenon after the January 1987 plenum.

The Social Initiative Club (KSI) and Perestroika in 1987 advanced the idea of organizing a conference. Members of some fifty groups convened in August and several issued a joint declaration asking for perestroika from below. Some argued for ecological concerns while others commemorate the victims of Stalin's terror. The nineteenth party conference endorsed these movements, though Gorbachev was critical of extremists who do not accept the party's dominant role.[72]

There are several types of such organizations. Some are apolitical, and are kinds of youth sub-culture organizations like rock fan clubs. There are some deviationist movements such as 'Lyubertsy'. Others are concerned with the preservation of the country's cultural heritage. Religious groups are also to be found. Ecology movements are popular, taking up relevant environmental issues.

Another new phenomenon is the emergence of political organizations. These can be categorized into six groups: (1) Groups like the 'Democratic Union', which have come out against Leninism and the October Revolution;[73] (2) groups like Pamyat and the Karabakh committee, which raise nationality issues; (3) People's Front-type organizations, which favour pressing for perestroika from below;[74] (4) discussion clubs or political clubs which aim at explaining the need for democratization and glasnost – Democratic Perestroika in Moscow is an example;[75] (5) issue-oriented organizations like 'Memorial', which seek to gather information on and commemorate the victims of Stalin's terror;[76] (6) groups which aim to democratize the 'formal institutions' like the Komsomol and trade unions.[77]

Some organizations cut across these categories. For instance, the Estonian People's Front, which is in part a nationalist movement, has now almost taken control of the party.[78] Some political scientists favour uniting these groups under an umbrella organization. Others have proposed that their existence should be guaranteed by decree or by a law on associations. Preparations are now under way to grant them legal status.[79]

Social scientists like Migranyan and Ambartsumov regard these informal groups as new social movements which constitute a 'socialist civil society'. Indeed, Soviet political scientists began to discuss 'civil society' in the Soviet Union in 1987, a concept to which Gorbachev's adviser, Abalkin, adopted a positive attitude in his speech at the nineteenth party conference.[80]

According to the sociologist Rumyantsev, these groups developed from the contradictions between 'true socialism' and a 'totally regulated society' or 'monopolistic bloc of power'.[81] They also represent interests in society in general. In other words, they defend their own interests, some of which may be in contradiction with one another or with the general interest. These autonomous people's organizations themselves seek social consciousness, the lack of which may result in conservatism on the one hand and radicalism on the other. They are conveyor belts between the 'first society' and the 'second society', to use a term coined by the Hungarian sociologist Hankiss.[82]

Of course, these avant-garde organizations are only a tiny phenomenon, except in the national minority regions, and their importance should not be exaggerated. So far they are confined to Moscow and other large cities and some of the republics. Nevertheless, there are 40,000 of these politicized civil movements. This explains the negative attitude of some politicians, who fear they may turn into a 'second party'. Most Komsomol officials are naturally unhappy about them because of 40 to 50 per cent of their own members are also positive towards these movements,[83] though some, as those in Novosibirsk, tend to take a more positive stance. Medvedev's positive comments in November 1988 provided another endorsement of informal groups; a new law on glasnost and associations was in preparation in 1989.[84]

Prospects

There are two schools of thought on the future of perestroika. On the one hand, some people point out that urbanization in the Soviet Union means that almost two-thirds of the population now live in cities where educational and cultural levels are high; consequently, circumstances are favourable for the Gorbachev reforms to rally support, provided they succeed in eliminating shortages of foodstuffs and certain other commodities. These people argue that a Soviet-type civil society will develop and flourish.[85]

But there is strong opposition to this line of argument, in that Soviet society has no tradition of democracy; it has a complicated ethnic and social structure and a huge bureaucracy which would destroy any embryonic civil society. According to this view, the political system is too rigid to be transformed and the one-party system deters any sign of an 'abnormal' pluralistic tendency. Also, civic initiatives are strongly motivated by the nationalistic sentiments and are not necessarily democratic. It was noted in 1988 that public support for perestroika was tending to decline: another indication of the limits of 'revolution from above'.[86]

This is a difficult question to address. Still, Soviet society is now more articulate and sophisticated than it was in the 1960s or 1970s, to say nothing of the 1930s to 1950s. Soviet citizens are more oriented towards civic life, and the Soviet media are adapting to the people's preferences and interests, rather than merely disseminating indoctrination from above. A careful analysis of Soviet affairs would show that the topics discussed under glasnost had already been touched on in the 1960s and 1970s. In this respect, the changes now recognized as under way in the USSR are a culmination of the changes begun two decades ago. The prospects for economic reform may be difficult to assess but political and agricultural changes in Soviet society are likely to gather momentum, as is happening in the soviets now. Yet to paraphrase Karl Marx, it is not politics, but the economy, which will settle the fate of perestroika.

Notes

1. Nobuo Shimotomai, 'The reform movement: power, ideology and intellectuals', in P. Juviler and H. Kimura (eds), *Gorbachev's Reforms: US and Japanese Assessments* (New York: Aldine de Gruyter, 1988), pp. 63–79; Nobuo Shimotomai, *Gorbachev no jidai* [Gorbachev's Era] (Tokyo: Iwanami, 1988).

2. M. S. Gorbachev, *Perestroika i novoe myshlenie* (Moscow: Politizdat, 1987), p. 59.

3. See Yu. Afanas'ev (ed.), *Inogo ne dano* (Moscow: Progress, 1988). See also the interesting discussion on socialism in *Voprosy filosofii*, 11 (1988): 31–71.

4. *Pravda*, 2 July 1988.

5. V. Medvedev, economist and former secretary of Leningrad gorkom, was appointed Rector of the Social Science Academy of the party in 1978. His criticism of Butenko over 'contradictions of socialism' seemed rather orthodox (*Voprosy istorii*, 2, 1984), but some reformists deny that he was conservative. His statement at the end of 1987, and especially his first speech after being appointed chairman of the ideological commission of the Central Committee, showed him to be progressive, although some still doubt that he is a radical reformist. *Pravda*, 5 Oct. 1988; *Kommunist*, 17: 3–18.

6. Shimotomai, *Gorbachev no jidai*, (fn. 1), p. 30.

7. Ibid., p. 60.

8. *Kommunist*, 17 (1988): 3–18. On the structure of the newly organized ideological department, see *Pravda*, 20 Feb. 1989.

9. *Kommunist*, 2 (1988): 93–102.

10. *Kommunist*, 12: 57–9; 1 (1989): 113–17.

11. *Argumenty i fakty* sometimes gives unpublished information but seems less progressive than *Moscow News* and others. For example, when 'new thinking' in the nuclear age was debated between writers like Adamovich and the military, they interviewed Volkogonov, who was orthodox on this, though he seems moderately progressive on Stalin. *Argumenty i fakty*, 25 (1987).

12. *Voprosi istorii KPSS*, 2 (1988). See discussion on Butenko's usurpation thesis – 7 (1988): 139–41. By the latter half of 1988, this journal also followed the general line of radicalization.

13. *MEiMO*, 3 (1988): 15–26. Ligachev emphasis on the class approach in international affairs (*Pravda*, 7 Aug. 1988) was intended to criticize Shevardnadze (*Vestnik MID SSSR*, 15 (1988): 27–46), but was rebutted by Yakovlev (*Pravda*, 11 and 13 Aug. 1988) and Medvedev (*Pravda*, 5 Oct. 1988).

14. *Novoe vremya*, 32 (1988). *Vek XX i mir* is run by ex-dissidents. *Sputnik*, a popular Soviet magazine, was banned in the GDR at the end of 1988 because the famous Soviet writer raised in it the issue of the responsibility of Stalin for the rise of Hitler (*Sputnik*, 11 (1988): 135–8; *Neues Deutschland*, 25 Nov. 1988).

15. Rural writers like Alekseev, and to some extent Mozhaev, Rasputin, Belov and Astaf'ev are more or less critical of the internationalist tendency of *Novyi Mir*. They see collectivization as the responsibility of non-Russians like Stalin and Kaganovich. See the speech by Bondarev at the nineteenth party conference: *XIX Vsesoyuznaya Konferentsiya KPSS, steno. otchet* (Moscow: Politizdat, 1988), p. 225. Seven writers of this tendency wrote to *Pravda*, criticizing *Ogonek* (*Pravda*, 18 Jan. 1989).

16. *Kommunist*, 14 (1988): 25.

17. *Vestnik AN SSSR*, 1 (1988): 41.

18. *Vestnik MID*, 15 (1988): 41.

19. *Pravda*, 16 March 1988.

20. *Obshchestvennye nauki*, 5 (1988): 178–82.

21. *Mezhdunarodnaya zhizn'*, 5 (1988): 160; 9: 30.

22. Personal information from the Institute of State and Law (IGPAN) in July 1988. See also V. Shlapentokh, *The Politics of Sociology in the Soviet Union* (Boulder and London: Westview, 1987).

23. *Kommunist*, 8 (1987): 102–11.

24. *Sotsiologicheskie issledovaniya*, 5 (1988): 6–24.

25. *Sotsiologicheskie issledovaniya*, 5 (1988): 8.

26. *Sotsiologicheskie issledovaniya*, 5 (1988): 7, 18–19; Afanas'ev, *Inogo ne dano*, (fn. 3), p. 39.

27. *Sotsiologicheskie issledovaniya*, 5 (1988): 15–19.

28. *Kommunist*, 17 (1988): 12–13.

29. *Sovetskaya Rossiya*, 13 March 1988. Apparently Ligachev was involved in advancing this ex-communist's letter. About thirty local papers reprinted this article. See Afanas'ev's article in *Pravda* on 26 July 1988. The counter-attack was heralded by *Pravda* on 5 April 1988.

30. V. Medvedev announced in December that *Gulag* would not be published in the USSR, though some writers like Astaf'ev were openly calling for his rehabilitation (TV programme, 29 July 1988). Mozhaev also called for his rehabilitation (*Vek XX i mir*, 1 (1989): 4–7).

31. *Nauka i zhizn'*, 8 (1988); *Teatr*, 8 (1988); *Moskovskie novosti*, 24 (1988); *Neva*, 7 (1988) (Koestler).

32. *Moskovskie novosti*, 9 Nov. 1986; *Voprosy istorii*, 9 (1988). See roundtable on the NEP, particularly speech by Danilov.

33. *Pravda*, 3 Nov. 1988.

34. *Znamya*, 1 (1988). See *Pravda*, 10, 13 Jan. 1988; 15 Feb. 1988.

35. *Voprosy istorii*, 3 (1988).

36. Young historians' meeting to set up a conference; see *Komsomol'skaya Pravda*, 4 May 1988.

37. *Vestnik AN SSSR*, 1 (1988): 39; *Pravda*, 16 Aug. 1988; 16 Sept. 1988.

38. R. W. Davies, 'Soviet history in the Gorbachev revolution, the first phase', in *Socialist Register 1988*, 1988. Nobuo Shimotomai, 'New interpretation of the NEP and the Stalinist system under glasnost', AAASS address 18 Nov. 1988; Mark von Hagen, 'History of politics under Gorbachev', *The Harriman Institute Forum*, 11 (1988).

39. The membership of this commission was first announced in *Pravda*, 19 Aug. 1988; it was slightly reshuffled later in 1988 (*Pravda*, 2 Dec. 1988).

40. On Bukharin, see S. Cohen, *Bukharin and the Bolshevik Revolution* (New York: Random House, 1973). See also my article in *Asahi Journal*, 42 (1978). On Tomsky, see *Voprosy istorii*, 8 (1988). For more detail, Nobuo Shimotomai, *Soviet Politics and Trade Unions* (Tokyo: Tokyo University Press, 1982, in Japanese). Take the example of the rehabilitation process of Bukharin; on 21 Jan. 1986, *Pravda* mentioned his name, though in a negative way. On 21 Jan. 1987 Moscow's TV first portrayed Bukharin in a semi-documentary film by Shatrov, a relative of Rykov (Second Chairman of the People's Commissariats and Bukharin's accomplice). He also described how oppositionists, including Bukharin, debated in the Brest-Litovsk Treaty issue, the first public rehabilitation of them. Though intermittent reports suggested he might be rehabilitated on the seventieth anniversary of the October Revolution, Gorbachev could only mention him in the context of his alliance with the orthodox against Trotsky.

However, some were bold enough to take a further initiative. *Kommunist* printed his article 'Lenin's testament' in January 1988. The supreme court and eventually the Politburo commission also concealed the alleged accusation of 1938. *Ogonek* and other media printed his wife's memoirs while there appeared political clubs named after Bukharin. Eventually, in June 1988, the Politburo rehabilitated him as a party member. A *Kommunist* article characterized his view as an alternative to Stalin's extremist strategy, while *Problems of History* and other journals printed his work. On his hundredth birthday, 8 Oct. 1988, Zhlavlev and Nosov, rather cautious historians of the Institute of Marxism-Leninism, portrayed him as a true Leninist: *Pravda*, 21 Jan. 1986; TV programme on 21 Jan. 1987; *Sovetskaya kul'tura*, 6 Oct. 1988; *Kommunist*, 13 (1988); *Voprosy istorii*, 7 (1988); *Nauka i zhizn'*, 10 (1988).

41. *Karsnaya zvezda*, 23 July 1988; *Voprosy istorii*, 3 (1988).

42. *Argumenty i fakty*, 42 and 43 (1988).

43. *Kommunist*, 13 (1988); *Voprosy istorii*, 7 (1988). Some oppositionists like Shlyapnikov have already been rehabilitated as historical persons and are soon likely to be so at the party level.

44. *Argumenty i fakty*, 14 (1988).

45. *Pravda*, 16 Sept. 1988. See also N. Shimotomai, 'A note on the Kuban affair', in *Acta Slavica Iaponica* (Sapporo: Slavic Centre, 1983), Table 1, pp. 39–56.

46. TV on 18 Oct. 1988; Orbita 1.

47. *Sovetskaya kul'tura*, 6 Aug. 1988.

48. *Pravda*, 6 Jan. 1989.

49. *Pravda*, 2 Sept. 1988; *Moskovskie novosti*, 41 (1988); and *Ogonek*, 1 (1989).

50. *Kommunist*, 13 (1988): 108.

51. *Mezhdunarodnaya zhizn'*, 5 (1988): 147–59; *Vestnik narodnogo fronta* (Estonia), 1 (1988). See also *Literaturnasya gazeta*, 52 (1988).

52. *Sputnik*, 11 (1988); *Neues Deutschland*, 25 Nov. 1988.

53. *Sovetskaya kul'tura*, 2 Sept. 1988. See also Yu. Polyakov in *Literaturnaya gazeta*, 40 (1987). The term 'totalitarianism' is no longer taboo in Soviet social science. *Sovetskaya kul'tura*, 26 April 1988 (N. Popov); *Oktyabr*, 4 (1988) (Kapustin); *Pravda*, 3 Feb. 1989 (G. Shmelev).

54. *Nauka i zhizn'*, 4 (1988): 46–53.

55. *Sovetskaya kul'tura*, 2 Nov. 1988; *Nauka i zhizn'*, 5 (1987).

56. Afanas'ev, *Inogo ne dano*, (fn. 3); *Voprosy istorii*, 11 (1988).

57. Nobuo Shimotomai, 'Soren-Seijiteki shiko no Fukken', *Sekai*, 11 (1988). See also A. Polan, *Lenin and the End of Politics* (London: Methuen, 1984).

58. The term 'deformation of socialism', which is now common in perestroika documents, was first used by A. Butenko in 1982. See A. Butenko, *Sotsializm kak Mirovaya sistema* (Moscow: Politizdat, 1984); *Vlast' naroda posredstvom samogo naroda* (Moscow: Mysl', 1988); *Argumenty i fakty*, 17 (1988).

59. *Kommunist*, 14 (1988): 62. Academician Fedoseev allegedly advanced this idea in the 1940s but was criticized by the conservatives.

60. N. Shimotomai, *Soviet Contemporary Politics* (Tokyo: Tokyo University Press, 1980).

61. *Literaturnaya gazeta*, 14 (1986).

62. *Znamya*, 4 (1987): 162–87.

63. Afanas'ev, *Inogo ne dano*, (fn. 3), pp. 97–121.

64. *Pravda*, 3 Nov. 1987.

65. *Sovetskaya Kul'tura*, 6 Aug. 1988.

66. M. Gorbachev, *Revolutsionnoi perestroike-ideologiyu obnovleniya* (Moscow; Politizdat, 1988), pp. 17–18.

67. *Nash Sovremennik*, 1 (1987); *Sovetskoe gosudarstvo i pravo*, 5 (1988); B. Kurashvili, *Ocherk teorii gosudarstvennogo upravleniya* (Moscow: Nauka, 1987);

108   *Perestroika: Soviet domestic and foreign policies*

Kommunist, 8 (1988); R. Medvedev, *Kniga o sotsialisticheskoi demokratii* (Amsterdam: Gertsen Foundation, 1972).

68. *Kommunist*, 8 (1988): 29.
69. *Moskovskie novosti*, 10 April 1988; *Sotsiologicheskie issledovaniya*, 5 (1988).
70. *Vek XX i mir*, 6 (1988): 18–21. The term 'civil society' seems to have appeared in *Voprosy filosofii*, 8 (1987): 75–91. See also *MEiMO*, 11 (1988): 5–18.
71. Afanas'ev, *Inogo ne dano*, (fn. 3), pp. 188, 210–17; *Otkrytaya Zona*, organ of the Demokratic Perestroika, 7 (1988); *Argumenty i fakty*, 31 (1988). According to an Institute of Sociology survey, about 10–13% of the younger generation are active participants and more than 50% are sympathizers. These trends are particularly strong in the cities of over 1 million where more than 30–40% of the Komsomol generation are participants (*Inogo ne dano*, (fn. 3), p. 223).
72. Shimotomai, *Gorubachev no jidai*, (fn. 1), p. 143.
73. *Otkrytaya zona*, 7: 117.
74. *Otkrytaya zona*, 7: 84, 89.
75. *Otkrytaya zona*, 7.
76. *Ogonek*, 4 (1989): 29.
77. *Sotsiologicheskie issledovaniya*, 5 (1988): 14.
78. See *Literaturnaya gazeta*, 49 (1988) for People's Front in Kazakhstan.
79. Gorbachev's speech at the UN. Incidentally, the law on glasnost had already been drafted by the commission headed by the late Vasiliev of IGPAN but was not yet ratified (*Sovetskoe gosudarstvo i pravo*, 2 (1988): 146–7).
80. *Voprosy filosofii*, 8 (1987): 75–91. See also *MEiMO*, 11 (1988): 5–18, especially E. Migranyan, *XIX Vsesoyuznaya Konfrentsiya KPSS*, 118.
81. O. Rumyantsev, *O samodeyatel'nom dvizhenii obshchestvennykh initsiativ* (Moscow: IEMSS, 1988).
82. *Social Research* (Budapest), 55 (1–2) (1988): 13–42.
83. *Pravda*, 2 Sept. 1988; *International Herald Tribune*, 13 Feb. 1989. But according to one sociologist, only 18 among the 2,500 Moscow informals are 'anti-social' or 'extremist' (*Sotsiologicheskie issledovaniya*, 5 (1988): 13).
84. *Kommunist*, 17 (1988): 14.
85. M. Lewin, *The Gorbachev Phenomenon* (Berkeley: University of California Press, 1988).
86. *Moskovskie novosti*, 29 May 1987; *Argumenty i fakty*, 32 (1988).

5

Gorbachev's Economic Policies
after Four Years

Philip Hanson

Introduction

Perestroika means, to its author, more than economic reform. In
the first place, it is intended to be more than economic change; it
is seen by Gorbachev as a transformation of attitudes in Soviet
society and of the management of Soviet politics, as well as a
transformation of economic performance. In the second place, Gorbachev describes the economic part of perestroika as consisting of
more than the reform of the economic system. It starts with a
reassertion of discipline, followed by changes in priorities; it
extends (and Gorbachev in 1987 described this almost as if it was
no more than on a par with changing priorities) to 'a radical transformation of the economic mechanism' – that is, to reform.[1]

The tighter discipline, faster investment growth and concentration of investment on the cluster of electronics-based technologies are important elements in Gorbachev's policies. They have,
I think, contributed to the modest improvement in economic
growth in 1985–8 over 1981–5, at a time when the growth of capital
and labour inputs into production was slowing (see Table 5.1).
They have also, however, hindered the start of economic reform
proper. This point seemed to have been accepted by at least some
of the leadership in late 1988.

By the end of 1988 several of these policies were being revised.
There was a shift back to more 'consumerist' priorities with the
adoption of several decrees on the consumer sector and higher
consumer goods targets.[2] In October there was a decree greatly
softening the anti-alcohol campaign.[3] Meanwhile the reform debate
and the reform legislation had become more radical between 1987
and 1988.

As these conflicts between reform and policy were being
acknowledged, two difficulties about the reform itself were emerg-

Table 5.1   *Soviet economic growth since 1965: sectors, inputs and outputs (% pa growth rates)*

A   Soviet official measures

	1966–70	1971–5	1976–80	1981–5	1986[a]	1987	1988
NMP produced	7.7	5.7	4.2	3.5	4.1	2.3	4.6
NMP utilized	7.1	5.1	3.9	3.2	3.6	–	–
Gross industrial output	8.5	7.4	4.4	3.6	4.9	3.8	–
Gross agricultural output[b]	3.9	2.4	1.7	1.1	5.1	0.2	–
Investment[b]	7.4	7.2	5.2	3.2	8.0	4.7	–
Capital stock	7.5	7.9	6.8	6.0	5.3	5.0	–
Electric power	7.9	7.0	4.5	3.6	3.6	4.1	–
Three main fuels[c]	5.2	5.4	4.2	2.5	4.6	3.1	–

B   CIA estimates[d]

GNP	5.1	3.0	2.3	1.9	3.8	0.5	
Industrial output	6.4	5.5	2.7	1.9	2.5	1.5	
Agricultural output	3.6	−0.6	0.8	1.2	8.2	−3.1	
Investment	5.5	4.3	4.3	3.5	6.0	4.7	
Capital stock	7.4	8.0	6.9	6.2	5.5	5.3	
Labour (man-hours)	2.0	1.7	1.2	0.7	0.4	0.4	
Per capita cons.	5.3	2.8	1.9	0.5	−2.0	0.7	

Notes: General: All output series and the investment and capital-stock series are, in principle, in constant prices, i.e. denote 'real' changes. The Soviet official series, however, are known to contain an element of hidden inflation and therefore to be upward-biased. See also note (*a*).

(*a*) Soviet reported growth rates for 1985 and 1986 are more than usually upward-biased. See Philip Hanson, 'Plan fulfilment in 1986. A sideways look at the statistics', *Radio Liberty Research Bulletin* RL 76/87 (26 Feb. 1987); Jan Vanous in *PlanEcon Report* (11 Feb. 1987).

(*b*) For five-year periods, the growth rates shown are those between the total for the period and the total for the preceding five-year period.

(*c*) Oil + gas + coal; author's estimates in terms of standard coal fuel units.

(*d*) At 1982 rouble factor cost. 1987 figures are preliminary. *Sources: Narodnoe khozyaistvo SSSR* (various years); *Pravda* (24 Jan. 1988); CIA, *Handbook of Economic Statistics 1986*; Laurie Kurtzweg, 'Trends in Soviet Gross National Product', in US Congress Joint Economic Committee, *Gorbachev's Economic Plans*, Washington DC, US Government Printing Office, 1987, vol. 1: pp. 126–66; CIA/DIA, 'Gorbachev's Economic Program: Problems Emerge', report to the Subcommittee on National Security Economics of the US Congress Joint Economic Committee, 13 April 1988; *Pravda* 28 Oct. 1988, pp. 1–2; *Strany-chleny SEV v 1988*: 26.

ing more clearly. First, it was felt in Moscow to be increasingly difficult to implement real organizational changes. Second, the lack of a clear and agreed vision of reform became more obvious.

Few people of influence in Moscow have a clear idea of what the new system should be like. Fewer still have any clear programme for moving, in stages, from here to there. Probably most reformers share the following general belief that an economy in which the managers of most production units most of the time worry mainly about customers, and competitors will deliver more prosperity in the long run than an economy in which most managers most of the time worry mainly about the 'higher authorities'. How to achieve this happy state is not clear.

Experience in Hungary, Poland and China shows that turning an administrative economy into a competitive economy is very hard. Moreover, the Soviet Union has several handicaps that Hungary, Poland and China do not: notably, a potentially severe nationalities problem and much longer habituation to a non-market system.

The State of Play at the End of 1988

On the face of it, Gorbachev's radical economic policies are going ahead successfully. Officially, total production in 1988 was expected to be about 4 per cent above 1987. These numbers refer to what is known in the West as net material product, or NMP. That is the Soviet-style definition of national output; it excludes depreciation and most services and is therefore different from the Western-style GNP measure of a nation's output. This means that the Soviet official measure of output in 1988 was about where it was planned to be according to the 1986–90 plan: around 14 per cent above 1985. On this basis, performance in 1986–8 inclusive looks slightly better than in 1981–5, at 3.7 per cent a year growth against 3.5 per cent. Moreover, the services sector, largely excluded from the NMP figures, has been growing considerably faster than material production. That means – and again, it must be said that this is the first impression, from the official figures – that national output in the Western (GNP) sense ought to have been growing at more than 3.7 per cent.

The five-year plan target for 1989 (or, to be precise, what we are now told it originally was) could be reached by a modest 3.4 per cent increase. Food output is reported to be growing somewhat faster than population; there is no balance of payments crisis; the level of external debt is modest, and (good news for East–West traders) imports from the West have been increasing quite strongly: some 15 per cent up in the first half of 1988 over the first half of 1987.

In the background are the political reforms and the bold measures in foreign policy. Gorbachev seems set to install himself in a specially powerful position as a new type of Soviet president, with a degree of independence from his Politburo colleagues that has not been matched by a Soviet leader since Stalin. Unlike Stalin, he looks determined to use his powers in a reforming, Westernizing and peacemaking direction. His flexibility on defence policies has been demonstrated most recently in unilateral conventional arms cuts, including a reduction of half a million over two years in troop numbers.

That particular cut may be marginal to the military balance, and it is certainly not substantial in relation to the economy. Still, it should add about 0.2 per cent a year for two years to the civilian labour force, which is not negligible when growth of labour inputs had slowed to 0.4 per cent a year in the absence of such cuts. As a sign of his general approach, moreover, moves like this strengthen impressions based on other evidence of an effort to shift at least some resources from military to civilian uses.

All this suggests a healthy economic picture. Even if the NMP growth figures are adjusted for concealed inflation and made comparable to Western real growth GNP numbers, the signs are that growth is of the order of 2.5 per cent a year under Gorbachev so far: not very impressive by international standards for a medium-developed economy, but surely respectable enough for such an economy when it is undergoing radical reform after growing at less than 2 per cent a year in the early 1980s. Why, then, is there so much gloom among the commentators over the state of the Soviet economy and its medium-term prospects?

The answer lies partly in the state of the reform, and partly in the confused state of macroeconomic policy and priorities. There is a pessimistic mood about the reform among the Moscow intelligentsia, which may be exaggerated but which has been communicated much more swiftly and accurately to Western analysts than it would have been in the past, when contact was so much more restricted.

The reasons for the pessimism in Moscow are briefly as follows. To begin with, the shortages of food and other consumer goods in the shops seem to have worsened, and there is a fear that 'the people' will fail to support continued reform if reform does not deliver the goods. A third of the Russian republic currently has rationing of meat and dairy produce – a situation not much different from that of 1981–2. The 1987 law on the state enterprise, the centrepiece of the package of reform measures designed to decentralize the state sector, is now widely seen as inadequate. State enterprises remain tied to the 'higher authorities' (usually branch ministries), and they remain, broadly speaking, as disinclined as ever to cut costs on their own initiatives or to innovate.

The fact that prices are still centrally controlled (with a marginally larger number of exceptions than before) is part of the problem. It now looks increasingly unlikely that the reform of industrial wholesale prices in 1990–1 will include much decentralization of price-setting or bring the structure of wholesale prices close to the structure of world market prices, except in so far as internal real energy prices are raised. The politically more sensitive issue of retail prices, where an elimination of food subsidies would raise state food prices by an average of around 40 per cent (see Annex 5.1, page 118) now looks like being addressed only later in the 1990s, and then (no doubt sensibly) in stages. The transition of state enterprises to trading with one another instead of having their materials, bought-in components and equipment centrally allocated to them, is also hanging fire. Some transfers to the new 'wholesale trade' arrangements indicate the problems: enterprises that have to find their own customers often find they have unsellable products (at existing prices), and producers 'free to choose' their own suppliers of inputs often simply cannot get (at existing prices) the items they want. Yet if prices were simply decontrolled they would go through the roof – or so, at least, most people believe.

The bold attempts during 1988 to change the ownership system and introduce a substantial, legalized non-state sector are potentially more promising, but face enormous obstacles: hostility from local officials; difficulties for the new non-state firms in buying the inputs they want when so much is still centrally allocated; encroachment on their activities by the criminal underworld, practising new skills in laundering money and running protection rackets; and above all the uncertainty of both potential entrepreneurs and potential full-time private-sector employees about the durability of the new liberalism. The pressures to make quick profit out of shortages and not invest significantly are great. The result is popular resentment of 'profiteering' by the new cooperatives, which bolsters the support for new politicians.

Behind these severe difficulties in changing the system lies a set of circumstances that is partly of the Gorbachev leadership's own making. There is strong inflationary pressure fuelled by a large and latterly increasing budget deficit. In 1989 the declared deficit will be, I estimate, about 5 per cent of NMP or 4 per cent of GNP (see Table 5.2). The Soviet economy, in other words, now turns out to have a key problem in common with the US economy: a large and intractable budget deficit – indeed, one whose dimensions are worse than those of the US budget in relation to the economy as a whole. The addition to government debt, both long- and short-term, will be considerably larger than 4 per cent of GNP: perhaps as much as 12 per cent. Declining world oil prices have contributed to this, since favourable differences between foreign prices (at the official exchange rate) and domestic prices have in the past been a major source of government revenue. Probably more important, however, has been the effect of rising farm costs and therefore rising farm subsidies, given the fixed retail prices; this, in turn, has been exacerbated by a major loss of budget revenue from the cuts in alcohol sales enforced by the leadership's own anti-alcohol campaign.

Table 5.2 *Price distortions and money supply pressures in the USSR: some numbers: Plan 1989, billion roubles, current prices and % of national income*

NMP produced (estimated, approximate)	660	100.0
subsidies from state budget	103	15.6
of which, on food	88	13.3
turnover tax	104	15.8
budget income and expenditure arising from differences between Soviet and world prices, given the official exchange rate:([a])		
income	60	9.1
expenditure	29	4.4
net budget income	31	4.7
declared budget deficit	35	5.3
'resources of govt loan fund'	63	9.5
hence, apparent total govt borrowing	98	14.8

([a]) income = (?) Q_m (P_m − RP_{wm}) (?) excluding intra-FTO offsetting expenditure = (?) Q_x (RP_{wx} − P_x) excluding intra-FTO offsetting (usually negative)

Source (for numbers): derived from Gostev budget speech, Maslyukov plan speech and final Supreme Soviet amendments (*Pravda* 28 Oct. 1988; 2–5, 29 Oct. 1988; 2).

Additions to the supply of other consumer goods, to offset the fall in official alcohol supplies, were not made in 1986–7, and this worsened shortages in the shops, even though the absolute amount of consumer goods supplied probably increased a little.

The over-ambitious targets set in 1985–6 for industrial modernization, with little reliance on increased machinery imports, have added to the strain, and helped to generate money-wage increases over and above the productivity growth. The fall in the earning capacity of Soviet staple exports of oil and gas, both in Eastern Europe and in Western markets, has made resorts to imports politically difficult, given the continued reluctance to increase debt to the West. Joint ventures may be useful at the margin, but some 140 joint ventures so far have brought in less than a tenth of 1 per cent of the Soviet Union's annual flow of investment.

The plan for 1989 puts all state enterprises onto the new 'self-financing' basis. It also sets ceilings for the share of output that can be covered by state orders – the new equivalent of the old centralized allocation. For several industries these ceilings are low; for example, 25 per cent of output in civilian engineering. However, other devices for maintaining central control over the allocation of producer goods are springing up, such as a class of 'specially imported products', that will be controlled for the sake of 'economic balance'.[4] Only about one-seventh of intermediate output seems set to be freely traded – and even that may not materialize in practice.

The policy error of going for ambitious investment plans while trying simultaneously to reform the economic system seems to have been acknowledged by the policy-makers. There has been a retreat from the high investment priority asserted in 1985–6 and maintained, apparently, until about autumn 1988. At that time worries about consumer shortages increased. New consumer-goods targets have been added to the original (1985) plan for 1989. There has also been a shift towards importing somewhat more, with worries about the (low) debt level apparently somewhat relaxed. Importing on credit, however, seems likely to be restricted to capital goods, with a special emphasis on capital goods for the light and food-processing industries. And it is unlikely that Soviet debt levels will be allowed to increase greatly.

The reform process is therefore entering a delicate phase. There could be a loss of momentum if a critical mass of organizational change is not reached and if consumer welfare goes on stagnating. The hopeful signs are the continued determination to press ahead with changes. This was recently exemplified by the extension of foreign-trade rights to all states and cooperative enterprises and the creation of an internal hard-currency market.[5]

Conclusions

Policy-makers now face the following transitional problems:

1 If the branch ministries continue to exist, they will go on 'controlling' 'their' enterprises, since the ministries are held respon-

sible for what happens in 'their' industries. No move has yet been made to abolish these ministries.

2 If, despite (1), enterprises did get the freedom to set output levels and pursue profits, the results would not be efficient. So long as most prices are centrally fixed and far from supply–demand equilibrium, profits are a poor guide to resource allocation.

3 If the prices are decontrolled, many of them, including food prices, will go sky-high. Subsidies on food prices now exceed 10 per cent of national income (NMP). To make things worse, the highly concentrated structure of production (fewer manufacturing enterprises than in Britain) guarantees extensive monopoly power.

4 If materials, components and machinery cease to be centrally allocated and are instead freely traded among producers, many enterprises will in the short-to-medium term be unable to sell what they produce and may well be unable to obtain the inputs they want – at virtually any price. This is already happening in the attempted transition to 'wholesale trade in the means of production'. In other words, the structure of output and of capacity needs to change sharply. The adjustment problem would be akin to that of a capitalist market economy that has to shift at short notice to a war footing; in Britain in 1939–41, this adjustment was not left to the market.

5 There are obvious political problems about making adjustments quickly (factory closures and so on). But making them slowly brings the risk of failing to reach a critical mass of organizational change that would sustain confidence in the reform's momentum.

6 'Decentralizing', if it were done, would probably be inadequate to transform performance if the state still owned most resources. State-owned enterprises tend in all countries to be bailed out when in trouble, and thus to be spared the ultimate competitive stimuli. Recent Soviet legislation, especially on cooperatives and joint ventures, implies that policy-makers recognize this problem. But such recognition entails (many would argue) changes that go beyond 'market socialism'. How do you value assets, create freedom for market entry and exit, or allow productivity-enhancing patterns of capital flows between branches without a capital market? Faith in the centre's ability to enforce efficiency in current production or to allocate investment rationally has dwindled.

7 Expanding the private and cooperative sector (the coops are

just private firms with a Leninist name) helps to deal with problems (1), (4) and (6). But how do you privatize assets when there is no existing private corporate sector, including institutional investors, to buy them? Household financial assets are probably equivalent to less than a fifth of the 'productive' capital stock.

The obstacles to success are technical (deciding exactly what to do and how to do it) and political (the resistance and opposition of people who stand to lose status, to lose some economic security, to have to work harder or to lose (if only relatively) from changes in the established pattern of differentials).

Attachment to Marxist-Leninist principles is probably not an obstacle, but claims to ideological purity may be used as a tactic by those who object on other grounds. (These other grounds could include a genuine attachment to a 'safe', if poor, lifestyle – for others as well as for oneself. The traditional Soviet way of life, though hardly anybody votes for it with their feet, is not without its charms.) The officials seem to be preoccupied with the obstacles to change, and pessimistic about dealing with them.

A gradual opening to the world economy is part of the reformers' strategy. This is in my view to be welcomed by Western governments, but its success depends overwhelmingly on the success of the domestic reforms. There is a new and remarkable readiness on the part of at least some senior officials to listen to the views of Westerners about how reforms could proceed, especially those reforms that directly affect foreign trade. Dialogue about reform should in my view be encouraged, though without patronizing or pontificating from our side.

One way forward may be through the creation of special economic zones. These would need to be not just exporting enclaves but bridgeheads for the reform process (one way of tackling the 'critical mass' problem). Like all the various reform strategies, however, this has its attendant political problems: the Baltic states, for example, would in many ways be exemplary special zones, but there is a profound fear of encouraging their incipient separatism.

The chances of the Soviet economy becoming technologically dynamic, prosperous and internationally competitive before, at best, the early years of the next century, are in my view slim. But even incomplete reforms may achieve something: especially in the farm sector, where the scope for improvement is enormous and encouragement of some sort of family farming is being attempted.

Notes

1. M. Gorbachev, *Perestroika* (2nd ed.) (London: Fontana, 1988), p. 28.
2. *Izvestiya*, 21, 23 and 24 Aug. 1988.
3. *Pravda*, 26 Oct. 1988.
4. See the article by V. Moskalenko and others on a further reform experiment starting in 1989 at the Sumy science-production association, *Ekonomicheskaya gazeta*, 47 (1988): 12–13.
5. *Izvestiya*, 10 July 1988, p. 2.

Annex 5.1 Effects of removing the Soviet Food-price subsidy: rough estimates

A Estimates of food subsidies as percentages of household income, expenditure and food expenditure, 1986, from *Narkhoz 17–87*:

1 Household income (*N17–87* page numbers in brackets). Average wage in state employment (434): 195.6 roubles/month. Average numbers in state employment (411): 118.5 mn. Hence, total income from state employment = 278.1 billion roubles/year.

Average kolkhoznik income from social labour (435): 163 r/month. Average annual number of kolkhozniki at work (411): 12.4 mn. Hence, total kolkhoznik income from kolkhozy = 24.3 bn r/year.

Total pensions & *posobiya* (435): 63.9 bn r/year.

Other income (mostly private sources), say, 15% of the sum of the above: 54.9 bn r/year.

Hence, total of the above: 421.2 bn r/year.

Taxes on population (628): 31.2 bn r/year.

Hence, post-tax household incomes in 1986: 390 bn r.

Increase in savings-bank deposits (448): 22 bn r. Hence, household expenditure in 1986: 368 bn r.
2 Food sales through state and cooperative trade (464): 156.5 bn r.
3 Approximate size of food-price subsidies in 1986 (various sources): 67–70 bn r.

B Some key relative magnitudes (total = 1) in 1986:

1 State food sales/disposable incomes: 0.401
2 State food sales/household expenditure: 0.425
3 Food subsidies/state food sales: 0.38–0.45

4   Food subsidies/disposable incomes: 0.15–0.18
5   Food subsidies/household expenditure: 0.16–0.19.

C   Some working assumptions for a trial calculation:

1   Price elasticity of demand for all food = 0.4.
2   Income elasticity of demand for food = 0.2.

Note to C: These elasticities are taken from estimates for the UK in 1960s and 1970s (R. Lipsey, *Introduction to Positive Economics*, 5th edition, 1979). The Soviet values are likely to be somewhat different. More important is the disequilibrium in Soviet consumer markets, with prices short of market-clearing levels. Price elasticities will be a guide only to movements along and shifts of the demand curve in relation to what Soviet households *seek* to buy at present prices.

D   Some trial calculations about the effect of removing subsidies, on the basis of 1986 data.

1   Subsidy abolished without compensation.
    (i) Food prices rise 38–45%.
    (ii) Overall cost of living rises by 0.425 × food price rise = 16–19%.
    (iii) Quantity of food sought by consumers in state and other shops falls by 0.4 × 38 to 45% = 15–18%.
    (iv) Expenditure on food rises by 0.82 × 45 to 0.85 × 38% = 32 to 37%. Expenditure on non-food falls by 24 to 27%.
2   Food subsidy switched from prices to incomes.
    (i) Disposable incomes rise by 15–18%.
    (ii) Quantity of food demanded rises by 0.2 × 15 to 18% = 3 to 4%.
    (iii) Hence, food expenditure as % old expenditure level, given new prices, rises from 56–58 to 58–60 (1.03 × 56 to 1.04 × 58). Non-food expenditure then, as % old total expenditure = 115–58 to 118–60, or 57 to 58% of old expenditure level, i.e., approximately unchanged in both nominal and real terms, but only 49–50% of the new level of total disposable income.

Annex 5.2   Indicators for monitoring change from 1989 (in likely chronological sequence)

Organizational
Creation of Special Economic Zones (SEZs). More encouraging if they are larger than a few towns, and not purely export enclaves. Could be regional + coops and joint ventures. Better if *not* defined on the basis of branches.

Extension of wholesale trade, fall in percentage of output covered by state orders (goszakazy): This could lead to problems and a retreat; encouraging if the extension proceeds over time.

Abolition of branch ministries. Best if a single Ministry for Industry replaces all industrial branch ministries, with an appropriately reduced staff.

Price reform. Major reforms ought to be through by 1992. In the case of industrial wholesale prices, a substantial share of 'contract' pricing, negotiated between buyers and sellers, should be involved. It is unrealistic to expect complete de-control early, but the revised (centrally set) structure of prices of key products and indices for product groups should come appreciably closer to the world market price structure reflected in Soviet trade with the West. On retail food prices, at least an absolute reduction in subsidies is needed.

Non-resident rouble convertibility. Unlikely before 2000 at best, but desirable.

Removal of administrative (central planners') control of imports. Might start early in SEZs.

Information Policy
Regular publication of money supply, meaningful budget data, balance of payments, reserves and debt series. Reform of price indices.

Performance
Money supply. Growth needs to be controlled early, though decent data needed before we can judge. Linked to control of budget deficit.

Share of officially acknowledged non-state sector in total output ought to rise to >10 percent of national output reasonably quickly (say, by 1993).

Farm imports: sustained fall in absolute volume needed soon.

Manufactured exports: sustained rise in Soviet share of OECD total imports of manufactures. Will not happen quickly, but is probably the best measure of success in the long run.

Note

Pending reform of statistics, official measures of output growth will not be good measures of success. Even without the data problem, radical reform requires major changes in the structure of output, and this will tend to slow growth for a time. An exception to this generalization is farm output, especially the physical output measures reported for individual products. These could improve early, and it will be a good sign if they do. (To some extent, they have already done so.)

6

The Soviet Union: A Player in the World Economy?

Akio Kawato

The economy of the Western world is undergoing possibly one of the most profound transformations experienced since World War II. The United States no longer dominates international economics: its declining productivity, together with an inclination to over-consumption, has exposed the dollar to speculation in international currency markets. Consequently, to prevent any major economic disruption, coordination of economic policy among the industrialized nations of the West is now indispensable. Furthermore, increasing divergence of productivity rates among industrialized countries has encouraged some of them to form economic blocs, thereby accelerating the disintegration of the established order. As a result of these recent developments the international economy now finds itself at a crossroads. However, this is not to say that the capitalist economic system as a whole has lost its vitality: technological innovation is advancing ever more rapidly, and in the Pacific area new markets are expanding. In most Western countries, high levels of both consumption and investment continue and, in spite of high unemployment rates in some West European countries, there is no serious threat of social unrest. In the capitalist economic system, the trend towards economic deregulation, together with the modernization of telecommunications, has diminished the significance of borders between states; the 'borderless economy' is gradually emerging in the shape of free capital flows, international cooperation among large enterprises and international mergers and acquisitions. In the West, wars fought to win new markets are a thing of the past; the balance of power is no longer determined by military force but by economic strength. In such an economic environment, the Soviet Union is in an awkward position since the source of its power has traditionally been military rather than economic strength. Its stagnating economy no longer has many admirers abroad; it has, on the contrary, discredited socialism.

President Gorbachev has embarked on a sweeping overhaul of the economic system, even proclaiming that the global economy is being 'unified' and that the Soviet Union should take a more active part in this process. If he succeeds in his endeavour, his reforms will achieve the greatest revolution ever seen in the history of the Soviet economy. Discussion in the West is now focused on how to deal with this fresh wind from Moscow. Supporters of perestroika argue that it is high time to 'incorporate' the Soviet Union into the global economy: by so doing, we could transform this formidable military power into a docile mercantile partner and thus achieve permanent stability in the world. Indeed, some even speak of the necessity of 'helping perestroika'. However, encouraging as the developments in the USSR may be, the West should not embark upon any hasty, unconsidered course of action. Little evidence of real change in the Soviet economy has been seen so far and the prospects of success are uncertain; indeed, the kind of incomplete reforms witnessed thus far could eventually be counter-productive. The Soviets are in serious trouble and are appealing for international economic cooperation, but in reality their economy is ill-prepared for this kind of ambitious step: it is neither flexible nor open enough and, furthermore, has little to offer the West. Soviet exhortations to international economic cooperation are therefore little more than a cry for help. Without unnecessarily antagonizing the Soviet Union, it must be acknowledged that the West cannot afford to help the Soviets out of trouble. Its needs are limitless and its economic system cannot exploit foreign assistance effectively. What is more, its dreadful military machine is, by and large, still intact. The purpose of this article is to evaluate the opportunities which exist to incorporate the Soviet Union into the global economy and the obstacles standing in the way of this.

Will the Soviet Economy Recover?

The Soviet Union's desire to play a more active role in the world economy seems to be genuine, and such a development will be welcomed in the West if the necessary improvements in its economy are brought about in a fair manner. But how far the Soviets can succeed will depend upon their own economic strength; in other words, how well the Soviets manage to revitalize and reform their own economy will determine the degree to which they can be integrated into the global economy. The outlook is not reassuring. The Soviet economy suffers from many scarcities and bottlenecks in the supply of materials and labour, problems which are aggravated by a lack of technological innovation and of efficiency in general. The path to economic reform is dogged by deadly political pitfalls, such as inflation, unemployment and widening income differentials, not to speak of the considerable and still widespread resistance to opening up the Soviet economy; it would be hard to imagine, for instance, a merger between the Soviet automobile manufacturers Volga and Volkswagen or Toyota.

Obstacles to Economic Development
By paying too much attention to the Soviet economic mechanism, we tend to overlook the fact that the economy itself suffers from many shortages and bottlenecks. The USSR has openly acknowledged a deficit, which runs at 7 per cent of its total budget. In addition, resources for investment have always been tight, due mainly to the rising cost of energy. The shortage of capital, however, could be easily overcome: it is widely known that the ill-managed lending practices of Soviet banks have flooded the economy with money. Furthermore, the Soviet Union has a large, untapped reserve of monetary resources – almost one-third of personal savings is not deposited in banks. These 'hidden' savings could be mobilized by issuing government bonds or liberalizing the stock exchange.

'Money can always be found, but not materials' – this is the most frequent complaint made by directors of Soviet businesses. The principal problem facing the Soviet economy is not shortage of money but of goods. Despite the fact that existing deposits of oil, coal and iron ore are being exhausted and their productivity is rapidly declining, conservation of energy and materials has not yet become a priority for Soviet entrepreneurs, as the failure to meet annual conservation targets demonstrates. For one unit of production, Soviet industry consumes 1.75 times more iron and 1.53 times more energy than the Western average.[1] Shortage of electricity is also a perennial problem in the USSR; voltage fluctuates between 240 and 200 volts, and frequency sometimes drops to 49 kHz, which can damage electronic devices and disrupts their normal functioning.[2] Chernobyl has exacerbated the problem by delaying the construction of nuclear plants. Another problem is the shortage of labour: fresh influxes of labour have decreased from 11 million during 1976–80 to 3 million during 1981–5 (of whom 2.5 million came from Azerbaijan and Soviet Central Asia).[3] Poor transport and communications networks constitute yet another hindrance to economic development. The Soviet Union is proud of its brilliant tradition in science, but the fact remains that the fruits of these labours are seldom utilized in civilian production. The non-military economy is also burdened with Soviet directors' preference for meeting quantitative targets as opposed to improving product quality by introducing technological innovation: indeed, sometimes they are physically incapable of introducing new technology because Soviet machines are not designed to carry out delicate processes and because they lack the necessary high-quality materials. There are now signs that the Soviets are even beginning to lag behind in basic research, an area in which they have traditionally excelled. This is due to lack of sufficient computers in terms of both quantity and quality. Obsolete machinery is therefore a serious problem in the Soviet economy: almost half of its plants are more than twenty years old.[4]

Gorbachev is trying to overcome this handicap by accelerating the renovation of equipment and pumping more resources into the machine-building sector but, ironically, this comprehensive wave of renovation has itself incurred a shortage of machinery. Furthermore, most 'new' machines are not much more efficient than their predecessors.

Is a Market Economy Possible in the Soviet Union?

The key problem in the Soviet economy is the shortage of raw materials (*defitsit*): this shortage necessitates the central distribution of materials, hampers competition and, accordingly, does not provide incentives to improve quality or introduce new technology. The *defitsit* has been produced by the protectionist nature of the Soviet economy: in the Soviet Union, unprofitable businesses (about 13 per cent of the total)[5] and internationally uncompetitive sectors are maintained by government subsidy – which means, in part, by the profits of successful businesses. Another consequence of the absence of competition is waste of materials, which of course exacerbates the *defitsit* problem. Central distribution has deprived Soviet enterprises of incentive to show initiative and innovation. Businesses are run not according to the principles of entrepreneurship but of bureaucratism. They avoid responsibility and risk, and react not to the demand of the consumer but to the commands of central bureaucracy. Marketization of the economy and the introduction of competition can only be effected where there is flexibility on the supply side: if the supply of materials is tight or centralized, firms will not be able to react quickly to a shift in the market or, conversely, to expand production of competitive goods. But creation of such flexibility would be a difficult task for the Soviet economy. The Soviets contend that current reforms will force firms to conserve materials because most of the profits are no longer required to be turned over to the state but are left to businesses to dispose of at their discretion. However, this claim has yet to be verified: since industries collect more bonuses by fulfilling production quotas than by conserving materials, conservation targets have consistently not been met. One benefit of disarmament has been that some resources are now being diverted from the military to the civil economy, a development discussed by Julian Cooper in Chaper 7. But this redistribution of resources will not prove to be a panacea for the Soviet economy because the military will most probably try to keep the better scientists, along with high-quality materials and machine tools.

It is an established tradition in the Soviet Union that the consumer-goods sector of the economy is allotted second-class resources. The best way to overcome this *defitsit* would be to reduce or liquidate uncompetitive sectors and businesses. However, this would involve immense social sacrifice and is fraught with political risk: the authorities would be faced with the gigantic task of economic restructuring, complicated by the severe social problems arising from mass unemployment and bankruptcies on a hitherto unprecedented scale. Since prices in socialist economies are severely distorted by all manner of subsidies, all major economic reforms should be preceded by drastic price reform. As a result of frequently arbitrary pricing, some prices guarantee unjustifiably large profit margins while others do not even cover production costs. Under the present system, it is impossible to judge which enterprises are unprofitable and which sectors are internationally uncompetitive; to correct this, state subsidies should be reduced and market prices introduced. These measures will inevitably incur inflation, as was the case in Poland and Hungary, but this is an inescapable stage on the way to economic reform.

As we have seen, the transition from a protectionist, centralized economy is accompanied by almost unendurable sacrifice and considerable political risk. The Gorbachev administration has embarked on a very bold reform course; the centralized system is to be liberalized and private economic activity encouraged. In the agricultural sector the rent (*arenda*) system is being introduced, which is tantamount to individual land ownership. In his eagerness to reform, however, Gorbachev has put the cart before the horse: he has granted independence to businesses without first introducing price reform and liberalizing the distribution of raw materials, inadvertently unleashing monopolistic tendencies in the economy. Firms now produce fewer goods with low profit margins and arbitrarily raise prices under the pretext of providing new products. Consequently, some household goods have become unobtainable and inflation is beginning to bite. As stated above, businesses are now accorded more jurisdiction over the disposal of their profits, but consumers are disappointed at the lack of goods to spend their money on.

Private economic activity is growing, but is hampered by heavy taxation, harassment by local officials and shortage of necessary materials. The 'co-operative restaurants', much applauded by the Western media when they opened, have turned out to be luxuries which only the rich can afford and now excite only resentment among the general population, especially as they tend to buy up much of the scarce supplies of meat and vegetables in the state wholesale shops. The problem is that most of the Soviet people have lost whatever skills in private economic activity they still possessed at the time of the New Economic Policy (NEP). The *arenda* system is unpopular among the peasants because it has resulted only in harder work and unstable incomes; they have lost a secure existence on the collective farms and have not yet acquired the skills needed to succeed at private farming. Having realized the error of granting more autonomy to the business sector before reforming the price system and materials distribution, Gorbachev is now trying to correct his mistake by declaring that the supply system should be liberalized by 1990 and price reforms completed by 1991. Measures are being taken to close unprofitable enterprises or rent them to cooperatives. The future of the Soviet economy will depend on whether these aspirations can be translated into reality. So far, the prospects are not encouraging. Liquidation of unprofitable businesses is proceeding but on a limited scale and only small firms are affected. Ministries resist the closure of 'their' enterprises because of fear of disgrace, and also it makes the task of meeting production quotas more difficult. The difficulty of enforcing the liquidation of unprofitable businesses is underlined by the fact that even in Hungary, where the leadership is committed to rigorous reforms, the process of liquidation has tended to lose momentum. The renting of unprofitable enterprises to cooperatives has not always been a complete success either; workers sometimes resent it because it makes labour more intensive. Merging unprofitable businesses into larger ones is another solution, but is at best only a makeshift policy, not a long-term strategy.

In sum, then, there does not appear to be much hope of alleviating the shortages of consumer goods. There will continue to be insufficient competition in the Soviet economy, with the result that

the improvement of product quality and the introduction of technological innovation will take place slowly. In such circumstances,
three scenarios can be proposed: (1) most of the reform efforts will
be sabotaged and the old system will survive; (2) the authorities
will succeed in enforcing economic reform, at least superficially,
but this will ultimately bring about economic chaos; (3) the administration will slow down the tempo of reform in order to avoid
economic disruption. In none of these scenarios does the Soviet
economy become either liberalized or revitalized enough to be able
to participate seriously in the global economy.

The Soviet Union: a Player in the World Economy?

Changing Ideology
Faced with such gloomy prospects for the economy, Gorbachev has
directed his attention outward and revised the traditional approach
to the world economy. In this regard Soviet ideology has undergone
a thorough revision. The world, once clearly divided between
socialists and capitalists, has suddenly become united, and interdependence is now the key word. The Soviet Union has even become
a quasi-member of OPEC, declaring in March 1989 that it would
reduce oil exports by 5 per cent. At the party plenum in January
1987, Gorbachev stated that 'the world today forms a single entity.
All nations are interrelated and interdependent in spite of all their
fundamental differences. The globalization of economic activities,
the revolutions in science and technology and the dramatic new role
of telecommunications have all contributed to this phenomenon.'
Gorbachev considers foreign trade to be an integral part of the
Soviet economy, and not merely, as used to be the case, a means
of compensating for domestic shortages. He now says openly that
active participation in foreign trade will introduce competitive
thinking into the Soviet economy. The objectives of the 'internationalization' of the Soviet economy are as follows: (1) the Soviet
Union needs advanced Western technology, otherwise it will be
left behind in the contest for technological superiority now being
fought in the West. Technical research and development is very
costly but international cooperation and the division of labour thus
effected could reduce costs substantially for the Soviet economy. (2)
The Soviet administration is trying to restructure exports, stressing
above all the need to export more manufactured goods. This would
be much more lucrative than simply exporting energy resources
and would force Soviet businesses to become more competitive.

When the fall in oil prices reduced foreign currency income by $8 billion, thus aggravating the budget deficit (I estimate that at least 10 per cent of Soviet revenue comes from oil exports), Soviet leaders could not help but appreciate how deeply their economy is affected by developments at the international level. However, there is still a long way to go before the Soviet Union can become a major player in the world economy: trade with the West is still marginal (about $50 million) given the size of the economy, amounting to only 2.5 per cent of GNP, and exports to capitalist countries, as a proportion of total exports, have declined from 32.6 per cent in 1980 to 20.2 per cent in 1988. This was due mainly to the fall in oil prices. The Eastern bloc's share in trade with the West has decreased from 2.37 per cent in 1980 to 1.95 per cent in 1987.[6] A further difficulty is the fact that the Soviet domestic market is still largely closed to outside trade, due to the inconvertibility of the rouble and the lack of foreign currency.

(a) Increasing Exports of Manufactured Goods   In order to become an economic force to be reckoned with at the international level, the Soviet Union must increase its exports of manufactured goods. Its present export structure is heavily dependent on the export of raw materials; it is inefficient and fails to provide a good enough basis for closer integration into the global economy. The percentage of manufactured goods as a proportion of total Soviet exports has declined from 21.6 per cent in 1980 to 20.9 per cent in 1986; in both 1986 and 1987 exports of machinery and equipment fell by 1 per cent in 1985 prices.[7] Furthermore, there is a structural imbalance in Soviet manufactured goods exports, making them vulnerable. Exports of consumer goods are very small, less than 3 per cent of total exports, while the bulk of manufactured exports is machinery and equipment. About 70 per cent of exports of manufactures to the West is made up of four groups of commodities: motor cars, power plant, technical instruments and laboratory equipment, and railway rolling-stock, with motor cars making up 46 per cent of this figure.[8] However, since 1987 there have been some hopeful signs. The proportion of manufactured goods in Soviet exports rose to 21.5 per cent in 1987. Soviet exports to industrialized capitalist countries have grown by 5 per cent, as opposed to only 0.1 per cent for total exports.[9] But further analysis is necessary to determine whether this indicates a substantial new trend, since some increases may be due to such unfair trade practices as dumping or counter purchase.

(b) Direct Trade with the West Trading procedure in the Soviet Union has been liberalized to provide a more stimulating business environment and to get rid of bureaucratic interventionism. From 1987 onwards, twenty ministries and seventy enterprises have been authorized to conduct foreign trade without the intervention of the Foreign Trade Ministry, and from April 1989 this right was extended to all internationally competitive businesses.[10] As of 1987, 19.5 per cent of all trade was done according to this new formula.[11] This certainly represents liberalization, but liberalization is not without its own problems, as we shall see below. Foreign business-men are now forced to travel vast distances in order to negotiate with their Soviet counterparts, and many Soviet businessmen suffer from a permanent shortage of skilled personnel who are experi-enced in foreign trade.

Thus far liberalization has been incomplete. For instance, firms are not allowed to dispose of all their foreign income as they see fit: only one-quarter of the car manufacturer Volga's foreign currency income is left at the firm's own disposal, and even then permission from the Foreign Trade Ministry is required (now the Foreign Economic Relations Ministry).[12] Such conditions are hardly conducive to increasing exports. There are limits also to what Soviet industry can cope with; for example, if an export becomes popular abroad, businesses cannot respond appropriately to the increased demand because of scarcities of materials. Conversely, the drive to increase exports occurs sometimes at the expense of domestic consumption. Muscovites now complain that it has become more difficult to purchase a car under perestroika, since more are now exported. Exports of passenger vehicles increased sharply from 20 per cent of total exports in 1985 to 23 per cent in 1986.

(c) Joint Ventures The adoption of the Law on Joint Ventures in January 1987 caused a sensation in the West. Until then it had been inconceivable that a Soviet administration firmly committed to public ownership of the means of production should permit joint ventures with Western capitalists. Even now, the Soviet consti-tution does not provide for such forms of property, making the concept of a joint venture actually unconstitutional. The aim of joint ventures is to attract foreign capital without incurring more debt and to acquire new technology and Western management skills. But this is not a new idea; even in the Brezhnev era, the Soviets insisted on 'industrial cooperation', which went far beyond simple trade and required foreign enterprises to become closely

involved in management and technological research and development.

The Soviet Union's active encouragement of joint ventures recalls the 'concessions' offered to foreign firms during Lenin's NEP. Like Gorbachev, Lenin then attempted to rescue the Soviet economy by injecting foreign capital and technology, but his efforts to persuade conservative colleagues of the merits of this scheme did not pay off and only a few foreign industralists took up his offer.

Now, as then, the number of joint ventures in the Soviet economy is low: at the beginning of 1989 they numbered 164, but Western investment in them comes to only about $500 million.[13] The reasons for this are many. Most foreign firms are concerned about possible restrictions on repatriation of profits, while poor infrastructure and unreliable supplies of materials are further drawbacks. Yet another barrier is the Soviet authorities' preference for export-oriented joint ventures, whereas Western businessmen tend to be more interested in the domestic market.

In order to remedy these deficiencies, the authorities adopted a new strategy in December 1988. From that point onwards, the foreign partner in a joint venture could hold up to 99 per cent of the capital, and foreigners could also become directors of joint ventures. Joint ventures for domestic production were also sanctioned by the new measures. But in spite of these improvements, conditions are still not favourable for the establishment of joint ventures. Frequent changes in the economic legislation and the instability of the rouble deter would-be investors. Therefore, the impact of joint ventures on the economy is likely to be limited.

(d) Free Trade Zones Although successful experiments with free trade zones in China have made these fashionable among Eastern bloc countries, socialist policy-makers are as yet cautious about their eventual utility. The reservations most commonly expressed are either that 'greedy Western capitalists' will rush in to exploit the newly established free trade zones, or that (should the greedy capitalists fail to materialize) Western governments will discourage investment in socialist free trade areas. Western investors interested in such free trade zones would be faced with problems similar to those associated with joint ventures: investments could be jeopardized by poor social infrastructure, unreliable supply of materials or arbitrary interventions by local officials. In such a hypothetical free trade area, Eastern bloc countries would have to compete with one another to provide as favourable conditions for investment as possible. This is especially true today, given the emergence of such

attractive locations for investments as Spain, Portugal or the Newly Industrialized Economies countries. All in all, it appears unlikely that free trade zones will become feasible in Eastern Europe. So far the Soviet Union has failed to establish even one such area, and where there are possible candidates, they lack the proper qualifications. The countries of the Soviet Far East have no proper infrastructure and labour is in short supply, while the resurgence of nationalism in the Baltic states has made the area unstable and therefore unattractive to investors.

(e) Accession to International Economic Organizations   The Soviet Union's expressed desire to join organizations such as GATT also caused rather a sensation in the West: it was felt that the Soviets, who had participated in the founding of the IMF but later withdrew because of the cold war, had finally offered proof of their willingness to join a Western 'club'. However, this is no romantic pipe dream on the part of the Soviet Union: they have concrete objectives in applying for membership of GATT, among which are the expansion of manufactured goods exports and the acquisition of Most Favoured Nation status which membership would bestow, and which would make its exports less vulnerable to arbitrary import restrictions. The difficulty here is that the Soviet economy is not 'compatible' with GATT. GATT is a network of concrete obligations and mutual concessions, which means that, in order to join, the Soviet Union would have to abolish its complicated multiple exchange rates, lift quantitative restrictions and suspend government subsidies. The accession of some of the Eastern European countries to GATT did not cause much disruption as their economies are small, but the accession of an economy the size of that of the Soviet Union could cripple GATT. Another impediment to its accession is that GATT is now preoccupied with major issues such as the Uruguay Round and the accession of China. At present, GATT has not much opportunity to discuss the USSR's accession, which is neither urgent nor of advantage to the organization. Unless the Soviet economy becomes strong enough to become truly open to international business, its accession to GATT would benefit only the Soviets themselves. The West should therefore carefully weigh hoped-for political gains against the likely economic burdens before admitting the Soviet Union to GATT. Fortunately for the West, the Soviets are in no hurry to join GATT. They are fully aware that their economy could not yet absorb such a move, which would have to be preceded by modification of their price and tariff system. As for the IMF, they have yet to express any interest in joining.

The Soviet Union is indeed adapting its foreign trade system, albeit slowly. As mentioned above, direct trade is now allowed, and reforms have been announced for the tariff system: by 1990 new tariff rates will be enforced, and regulations concerning non-tariff barriers will be elaborated from 1989 onwards.[14] Multiple exchange rates are to be abolished and the rouble devalued. However, whether these reforms will succeed remains to be seen.

(f) Relations with the EC   The CMEA Secretariat and the EC Commission adopted a Joint Declaration in June 1988. The Soviet Union now has an ambassador to the EC and is about to conclude a trade agreement with the Community it once regarded as an enemy. Will these developments provide a solid basis for closer economic ties with the West? It must be said that the likelihood of this happening is not great, mainly because the Joint Declaration is a purely formal document and involves neither rights nor obligations on either side. It is, rather, a propaganda piece. The EC Commission, however, instead of being taken in by such propaganda, has won Soviet consent to pursue a bilateral strategy in concluding trade agreements with Warsaw Pact countries, which means that it can adopt a differentiated attitude to each Eastern bloc country, depending upon how far their reform measures have advanced. This is a victory for the economic strength of the West. The EC's trade agreement with Hungary is the most generous so far, including, as it does, the extensive abolition of quantitative restrictions. However, the EC will not lift all restrictions, even for Hungary, since the Community could not absorb a flood of imports from Eastern Europe. Since the Soviet Union is incapable of increasing its exports to the West as much as it would like, due to the lack of competitive goods, the enhanced integration of the EC in 1992 will not necessarily strengthen economic ties between the EC and Comecon, but it might exert psychological pressure on Soviet bloc countries to reform their economic systems.

(g) Borrowing from the West   As the measures described above have yet to bear any fruit, the Soviet Union has resorted to increased borrowing in the financial markets of the West. Western banks are responding positively to Soviet approaches – for them, the Soviet Union is one of the few countries to which they can lend money safely. In 1988 the Soviet Union achieved a debt service ratio of 21, much lower than the average of 42 for the other East European countries. Not surprisingly, therefore, Soviet indebtedness to the West is growing. At the end of 1988 its estimated net

debt in convertible currencies stood at about $23 billion; in 1984 it was $11 billion, the lowest figure for the last ten years. The Soviet Union has even begun to issue bonds in Western markets, breaking a tradition which has survived since the Revolution: in 1988 they issued bonds for 100 million Swiss francs and 500 million Deutschmarks.[15]

This new trend in foreign borrowing will not increase unchecked: it will not reach pre-revolutionary levels, when foreign funds financed almost 40 per cent of total Soviet investments. The Soviet press is already reporting popular concern about the rapid increase in foreign borrowing, and the administration itself is showing restraint. The much-advertised lending by Western banks in 1988 (the credit extended was reported to amount to about $9 billion) has been disbursed only slowly, with some contracts not even being included. At current levels, foreign borrowing will not be able to do much to revitalize the Soviet economy to any great degree: the Soviet Union's annual investments total $300 billion and the potential need for finance to improve infrastructure is immense.

What is more, funds from foreign borrowing are not used efficiently: imported goods are often embezzled or wasted through careless transportation and imported plants are not operated efficiently. *Pravda* reported that in one imported chemical plant 3.5 times as many engineers and workers were working compared to its Western equivalent.[16] Furthermore, secrecy and lack of precision instruments and high-quality materials prevent the diffusion of high technology. The Soviet administration is now compelled to use foreign currency to import consumer goods in order to avert a popular backlash against perestroika, which means that foreign money will not be used to prevent an economic crisis but merely to afford a brief breathing space.

(h) The Asian Dimension　The Soviet Union has recently become more interested in the Pan-Pacific basin area than heretofore. Gorbachev stated his interest in this area in major speeches in Vladivostok in July 1986 and Krasnoyarsk in September 1988. What attracts the Soviets to this area is its potential for economic development. In this rapidly growing region, it is anxious to gain more political as well as economic influence, as can be seen by its current eagerness to join the PECC (Pacific Economic Cooperation Conference) and the Asian Development Bank. However, it is not at all certain that the Soviet Union can become a major partner in this region. The population of the Soviet Far East makes up only 2.5 per cent of the Soviet Union's total population. Soviet trade with its four

major partners in this area (Japan, China, Vietnam and North Korea) amounts only to 5.9 per cent of total trade and is only 2 per cent of the total turnover of the Pan-Pacific region.[17] So far, the Soviet Union is a negligible partner in this region.

In August 1987 the Soviets adopted a programme, grandiosely entitled 'The Long-Term State Programme for Complex Development of Production Capability in the Far East Area until 2000'. It foresees 200 billion roubles' investment for the coming fifteen years (twice as much as for the period between 1970 and 1985). According to its projection, production of machinery will also increase by 3.9 times, petroleum by 3.1–3.8 times, electricity by 2.6 times, and foreign exports will triple. If the goals of this programme are fulfilled, this would certainly provide a solid basis for serious Soviet participation in the Pan-Pacific economy. However, in an interview with *Izvestiya* on 4 September 1988, the main author of this programme, Dr Minakir, vice-director of the Economic Research Institute of the Far East Branch of the Soviet Academy of Sciences, disclosed with the utmost frankness the impracticability of this programme. He complained that it was merely an uncoordinated summing up of ideas presented by the ministries concerned. The goal of this programme, the improvement of infrastructure by 100 per cent in fifteen years, is completely beyond the Soviet Union's means. Instead, he contended that while machinery will be produced in large quantity, there will not be enough foreign customers, apart from the socialist countries, and the Soviet Far East will not be opened to tourism because of the reluctance of local officials, since many areas are 'militarily sensitive'.

The outlook for rapid economic development of the Soviet Far East is therefore not good: it is generally short of labour and production infrastructure, and the Soviets themselves are not ready to pour resources into the region – at least for another ten years. Their main concern now is the modernization of production equipment and the improvement of the infrastructure of the western half of the Soviet Union, where serious problems have to be tackled: supply of raw materials from mines is guaranteed only until 2000, and the much advertised BAM Railway is not yet in operation, having already been criticized as a colossal waste of resources. The capitalist economies in the Pacific basin have no urgent interest in undertaking projects in Siberia. The Japanese demand for raw materials will be satisified for years to come by long-term contracts with other countries; they therefore see no need to spend astronomical amounts of money in Siberia. Furthermore, as long as the territorial dispute over the Kurile Islands remains unresolved, the

Japanese government will hardly feel inclined to support Siberian projects.

The Soviet Union is now trying to force Japan into economic cooperation by playing the 'Korean card'. South Korean enterprises are showing increasing interest in trade with the Soviet Union to compensate for shrinking US markets. While generally endorsing such a move, the Korean government has adopted a rather cautious attitude to joint projects with the Soviet Union in Siberia. The chief obstacle to increased economic cooperation is political: as long as the Soviet Union does not officially recognize South Korea, the South Koreans are not likely to embark upon large-scale economic cooperation in Siberia. Soviet military assistance to the North is another impediment to economic cooperation between the two. In spite of all the sensational estimates, Soviet–Korean trade is only one-tenth of the trade between South Korea and China. Economic constraints also inhibit the rapid growth of Soviet–Korean trade: South Korea has only limited financial resources, and its markets could not absorb the vast quantities of raw materials which Siberia would wish to export.

Other NIEs do not hold out much prospect of successful economic cooperation with the Soviet Union either. Taiwan has as yet not even allowed direct trade with the Soviet Union, and trade with the ASEAN countries has always been marginal, since the Soviets do not have much to offer in the way of suitable exports. In its current economic state, the Soviet Union is not yet qualified to join the Pacific club. If the Soviets are allowed to 'slip in', they will benefit at our expense, both politically and economically.

(i) Convertibility of the Rouble   The culmination of all economic reforms would be the convertibility of the rouble: only with full convertibility will the Soviet Union be able to embark seriously on the internationalization and revitalization of its economy. However, convertibility will only be achieved with a sound economy and free trade, and progress towards this goal will necessarily be slow. First of all, Soviet prices will have to be brought into line with international market prices. Furthermore, subsidies to certain commodities will have to be suspended and the prices amended to reflect exact marginal production costs.

The exchange rate must also be corrected, which will entail devaluing the rouble by perhaps ten times its present value, otherwise the Soviet economy would not survive the onslaught of a torrent of foreign imports and an astronomical trade deficit would inevitably accumulate. The difficulties involved in moving to full convertibility of the rouble are underlined by the case of South Korea, which, despite its flourishing economy, has only recently begun to make progress towards the convertibility of the won. The Soviet Union is gradually implementing measures to bring about convertibility of its currency: in December 1988, a decision was taken to devalue the rouble by 200 per cent, starting in 1990, and to introduce a new rate in 1991.[18] In 1989, an open auction of foreign currencies was allowed. All this constitutes nothing other than an official admission of the black market rate.

(j) Cooperation within the Council for Mutual Economic Assistance (CMEA) In conjunction with its commitment to becoming more deeply involved in the Western economy, the Soviet Union is simultaneously trying to improve the efficiency of the CMEA, obviously with regard to the possible economic benefits which might accrue to itself. Since 60 per cent of Soviet trade is with Comecon countries, this concern is understandable. The main prescriptions for reinforcing the CMEA are intensification of cooperation in science and technology; the establishment of joint ventures and so-called 'direct links' between CMEA enterprises; joint exploitation of energy sources and convertibility of the 'transferable rouble'.

The Soviet Union is also anxious that other CMEA members provide consumer goods of better quality than heretofore. However, most other Comecon countries are more eager to expand their trade with the West since only from the West can they acquire the advanced machinery and technology they desperately need. They comply with Soviet pressure to improve cooperation within the CMEA, but unwillingly, out of political obligation rather than for their own economic benefit. The 'Complex Programme for the Development of Science and Technology up to the year 2000', adopted in June 1984, has achieved little, and the number of 'direct links' among CMEA countries has increased only on paper.

Relations among the CMEA countries are hampered by red tape and lack of advanced telecommunications equipment. Uncoordinated price systems are an obstacle to convertibility of their currencies. In October 1987 they agreed on the introduction of partial convertibility of the transferable rouble, limited to convertibility in transactions among joint ventures and 'direct links', but without the participation of Romania and the GDR. Romania has maintained its traditional reserve toward any attempt to strengthen CMEA integration, and the GDR is afraid that its commodities will be bought up by poorer colleagues, without proper counteroffers. Along with the failure to improve cooperation within the

CMEA, the turnover of trade among CMEA members has been declining, due mainly to the fall in the price of Soviet oil. After constant growth up to 1986, Soviet trade with Comecon countries showed a 0.5 per cent decline in 1987. In contrast to the first half of the 1980s the Soviets now have trade deficits with some CMEA members. At the forty-fourth plenum of the CMEA in July 1988, the establishment of an 'integrated market' was agreed as a goal: this would mean free movement of goods, services, capital and labour.[19] But only the future will reveal exactly when this integrated market might actually come about.

Conclusion

All in all, the outlook for the Soviet economy is rather grim. Although only in its very initial stages, economic reform has already caused disruption, and further liberalization could lead to chaos. But if fear of social unrest causes perestroika to falter now, then the Soviet economy would regress to its state under Brezhnev, or worse. In any case, the Soviet people are now more sophisticated and conscious of their rights than under Stalin, and would not tolerate such a set-back; an increase in social friction appears increasingly likely. Such is the dilemma now facing the Soviet authorities. Importing Western technology can offer only slight relief, and even this option is constrained by limited foreign currency reserves as well as the COCOM regulations restricting technology transfer. In such circumstances, serious involvement of the Soviet economy in the international system is inconceivable. If it were a result of the Soviet Union's own efforts and at its own cost, such involvement would be welcomed, but as things stand now, there is no reason to 'help' perestroika, at great cost to ourselves, by extending subsidized credits or allowing Soviet products to be dumped on our markets. (The Soviet economy has to a certain extent become incorporated into the international economy, and this has been achieved without the type of aid described above; furthermore, the Soviet Union is already compelled to moderate its activities abroad in order to preserve good relations with the West.)

We should therefore interpret Gorbachev's conciliatory attitude as an appeal for help and not as an expression of generosity towards the West; the Soviets are in the weaker position. However, this does not mean that we should exploit this opportunity to 'corner' the Soviet Union: on the contrary, we should make progress in disarmament so that the balance of power can be maintained at as low a level as possible. Equally, economic relations should be dealt with on a basis of mutual benefit and costly forms of assistance avoided in favour of practical and relatively inexpensive measures such as the transfer of capitalist management methods.

East–West relations now seem to be moving towards stabilization and *rapprochement*. However, this superficial phenomenon is being fuelled by the erosion of the (bipolar) political system we have had since 1945. One of the two pillars of this system, the Soviet Union, is threatened by economic chaos and nationalist unrest, either of which could some day become serious enough to jeopardize the economic and political stability of the whole world. If this were to happen, the West might find itself faced with the immediate problem of deciding whether or not to help the Soviets out of trouble. Even in this type of 'worst case', Western aid to the Soviet Union should involve certain conditions; for instance, the Soviet Union would first have to relinquish some of the unfair advantages (territorial gains) it has enjoyed since World War II. Otherwise, Western aid would merely result in reviving a superpower which occupies the northern half of the Eurasian land mass. Relations with the Soviet Union must always take geopolitical as well as ideological considerations into account. A strategy of crisis management to cope with the instability which could result from the decline of the Soviet economy must now be on the agenda for the West.

Notes

1. *Sotsialisticheskaya industriya*, 22 March 1983; Slyun'kov's Speech at the Party Central Committee Meeting on 6 June 1987.
2. *Izvestiya*, 21 Sept. 1986.
3. *Trud*, 28 Aug. 1984.
4. *Pravda*, 8 March 1987.
5. *Izvestiya*, 12 Oct. 1986.
6. United Nations Material. UN TD/B/1195/Add. 1, 89.2.20.
7. *Izvestiya*, 18 Dec. 1987.
8. *Vneshnyaya torgovlya*, 11 (1988).
9. *Vneshnyaya torgovlya*, 3 (1988).
10. *Ekonomicheskaya gazeta*, 51 (1988).
11. *Vneshnyaya torgovlya*, 3 (1988).
12. *Pravda*, 10 March 1986.
13. *Vedomosti Pravitel'stva SSSR*, 1 (1989).
14. *Ekonomicheskaya gazeta*, 51 (1988).
15. *Nihon keizan sinbun*, 24 Nov. 1988.

16. *Pravda*, 8 March 1987.
17. 1985 figures. Tatsuo Kaneda, *Soviet New Economic Policy and the Asian Economy*, 1988.
18. *Ekonomicheskaya gazeta*, 51 (1988).
19. *TASS*, 18 July 1988.

7

Soviet Resource Options: Civil and Military Priorities

Julian Cooper

Perestroika and the Economy

Perestroika in the Soviet economy is a process of all-round modernization. It involves not only economic reform, but also a potentially far-reaching process of structural change and a reassessment of the priorities of the country's economic development. The goal of Gorbachev and his supporters is clear: they want to create an innovative, competitive economy able to secure high standards of living and welfare. It will be a socialist economic system, although the nature of the socialism is itself now under active review. This modernization process cannot but have an impact on the Soviet Union's potential military capability and the relationship between the military and civilian sectors of the economy.

Priorities of Perestroika

It is fortunate for the Soviet political leadership that there is a measure of complementarity between economic perestroika and the maintenance of the country's security. As is now recognized, national security cannot be seen in purely military terms. Gorbachev appears to appreciate that the best guarantee of long-term security is a dynamic modern economy able to provide its citizens with a standard of living comparable to that of the leading capitalist countries, coupled with a democratized political system. Such an economy also provides a sound basis for the maintenance of the country's military capability. But this congruence of longer-term aims does not rule out the appearance of transitional problems, with the potential of conflicts between civilian and military interests in the short run.

Taking a somewhat narrower view, the complementarities of civilian and military modernization can be seen from the perspective of trends in the development of technology. Decades of extensive development and the operation of the priority system have left the Soviet economy with an extremely uneven technological level. Able to supply goods of low- and middle-range technology in large quantity (but inadequate quality), outside the military sector it has difficulty in meeting demands for modern, high-technology products. This applies in a number of fields vital to the success of perestroika, including microelectronics and computing, new materials, lasers, and high-productivity, precision, manufacturing technologies. Enhanced capabilities in these fields would benefit the Soviet weapons industry by improving the domestic availability of advanced-technology inputs and also by reducing costs.[1] The creation of new-generation conventional weapons and the modernization of the Soviet Union's strategic capability will inevitably draw to some extent on those technologies and skills vital to general economic modernization: again, at least in the longer term, there is some congruence of interests of the two sectors. The present policy is thus one that keeps options open: to the extent that international conditions improve, the modernization drive can be directed increasingly to civilian purposes; but, if necessary, the basis will have been created to meet the challenge of a new generation of military technology.

The Two Sectors of the Economy

For a long time in the West the prevailing view of the Soviet defence industry was of an almost totally distinct sector of the economy with its own principles of operation, walled off from the civilian economy by virtually impenetrable barriers of secrecy. If this image were an accurate reflection of reality, the task facing Gorbachev would be even more formidable than it is. But over recent years it has begun to be appreciated that the boundaries between the two sectors are more fluid than previously believed, and that the principles of operation, though different in some respects, are not of a completely different order. Of particular importance to perestroika is the fact that the defence industry already has considerable experience of civilian work.[2]

Elsewhere the author has discussed the civilian production activities of the 'defence complex', as it is now known in the Soviet Union.[3] It has proved possible to establish the volumes of output of a range of civilian products, including industrial, agricultural and transport equipment and consumer goods: the results are summarized in Table 7.1. However, in addition the defence

Table 7.1 *The share of total Soviet output of civilian products from enterprises of the defence industry (% of total output in physical unit terms, unless otherwise specified)*

Product	1965	1970	1975	1980	1985
Crude steel (MOP, MOM, MSP)	(10)	(9)	(8)	(8)	(8)[a]
Inc. electric-arc steel[1]	55	53	53	50	49[a]
Metal-cutting machine tools (MAP, MOP, MM, MOM, MSP, MRP)	n.	(14)	(14)	(14)	(13)
Inc. NC machines	n.	(42)	(36)	(30)	(26)
Tractors	13	13	(14)	(15)	(15)
Irrigators (MSP)[2]	–	–	n.	9	12
Railway freight wagons (MOP)	n.	(33)	(30)	(27)	n.
Tramcars (MOM)	72	55	65	60	n.
Passenger cars (MOP)	–	11	10	10	(12)
Motorcycles and scooters (MOP)	73	69	68	(64)	(63)
Bicycles (MM)	44	37	(39)	(42)	(40)
Mopeds and motorized cycles (MM)	23	21	21	21	n.
Refrigerators (MOM, MAP, MM, MOP, MRP)	48	48	(48)	(48)	n.
Washing machines (MAP, MM, MOP, MSP, MOM)	(41)	(38)	(32)	(27)	(27)
Vacuum cleaners (MAP, MOP, MSP)	49	(42)	(46)	(43)	n.
Television sets (MPSS*, MRP, MOM, MEP)	100	100	100	100	100
Radios (MPSS*, MRP, MEP, MSP, MM, MOM (?))	100	100	100	100	100
Tape-recorders (MPSS*, MRP, MEP, MM, MAP, MSP)	(95)	(95)	(95)	(95)	(95)
Video-recorders (MEP*, MAP, MM, MSP)	100	100	100	100	100
Personal computers (MRP*, MEP)	–	–	–	–	(90)
Inc. home computers (MRP, MEP)	–	–	–	–	100
Clocks and watches (MM, MAP, MEP)	12	12	(11)	(14)	(19)
Cameras (MOP*, MAP)	100	100	100	100	100
Furniture (value terms)	n.	n.	n.	2	2
Consumer goods (MAP, MSP, MOP, MEP, MPSS only[3]) (value terms)	n.	n.	14	17	21

n. not known

* head ministry

[a] 1983

[1] Proportion shown is that produced outside the Ministry of Ferrous Metallurgy; somewhat overstates the share of the defence industry as there is limited production by civilian engineering ministries, notably the Ministry of Heavy and Transport Machine-building.

[2] Share of total deliveries to agriculture. Some irrigators are built at MOP enterprises, but the scale of production and deliveries is not known. The share shown refers to the shipbuilding industry alone.

[3] Date not available for MOM, MM, MRP and MSM.

MSM : Ministry of Medium Machine-building

MM : Ministry of Machine-building

MOM: Ministry of General Machine-building

MOP : Ministry of the Defence Industry

MAP : Ministry of the Aviation Industry
MSP : Ministry of the Ship-building Industry
MRP : Ministry of the Radio Industry
MPSS: Ministry of the Communications Equipment Industry
MEP : Ministry of the Electronics Industry

Source: J.M. Cooper, 'The scale of output of civilian products by enterprises of the Soviet defence industry', *CREES Discussion Papers*, SITS No. 3, University of Birmingham, Aug. 1988, pp. 2–3.

industry is responsible for a substantial proportion of the electronics, computer and communications-equipment industries. Recent developments have served to enhance further the civilian contribution. At the beginning of March 1988 the Ministry of Machine-building for the Light and Food Industries (Minlegpishchemash) was disbanded and most of its 260 enterprises transferred to the ministries of the defence industry. At a stroke the military sector has acquired major new responsibilities in a field now of vital importance to the overall success of perestroika.

It is generally accepted that from a technological point of view the defence industry is the most advanced sector of the Soviet economy, and this assessment has been reinforced by new evidence now becoming available as glasnost extends more deeply into the military sector. Without doubt this relative sector owes much to its priority material resource provision, but also to its human resources and management methods. While the defence complex obtains supplies of materials, equipment and components from civilian ministries, it is clear that it meets many of its own needs in order to ensure acceptable quality. As a Soviet designer (from a civilian enterprise) recently observed, it is the fact that the defence industry has its own 'captive' suppliers of components and parts – from hydraulic units to nuts and bolts – that goes far in explaining its ability to secure high-quality production.[4] A former defence sector chief designer, Val'kov, has described the structure of the defence industry in terms of a set of 'pyramids': each end-product weapons producer has its own stable pyramid of suppliers. He argues that this pyramid-like structure, formed originally in the 1930s, is now too rigid for the military sector to be the 'locomotive' of scientific and technological progress.[5] The drift of both articles is clear: the civilian economy should benefit much more from the experience and technology of the military sector, and the economic reform should develop in such a way as to create conditions making this possible. Val'kov is evidently convinced that these new arrangements would be beneficial to the defence industry itself, subjecting it to the pressures of economic competition.

The Defence Industry and Perestroika

How has perestroika affected the defence industry and what are the potential implications for the civilian economy? Very soon after Gorbachev became General Secretary, it became evident that he saw the military sector as a source of skills, managerial practices and technologies which could be employed to the benefit of civilian modernization. This was not entirely new: under Brezhnev there were periodic efforts to engage the defence industry to a greater extent in general economic life, and these efforts intensified under Andropov. But Gorbachev has been more resolute in his pursuit of the policy, and one gains the impression that his confidence in the ultimate success of perestroika rests in part on his appreciation that in the military and space fields the Soviet Union already has impressive technological achievements to its credit: the innovative potential is there; it must now be widely diffused.

Some of the forms of technology and skill transfers from the defence industry to the civilian economy have been discussed elsewhere.[6] As noted below, some of the key government and party economic posts are now filled by former military sector administrators, and measures have been adopted to increase the sector's contribution to the solution of a range of urgent tasks. Even before the dissolution of Minlegpishchemash, the latter included the production of medical equipment, agricultural machinery, food-processing equipment, educational technology, consumer durables and sporting recreational goods. In most cases the ministries concerned have relevant prior experience and it is not necessarily the case that anything more than minor resource reallocations are involved. However, this cumulative process must force the ministers and senior officials to concern themselves increasingly with non-military matters. With the transfer to the defence complex of the enterprises of the former Minlegpishchemash, the situation has taken a more radical turn.

Minlegpishchemash previously had primary responsibility for the development and manufacture of equipment for the food-processing industry, public catering, the textile and footwear industries, and a wide range of consumer durables and household goods. The ministry had 260 enterprises (many relatively small and backward), employed some 360,000 people, and had an annual output of 4–5 billion roubles, equivalent to approximately 5.5 per cent of the total output of the civilian machine-building complex.[7] Evidence is still far from complete, but it is possible to determine some of the new affiliations (shown in Annex 7.1, page 153). The ministries concerned are now expected to modernize the factories, in some cases with the aid of Western technology and joint ventures, and quickly develop and manufacture a wide range of new equipment up to the latest standards of technology. Between 1988 and 1995 the defence industry ministries are to produce equipment for the food industry to a total value of 17.5 billion roubles.[8] This effort is being overseen and coordinated by L.B. Vasil'ev, the former minister, who has retained his ministerial status as a new deputy chairman of the Military-Industrial Commission. Within the commission a new managerial apparatus has been created, and the ministries have created their own new directorates to manage the civilian production, each headed by a new deputy minister. This proliferation of new agencies has already attracted criticism.[9]

Events since March have shown some of the difficulties of engaging the defence industry in civilian tasks, but have also served to underline the determination of the authorities that the new measures should succeed. There have been the inevitable transitional organizational problems, projects have been delayed, new problems of secrecy have intruded (it is striking how often the formula 'enterprise of their former Minlegpishchemash' is employed to avoid identification of the ministry now responsible), and in some cases prices have risen dramatically. Many of these issues were aired at a session of the USSR Council of Ministers in October 1988, unusual for being the first session ever to be televised. This treatment appears to be a deliberate attempt to expose the defence industry to public opinion and break down its deep-rooted aversion to publicity.[10] Ryzhkov acknowledged the many difficulties but expressed his confidence that the correct decision had been made. Soon after the Council of Ministers meeting, in an unprecedented move, the minister for the nuclear weapons industry, L.D. Ryabev, discussed his ministry's civilian work in the pages of *Izvestiya*.[11] Then, to underline the party's concern, Ligachev and Baklanov in November 1988 met with leading representatives of the defence industry to stress the importance of a rapid improvement in the supply of equipment to the agro-industrial complex.[12] The defence sector now finds itself under severe pressure to produce results, and the evidence suggests that, even before Gorbachev's December 1988 United Nations speech, real resource reallocation was beginning to take place.

Another aspect of the impact of perestroika on the defence sector is the issue of economic reform. So far the sector has only partially experienced the measures adopted, but from 1 January 1989 it went over to the self-financing arrangements. While weapons production (and also some of the principal civilian goods) will be covered by state orders, the defence industry may find itself in the unaccustomed position of having to find orders to use some of its capacity. The description of the above-mentioned Val'kov implies an even more radical shift: the system of payment for weapons is to be changed in such a way that the forces themselves will have to pay for the systems they need and can afford, without the automatic state funding normal up to now. This, Val'kov believes, will reduce the 'appetite' of the military and, coupled with progress in disarmament, should lead to a 'significant reduction' in the use of production capacity, forcing the defence enterprises to seek order 'on the side'.[13] Even if the changes are not as dramatic as suggested by Val'kov, it is likely that the defence industry will find itself in more economically challenging circumstances and may experience new pressures to use its resources more efficiently and to reduce costs. Thus the economic reform could exert an impact favourable to a reduction of the military burden of the economy.

Resource Reallocation

An argument frequently employed in the West for a cautious approach to the Soviet reforms has been the apparent lack of firm evidence of any resource shift from military to civilian purposes. In the absence of official data on the scale of military expenditure, still promised once the price reform has been completed, Western analysts are heavily dependent on intelligence assessments of Soviet current military procurement. These estimates, based on technical means of data collection, are subject to a margin of error (as can be seen from the regular retrospective revisions in successive editions of the US DOD's *Soviet Military Power*) and have the limitation that they only cover end-product weapons; that is, the production of weapons system derived from development programmes initiated several years ago, in most cases probably predating the perestroika. This type of evidence can tell us little about real and planned resource shifts in relation to more recent or projected programmes. We are forced to seek alternative forms of evidence.

Before Gorbachev's UN speech, the firmest statement on Soviet total military expenditure was that of Deputy Minister of Defence for Armaments, Army General Vitalii Shabanov, who in an interview with the *Washington Post* in July 1988 said that military spending began declining after the start of the current Five Year Plan in 1986. A senior official accompanying Shabanov 'said more precisely that it had declined "slightly" each of the past two years'.[14] The meaning of this aim is unclear. Assuming Shabanov was correct in his declaration, then given the usual Soviet practice of discussing economic indicators in current price terms, it is not impossible that there was a more than 'slight' cut in real terms during the period 1986–8.

A second type of evidence, which some in the West have attempted to employ, is the allocation of investment between what are now known as the 'defence' and 'machine-building' complexes, the latter referring to the civilian engineering ministries. Such evidence has the advantage that it relates to current resource allocation priorities, but unfortunately the available data are inadequate to permit any firm conclusions to be drawn. A serious problem is that some of the technologies crucial to civilian modernization – in particular, microelectronics, computers and other information technologies – are developed and produced to a large extent within the defence complex. Thus a resource shift from military to civilian purposes could entail an *increase* in the investment share of the latter. With the transfer of the former Minlegpishchemash enterprises to the military sector, the intra-machine building investment shares become even more problematic. In the author's view, attempts to detect resource shifts from the currently available investment data are probably futile.

Additional evidence relates to the increasing involvement of the defence industry in the civilian economy. First, there was the INF treaty and its impact on Soviet weapons procurement. There are two aspects to this: the direct financial savings from the elimination of an entire category of weapons, and the transfer of R & D and production capacities to civilian uses. The reported financial saving in 1988 alone amounted to some 300 million roubles, redirected to civilian purposes.[15] It is known that enterprises responsible for building the missile and transporter systems covered by the INF treaty are expanding their civilian work. Thus the Votkinsk machine-building works, previously building the SS-20, SS-22 and SS-23, is increasing its already established production of machine tools, washing machines and trams, and organizing the manufacture of new products, including dairy industry equipment and control systems for off-shore drilling rigs.[16] The Nadiradze design bureau, responsible for the design of solid-fuel missiles, intends to use freed capacity to develop a new meteorological rocket, which, if successful, may be offered for export.[17]

Secondly, there is evidence of forms of defence sector involvement in the civilian economy which entail some redirection of resources away from military programmes. The most striking example to date involves the Ministry of Medium Machine-Building, which produces nuclear weapons. This ministry has taken over from the former Minlegpishchemash ten enterprises of producing equipment for the dairy industry. The minister, L. D. Ryabev, has indicated that while new construction will be financed from the state budget, modernization of these backward production facilities will be undertaken from the internal resources of the ministry, and also that two enterprises originally intended for weapons production are being re-profiled. By the end of the next Five Year Plan it is envisaged that more than 1,000 million roubles of capital investment will have been reallocated. More than forty enterprises of the ministry are being engaged in the new production, which suggests that some capacity is being re-profiled. In addition, the ministry has appointed twenty-five chief designers of milk-processing equipment, and Ryabev again implies that some scientific and technical resources are being switched to civilian work.[18] Unfortunately, similar details are not yet available for the other defence-sector ministries, but it is likely that a common policy is being pursued.

The evidence for a switch of resources from military to civilian purposes was beginning to accumulate before the announcement of force reductions. But following Gorbachev's UN speech it became clear that a sizeable resource reallocation is now envisaged. By the beginning of 1991 overall military expenditure is set to decline by 14 per cent; weapons by 19.5 per cent.[19] This declaration of intent was followed by a flurry of press articles on new civilian production at defence industry facilities. Examples include the Moscow 'Znamya Truda' works where the MiG-29 is built, now making sugar-packaging machines, the 'Molniya' association, responsible for building the 'Buran' space shuttle, making equipment for the textile industry, and the missile industry's central technology institute, now helping to modernize the local economy of Moscow.[20]

Stresses and Strains?

As pointed out above, while the military appear to have an interest in civil economic modernization it is unlikely that the current process of restructuring is proceeding without tensions and conflicts. The Soviet defence industry is having to face a series of new challenges which many must find profoundly unsettling after the long, stable 'golden age' of the Brezhnev–Ustinov regime.[21] Almost all the leading personnel of the defence complex have been replaced, and the top leadership of the industry no longer has the very close links with the General Secretary characteristic of the Brezhnev years – taken together these factors may well have reduced the complex's political influence; pressure for an enhanced civilian role has steadily intensified, and now glasnost is beginning to expose its work and shortcomings to public view.[22] The economic reform threatens further disruption and the industry faces the prospect of having to meet new technological challenges with less generous resource provision.

While these circumstances must be unsettling, especially those habituated to the 'relatively protected' conditions of the military sector, they must also offer new opportunities. Some who previously lived in the shadows of secrecy are now entering the public domain – not only Ryabev of the nuclear weapons industry and his fellow ministers, now appearing on television and discussing joint ventures with Western businessmen, but also lower-level engineers and designers, able to discuss and display publicly the industry's achievements in weaponry and space technology. Many personnel of the military sector are likely to welcome some relaxation of career constraints (on travel, publication, contact with foreigners and so on) and greater ease of contact with civilian organizations.

While there may be unease in the defence industry and possible conflict with the political leadership on the pace of change and the magnitude of the expected reorientation, an additional factor must be the attitude of the armed forces. Will they become restless, fearful that the defence industry will no longer be able to meet its basic obligation to supply modern weaponry? This issue goes beyond the limits of the present chapter in so far as it has to be considered within the broader context of doctrinal renewal and the disarmament process. However, it seems unlikely that the leadership would push the defence industry to the point that its basic capability came under threat, and the system probably has adequate safeguards to protect the defence complex's interests.

One safeguard of the military interest in the short run could be the fact that key posts in the Soviet economy are now occupied by former members of the defence industry. Since the death of Brezhnev such transfers have become such a matter of course and there is no doubt that a deliberate policy has been pursued. It may be not only the administrative skills and experience of these former military sector personnel that is appreciated by the leadership, but also their toughness and discipline, seen as essential during a difficult process of change. There may also be perception that such transferees, knowing the state of affairs within the defence sector, are well qualified to prevail upon it to contribute more to civilian modernization. However, it cannot be ruled out that the defence industry itself, and the military leadership, gain reassurance from the fact that their 'own' people are effectively in charge of the implementation of the economic reform.

Who are the key defence-sector transferees? Above all, Yurii Maslyukov, chairman of Gosplan, and his first deputy for general affairs, A.A. Reut. But other important figures include Voronin, chairman of Gossnab; Tolstykh, chairman of the State Committee for Science and Technology; Silaev, chairman of the Bureau of Machine-building; and in the Party Secretariat, Zaikov, Baklanov and the head of the new Social and Economic Department (which will presumably oversee the implementation of the economic reform), Vladimir Shimko, formerly Minister of the Radio Industry.[23] This represents a powerful group within the leadership, to which must be added Belousov, chairman of the Military-Industrial Commission.

Conclusion

As the process of restructuring is carried forward, the three dimensions noted in the introduction – economic reform, structural change and reassessment of priorities – are all beginning to affect the relationship between the military and civilian sectors of the economy. When Gorbachev first came to power it was generally believed that he wished to curb the growth of military expenditure, at least in the short run, in order to facilitate general economic modernization. In the West many interpreted this policy as one of securing a 'breathing space': a five-year period of relatively constrained military growth could be followed by renewed development in the 1990s, taking advantage of the technological modernization secured by the implementation of the policy. Some spoke of a 'deal' or 'understanding' with the military, according to which Gorbachev secured their support for perestroika. Now, three years later, this interpretation is increasingly open to question.

First, the general process of modernization, especially as it relates to the civilian machine-building industry, is proceeding more slowly than originally envisaged. This is hardly surprising, as the planned qualitative transformation within five years was excessively optimistic. While from the outset there was a clear intention to involve the military sector in the modernization process, in the author's view the extent of that involvement has now gone beyond the scale originally envisaged. Furthermore, the measures taken indicate a longer-term commitment, casting doubt on the 'breathing space' interpretation. Second, the logic of the economic reform process is such that the defence sector is likely to experience pressure for more efficient use of resources. This pressure, plus what appears to be a growing perception (increasingly voiced openly as glasnost deepens[24]) that the Soviet Union possesses a hypertrophied military sector, and also the evolving process of doctrinal renewal, work together in the direction of a longer-term effort to constrain resource allocations to the military. In short, what we may now be seeing is the beginning of a historic, long-term shift of priorities from military to civilian purposes. The outcome of this, like so much else, will depend on the overall fate of perestroika.

Notes

1. The latter point can be illustrated by the example of composite materials: they are finding increasing use in the Soviet defence industry, but only limited application in the civilian economy. As representatives of the aviation industry have acknowledged, the modest volume of output leads to very high production costs, and this probably accounts, at least in part, for their active campaign for the wide-scale adoption of composites in the economy at large. (See *Izvestiya*, 1 Sept. 1986; 12 Aug. 1987; and 2 Feb. 1988; *Pravda*, 8 July 1987.)

2. In this chapter the defence industry is defined as that part of Soviet industry administered by the nine ministries constituting the 'defence complex'; namely, those for aviation, ship-building, general machine-building (missiles), medium machine-building (nuclear weapons), machine-building (conventional munitions), defence industry (ground forces equipment), radio, communications equipment, and electronics.

3. See 'The civilian production of the Soviet defence industry', in R. Amann and J. Cooper (eds), *Technical Progress and Soviet Economic Development* (Oxford: Blackwell, 1986), pp. 31–50; and 'The scale of output of civilian products by enterprises of the Soviet defence industry', *CREES Discussion Papers*, SITS No. 3, University of Birmingham, Aug. 1988.

4. G. Pushkarev, 'O "sekretnykh" boltakh i "rezhimnykh" gaikakh', *NTR*, 17(80) (1988): 4.

5. Yu. S. Val'kov, 'Poslednii kozyr', *Sotsialisticheskaya Industriya*, 13 Nov. 1988. This article is one of the most remarkable examples to date of glasnost in relation to the work of the defence industry. Val'kov believes that it was a mistake to transfer the former Minlegpishchemash enterprises to the defence sector; in his view it would be better to use the sector's skills to supply advanced machine tools to the civilian economy.

6. See the author's 'Technology transfer between military and civilian industries', in US Congress, Joint Economic Committee, *Gorbachev's Economic Plans* (Washington, DC, USGPO), 1987, vol. 1, pp. 388–404; and P. Cocks, 'Soviet science and technology strategy: borrowing from the defense sector', *ibid*, vol. 2, pp. 145–60.

7. *Izvestiya*, 2 March 1988; number employed calculated from *Sotsialistcheskii*

Trud, 5 (1988), inside front cover; output based on 1984 marketed output of 4.1 billion roubles (*Planovoe Khozyaistvo*, 3 (1986): 88); share of civilian machine-building based on 1980 5.3%: S. I. Mozokhin and E. N. Tatarintseva, *Territorial'-naya organizatsiya mashinostroitel'nogo proizvodstva* (Moscow, 1984), p. 8.

8. *Izvestiya*, 2 Jan. 1989.

9. See *Planovoe Khozyaistvo*, 10 (1988): 71.

10. For the proceedings of this extraordinary event, see BBC, *Summary of World Broadcasts*, SU/0292 C6-C/10, 26 Oct. 1988.

11. *Izvestiya*, 9 Nov. 1988.

12. *Pravda*, 19 Nov. 1988.

13. *Sotsialisticheskaya Industriya*, 13 Nov. 1988.

14. *Washington Post*, 27 July 1988: A17-A18.

15. *Sotsialisticheskaya Industriya*, 17 Aug. 1988.

16. *Sovetskaya Rossiya*, 15 Dec. 1987; *Pravda*, 1 March, 13 March and 7 May 1988.

17. *Pravda*, 29 May 1988.

18. *Izvestiya*, 10 Nov. 1988. The manufacture of equipment for the dairy industry is not an entirely new activity for the ministry, as for many years it has made milk-processing plant.

19. *Pravda*, 19 Jan. 1989.

20. *Vechernyaya Moskva*, 13 Feb. 1989 (also the *Independent*, 20 Feb. 1989, which reports that the works intends to reduce its military production by 30% in 1989 and again by a similar amount in 1990); *Pravitel'stvennyi Vestnik*, 1 (1989): 12; *Moskovskaya Pravda*, 19 Feb. 1989.

21. I use this term because Ustinov was the effective overlord of the defence industry for the entire Brezhnev period, and under his leadership there was remarkable stability of leading personnel and very little public exposure of shortcomings.

22. On the changed relations between the defence industry and the political leadership, see the author's 'The elite of the defence industry complex', in D. Lane (ed.), *Elites and Political Power in the USSR* (Aldershot, Edward Elgar, 1988), esp. pp. 177–82.

23. For Shimko's appointment, see *Pravda*, 13 Nov. 1988. Before becoming Minister of the Radio Industry, Shimko worked in the defence industry department of the Central Committee. It is worth noting that, while the other industrial departments of the Central Committee have now been abolished, the defence industry department has been retained, Belyakov remaining as its head (*Pravda*, 19 Nov. 1988).

24. For example, Academician Sagdeev's remarkable claim that at least 70% of Soviet R & D personnel work in the 'closed', 'postbox number' sector of science. It was mainly within this closed sector, he believes, that the 'degeneration' of Soviet science began (*Novoe vremya*, 47 (1988): 27).

Annex 7.1 Enterprises of the former Minlegpishchemash

Some of the enterprises of the former Ministry of Machine-building for the Light and Food Industries have been allocated to defence-sector ministries as follows:

Equipment for the food-processing industry – all enterprises to the defence industry,[1] including:

Dairy and milk-processing equipment – 10 enterprises to MSM[2]

Meat-processing equipment – enterprises to MOP[3]

Some types of food industry equipment – MAP, MOM[4]

Equipment for non-alcoholic drinks industry – some enterprises to MOP[5]

Equipment for public catering – enterprises to MSP[6]

Refrigeration equipment for retail sector – enterprises to MRP[7]

Equipment for light industry – 108 enterprises transferred to defence complex[8] (MAP, MM, MOP, MOM, MSM, MSP), including:

    Textile machinery – MAP and MOP[9]

    Domestic refrigerators – MOM (now 'head' ministry?), MAP, and others[10]

Note: Abbreviations as in Table 7.1.

Sources

[1] BBC, *SWB*, SU/0292 C/6, 26 Oct. 1988 (Ryzhkov)

[2] *Izvestiya*, 10 Nov. 1988

[3] *Izvestiya*, 2 Jan. 1989

[4] *Pravda*, 4 and 5 Nov. 1988

[5] *Sotsialisticheskaya Industriya*, 18 May 1988

[6] *Sovetskaya Torgovlya*, 7 July 1988

[7] *East European Markets*, 1 July 1988: 13; *Sovetskaya Torgovlya*, 11 Oct. 1988

[8] *Pravda*, 28 Oct. 1988

[9] *Izvestiya*, 2 March 1988; *Pravda*, 2 July 1988

[10] *Pravda*, 2 July 1988; *Vechernyaya Moskva*, 3 Oct. 1988 (MAP).

8

Perestroika in the Soviet Military

Naomi Koizumi

Although perestroika came to the military sphere later than to other fields, the pressure to move rapidly has been considerable. As perestroika in the economy stagnates, so Gorbachev tends to take ever bolder foreign policy initiatives. The military, then, has to be prepared to move. What changes does Gorbachev require of the military, and how are they reacting to his demands? Through an examination of these questions I would like to analyse the present situation and future prospects of perestroika in the Soviet military.

Before proceeding to an analysis of development, it is worth noting that the armed forces are a multi-functional institution; they are a sub-unit of Soviet security, responsible in educational terms for the formation of patriotic citizens; they are an economic unit, in that there are military industries which have always been given top priority in resource allocation; and self-evidently, they are responsible for national security. Gorbachev's demands on the military reflect their multiple functions. Gorbachev's targets for each category are: (a) personnel policy: to appoint officers who favour perestroika to the staff; (b) social policy: to improve military discipline and morale; (c) economic policy: to reduce military spending while investing more in high-tech weaponry; (d) foreign policy: to implement arms-control agreements and revise military doctrine and military strategy.

The fourth category is the one which affects the West most directly, particularly the issue of whether the USSR has really revised its military doctrine. Much has been said about doctrinal changes, but what is Gorbachev's goal? In order to understand this subject we need to consider the meaning of the Gorbachev reforms in their historical context. Looking back over the history of Soviet military strategy, two periods of change are discernible. The first began immediately after Stalin's death and ended in the late 1960s. Its main theme was the introduction of nuclear weapons into Soviet military thinking. Although Stalin in fact promoted nuclear development, he did not admit the principle of an 'ultimate weapon', because the belief that one technology could change the course of history constituted a serious deviation from Soviet ideology. Nevertheless, the leadership after Stalin could no longer ignore the huge destructive capability of nuclear weapons, which gradually became a major element of military strategy. This process was completed by the beginning of the Brezhnev administration.[1]

The second period of change started in the late 1970s. The main concern of this time was how to plan the use of nuclear weapons, a subject which was becoming ever more difficult as the possibility of 'overkill' set in. It was the military technocrats who understood this concept and took it seriously. In their view, ongoing scientific innovation was imposing a change of emphasis towards the qualitative improvement of conventional weapons.[2] They are also sensitive to 'stagnant phenomena' in the military society. Then the early 1980s saw a marked deterioration in East–West relations as well as declining economic growth in the USSR. When modernized INFs were stationed in Europe and targeted at Soviet territory, nuclear war came to be perceived as a real possibility. The 'new thinking' developed out of this sense of growing crisis. Its advocates were civilian military specialists who appeared in the latter half of the 1960s with the establishment of academic institutes specializing in international relations. The movement grew further with the SALT negotiations in the 1970s. According to this 'new thinking', security should be attained by confidence-building, not by military means. Needless to say, it was Gorbachev who translated this theory into practical policy.

Gorbachev's reform movement corresponds to the second stage of this second period of change. If this interpretation is correct, Gorbachev's policy is broadly in line with the reforms necessitated by purely military considerations; that is, denuclearization. His 'new thinking', however, goes much further than the views of military technocrats and may therefore cause confusion in Soviet military policy-making.

With these considerations in mind, I would like to analyse Gorbachev's objectives and the military's reaction to them under each of the headings mentioned above. The military are assumed to comprise the following three groups: conservatives who favour the status quo; reformists who support the reforms for military reasons but are reserved about the 'new thinking'; and finally, the new thinkers. As military-related economic issues are treated in the chapter by Julian Cooper, this chapter will examine (1) personnel changes; (2) social policy; (3) military doctrine; (4) military strategy; and (5) arms control and disarmament.

1 Personnel Changes

Perestroika in the military requires in the first place the promotion of younger, more able and more energetic people who understand its necessity. In the words of Sukharukhov, Deputy Minister of Defence in charge of Personnel Affairs, it needs 'well-prepared and energetic cadres who are endowed with new feeling, are able to make a critical assessment of their own activities and are not afraid to take personal responsibility for their decisions and for carrying them out'.[3]

Let us look at the personnel changes in the military leadership since Gorbachev came to power in March 1985 from this perspective. Table 8.1 shows the number of personnel changes in the military leadership for each year (January and February only for 1989). The table shows a fairly high rate of change during the four years since Gorbachev took office. Perestroika has had some

Table 8.1 *Personnel changes in the military leadership*

	15 of MOD[a]	CINCs of 5 Forces	4 of MPD[b]	9 of GSO[c]	16 C.[d] of MD[e]	4 C. of GF[f]	4 C. of Fleets	4 C. of ThF[g]
1985*	2	2	2	0	3	1	2	0
1986	2	0	0	1	1	0	1	1
1987	4	1	0	3	7	3	1	1
1988	2	0	1	2	3	1	1	1
1989	2	1	0	1	1	0	0	0
Total	12	4	3	7	15	5	5	3
%	80	80	75	87.5	93.75	125	125	75

* The date of each inauguration is the one confirmed in the *Krasnaya Zvezda*.
[a] 15 include Minister of Defence, 3 first deputies, and 11 deputies.
[b] MPD: Main Political Directorate; 4 include a chief, a first deputy and two deputies.
[c] 9 include a chief, 3 first deputies and 5 deputies.
[d] C.: Commander.
[e] MD: Military District.
[f] GF: Group of Forces.
[g] ThF: Theatre Forces.

Sources: *Soren Geppou (USSR Monthly Report)*, The Soviet Division of the Japanese Ministry of Foreign Affairs, 1985, 3–1988.11, and other sources.

success in breaking the longevity of office prevalent in the Brezhnev era. For example, former Minister of Defence Sokolov took office in December 1984 and had been in the post for only two years and five months when he was replaced by Yazov in May 1987. By contrast, the eighteen years of Brezhnev's rule saw only two ministers of defence, each of whom died in office (Grechko was nine years in office and Ustinov eight years and eight months). Admittedly, Sokolov was aged 73 in 1984 and thus already too old for the post.

A tendency is also evident towards a rejuvenation of the military leadership. With Gorbachev's own appointment of Yazov, the Minister of Defence became 'ten years younger'. In December 1984 of the fifteen top military leaders, six were over 70 years old; Ustinov was 76 and dying. The retirement system is at present under discussion; the only office-holder over 70 is Shestopatov, Minister of Defence in charge of Construction and Billeting of Groups (72 years old). During the period under review, however, the average age declined by only three years: from 67.1 in December 1984 to 64.1 in February 1989 (this is the average for the fourteen top office-holders excluding the new appointee Kochetov). Yazov himself was already 64 when he took up the post. Nevertheless, the recent appointments of Moiseev (aged 49) and Robov (53) as Chief of the General Staff and First Deputy Chief of Staff, and of Arkhipov (55) as Deputy Minister of Defence are clearly the result of Yazov's personnel policy.[4]

Extensive personnel changes are clearly being carried out, but what do they mean? Are new thinkers being brought on to staff? Some reservations should be made here. As noted before, Gorbachev's military reforms are an extension of the changes which began in the late 1970s; that is, the move to denuclearization. At this time the military decided to shift the emphasis of their strategy to preservation of the second-strike capability and development of high-tech conventional arms, including precision-guided weapons. This was not a change of strategy, but a shift in emphasis. Analysis of how it came about is beyond the scope of this chapter. Assuming, therefore, that a consensus on this matter had been reached before Gorbachev came to power, we will continue the present analysis.

As far as Gorbachev's policy of military perestroika (the second stage of the second period of change) is concerned, two opposing groups are discernible in the armed forces. The conservatives see their vested interests in the continuation of the 'period of stagnation', with its waste, corruption and bureaucracy. They are conservative in ideological terms, negative about changes in military

policy and strongly distrustful of the West. By contrast, the reformists consider it absolutely necessary to reconstruct military society
through intensifying discipline and democratization under the single
command system, and to promote the military application of scientific innovations. Naturally, the reformists support Gorbachev's
perestroika of the military, and show some flexibility towards economic perestroika and changes in military policy. It is from among
such people that Gorbachev has selected the new leadership.

Concerning the reform of national security policy, however, the
reformists as well as the conservatives are very cautious about
Gorbachev's initiatives. Gorbachev's appointees – Yazov, Tretyak,
Robov and Akhromeev (former Chief of the General Staff and
now his military adviser) – are unanimous in calling for vigilance
against imperialist aggression and for the maintenance of parity
and reciprocity in arms control. It seems that the new appointees
are not necessarily new thinkers. But it is quite difficult to distinguish
between new thinkers and others, for the military have traditionally
been independent and closed, monopolizing military information
and expertise. There is a clear division of labour between them and
the party. In spite of the rigid civilian control system, the military
have been given authority to make their own decisions on strategy.
They have been inflexible to civilian pressure on military thinking.

Nevertheless, Akhromeev and Moiseev are undoubtedly capable
of flexible thinking. They say they are working on a revision of
military strategy and are studying how to repel aggression in accordance with defensive military doctrine focusing on 'estimating the
nature of aggression' and 'characteristics of the initial phase of
battle operations and military activities'.[5] This does not, of course,
necessarily imply any changes, but the articles quoted reject dogmatism and call for creative approaches, democratization and localiz-
ation of discussion in the military. If glasnost develops further in
the military, it is quite possible that the 'new thinking' will emerge
there as well.[6]

2 Social Policy

The phenomena of 'stagnation' in the military were criticized in the
army press even before the Gorbachev era. However, ending this
tendency is now perceived as more urgent because the reallocation
of resources has attracted the attention of political leaders. According to Primakov, immediately after its plenum of April 1985 the
CPSU Central Committee began to elaborate a new foreign policy
doctrine. He commented,

There were two main themes: the need to reduce trends leading towards thermonuclear war, and the need to optimize the ratio between the money allocated and the reliable defence of the USSR and its allies, in order to increase civilian production and accelerate social development in the USSR.[7]

The military have been instructed to save money. Whereas at the April 1985 plenum, the political leadership said the military received all the resources they needed for defence, by the twenty-seventh party congress in 1986 the formula was revised as 'the defence capability of the USSR is maintained at such a level that it can secure the peaceful labour and life of the Soviet people'.[8]

At its nineteenth conference in June 1988, the party went further and decided that in future military development in terms of technology, military science and personnel should be determined by qualitative parameters.[9] Six months after this decision a unilateral troop reduction of 500,000 was announced. The military leadership was made responsible for revitalizing the armed forces in accordance with the overriding need to reduce the budget and cut personnel. This is no easy task – not only for the USSR.

In his first speech as Defence Minister on Soviet Army and Navy Day, 1988, Yazov concentrated to a greater extent than his predecessors on problems in the military. He identified the following three 'stagnant phenomena': (a) lack of preparedness of the troops; (b) lack of discipline; and (c) inadequate social development.[10] Let us summarize the issues raised in the military publications following Yazov's classification:

(a)   lack of preparedness of troops
   – pre-draft education and education in military schools is inadequate; the educational level is so low that many graduates need re-education:
   – military manpower is used for local economic activities; training plans are frequently interrupted by the party's requests for labour;
   – young people are becoming less physically fit, and alcoholism and drug addiction among young people are increasing.
(b)   lack of discipline
   – conscripts try to evade military service often through the rampant practice of bribery;
   – military discipline has become lax, and violence in the armed forces is on the increase, with robbery, negligence, criminality, bullying of recruits and sadism by officers being reported;

- nationality problems are increasing with the growing proportion of Central Asians and Transcaucasians among new
  conscripts.
(c) inadequate social development
- the shortage of housing means frequent complaints of over-
  crowding, high rents and poor facilities.

Yazov identified the following three counter-measures in his
speech: first, the improvement of cadres' working methods; second,
the raising of educational standards; and third, the intensification
of discipline. But his proposals were quite abstract and undefined.
He said that since the trouble was caused by intellectual inertia and
negligence on the part of cadres, solutions would be found in
democratization, glasnost and the activation of human factors. As
for material incentives, Yazov only reported that the annual
resource allocation for soldiers had been raised from the beginning
of 1988.[11]

In 1988, following the above-mentioned decision of the nineteenth party conference, the Central Committee passed a resolution
on the intensification of military discipline. While the need for
perestroika in the military had first become less apparent because
of the need for budgetary and personnel cuts, the need to save
money had become ever more urgent: perestroika in the economy
had come to a standstill and the food problem required immediate
attention. Progress in disarmament was therefore indispensable.
The party's efforts, however, seemed to have produced meagre
results. The Politburo meeting on 12 October 1988 pointed out how
slowly the Central Committee resolution was being implemented,
and expressed particular concern at the evasion of military service,
relations among servicemen, violation of duty regulations and sab-
otage of military machinery. It instructed the Ministry of Defence
and the main political directorate to take additional measures to
intensify military discipline.[12]

3 Military Doctrine

The Military Encyclopedia, published in 1986, gives the following
definition of military doctrine: 'a systematic view adopted by a
state at a certain period of time, concerning the nature, goals and
characteristics of a possible future war, and the preparation and
means of the state and the military to fight the war'. Military
doctrine has two closely related and interdependent components:
socio-political and military-technical. The socio-political compon-

ent, covering the goals of a possible future war, the means of attaining victory, and the economic, social and legal basis of the conflict, reflects the nation's class nature and political objectives, and therefore has continuous validity. The military-technical component defines actual military development, advanced weaponry and training in its use, safety and tactics.[13]

The political component of Soviet military doctrine is based on Marxist-Leninist ideology. It is defined by the party at a high level, notably by the party congress – as, for example, with the rejection of the doctrine of the inevitability of war. But the military has had a say in decision-making on the military-technical component on account of monopoly over the necessary information. The situation led to 'a certain discrepancy' between the socio-political and military-technical aspects in the late Brezhnev era.[14] Under Gorbachev, however, civilian specialists in national security matters are gaining the right to a voice in decision-making on military-technical matters.

The relationship between military doctrine and military strategy may be expressed as follows:

(a)   military doctrine
  – socio-political aspect: (i) whether a war can be a political means (the relationship between war and politics); (ii) aggressiveness of capitalism (inevitability and imminence of war); (iii) the defence of socialism (by military means or political means? possibility of avoiding war);
  – military-technical aspect: (i) form of a future war (possibility of the use of nuclear weapons or of a limited nuclear war; initial phase of the war: nuclear or conventional?); (ii) military build-up (emphasis on nuclear or conventional weapons? superiority, parity or reasonable sufficiency?)
(b)   military strategy
  – deterrence or war-fighting? pre-emption or retaliation? targeting.

Regarding (a) the socio-economic component or aspect and the relationship between nuclear war and politics: of course the theory of relations between war and politics is based on Lenin's (Clausewitz's) dictum, 'war is the continuation of politics by other means'. But the invention of nuclear weapons with their huge destructive power forced the leadership to rethink this theory. The dictum raises two different ideological questions: first, can nuclear war be part of Soviet policy; that is, can the USSR attain a political goal by winning a nuclear war? And second, can nuclear war be part of the policy of the enemy; that is, is nuclear war possible? Although these questions have been highly contentious ever since nuclear weapons were first created, the then leadership decided in 1956 that nuclear war was not inevitable but possible, and in 1961 the party platform officially decided that a nuclear war could be won. Since then the Soviets have made every effort to acquire first-strike capability.

It was at the twenty-sixth party congress in 1981 that the formula was partially changed: 'To expect to attain victory in a nuclear war is dangerous madness.'[15] Shortly afterwards, Chernenko said, 'It would be a crime to think that a thermonuclear war is a "rational" continuation of politics.'[16] It was then that the Soviets first decided that a nuclear war could not be the continuation of their politics. This decision marked a radical revision of Soviet military doctrine and shows how denuclearization entered Soviet policy-making. However, the adjectives 'rational' and 'legal' that Chernenko used indicate the leadership's judgement that a nuclear war could still be an 'irrational' continuation of imperialist politics. In other words, in their view it could not be Soviet policy to start a nuclear war but it could still be imperialist policy; they should still be prepared for nuclear war.

These two beliefs form the core of Gorbachev's 'new thinking'. At the Geneva summit meeting in November 1985, Gorbachev and Reagan confirmed that there could be no victor in nuclear war; this belief was specified in the new edition of the party programme (1986). At the Peace Forum in February 1987, Gorbachev said that after Hiroshima and Nagasaki world war ceased to be an acceptable continuation of politics by other means.[17] A new theory on the relationship between war and politics was thus firmly established; but lively discussions followed Gorbachev's statement. Even new thinkers voiced the argument that if 'somebody' pushes the button, for him nuclear war is still an acceptable continuation of politics.[18]

What attitudes do the military take to this issue? Though at first negative towards the denial that a nuclear war could be won, the military have since approved it, as it has been found to be compatible with readiness for war. For example, Yazov said, 'a nuclear war cannot be the means to attain any objective, whether political, economic or ideological'.[19] However, the military attitude to the revision of the second theory, on the possibility of nuclear war, is also negative. They think that the idea that nuclear war cannot be won applies only when both the opposing sides endorse it. The view of the majority is that 'nuclear war ceased to be a continuation of politics not essentially, but functionally'; that is, in the sense that it can no longer be a means for politics.[20] And for the military the 'somebody' mentioned above can only mean the imperialists.

Regarding military doctrine (a) (ii), Soviet ideology adopted from Lenin the notion that capitalism was aggressive and antagonistic. The importance of this idea to military thinking lies in the implication that war is imminent. According to Leninism, as the crisis of capitalism deepens, militarized capitalists will first go to war with each other and then attack the socialist countries. Khrushchev revised this view of the inevitability of war, on the grounds that socialist countries could 'compel' capitalism to maintain peace through their powerful defence capability.

This revision was retained in the Gorbachev era. But new thinkers are characterized by their realism. The new observation that the crisis of capitalism was not deepening was incorporated into the revised edition of the party programme. It has also been argued that capitalism can grow without militarism.[21] As glasnost has progressed, the opinion has even been expressed that the regular army should be replaced by a militia.[22]

The military are resolutely against the argument that imperialism is not necessarily aggressive. The *Kommunist vooruzhennykh sil* carried arguments against a militia-based system under the heading 'The danger of aggression still exists'.[23] The rejection of the aggression argument undermines the military's *raison d'être*, so naturally they cannot countenance it. But military ideologues are bound by party decisions. Some new developments were observed in 1988. *Kommunist vooruzhennykh sil* published a review of Lieutenant-General Serebryannikov's book *V.I. Lenin on the Aggressiveness of Imperialism*. The reviewer, Colonel Tyshkevich, was convinced by Serebryannikov's overall analysis on the aggressiveness of imperialism, but concluded that he wanted to know more about how to contain this aggressiveness and whether the arms control agreements with such aggressive imperialists might not harm the interests of the USSR.[24] The point at issue is not the nature of imperialism, but how to deter imperialist aggression and prevent war – that is, how to defend socialism.

As far as the defence of socialism is concerned (item (iii) above), defence by military means follows from theories on revolution and historical inevitability. The defence of socialism was seen in terms of class interest, but not necessarily in terms of general human interests. Gorbachev takes a very different approach to this point. He said that in the nuclear age the pursuit of class interests by military means might lead to the annihilation of human life; therefore the defence of socialism must be realized by political means.

This change has been gradually absorbed by the military. In June 1986, the then deputy chief of the Main Political Administration, the conservative Volkogonov, wrote in his paper, 'The justest war', that the Revolution must be defended by military means; political means would be used but were only one factor in the achievement of victory; a war would be against class interests, which correspond to the interests of the overwhelming majority of the world's population, but a powerful military deterrent was still necessary.[25] However, in 1987 the reformist Serebryannikov said that both political and military means should be used for the defence of socialism although political means were the best for socialism.[26] In 1988, in answer to Tyshkevich's question, Serebryannikov revealed his theory of 'compelling the imperialists to accept peace' and 'preventing war'. He believes that in the modern world all factors – the pressure of potential peace, military-strategic parity between socialism and capitalism, and the imperialists' instinct for self-preservation – are converging to compel the West to accept peace. Nevertheless, more interestingly, he pointed out the function of the United Nations as a factor in 'preventing war'.[27]

However, the conservative faction remains powerful. For example, Skorodenko's paper in June 1988, while admitting the importance of political factors in the maintenance of security, still emphasized the need for military means since there is no effective political mechanism for preventing nuclear war.[28]

As far as the military-technical aspect is concerned, according to the military doctrine established in the latter half of the 1960s to meet the flexible response strategy of the USA, a future war will be started with conventional weapons, with escalation to a general nuclear war seen as a very high probability. The possibility of a limited nuclear war is also assumed but only using low-level battlefield nuclear weapons like those in Central Europe. This doctrine has not yet been changed.[29] The military leadership has been rethinking the escalation issue: if it is no longer possible to achieve victory in nuclear war, it would be better to win the war at the conventional stage, avoiding nuclear escalation. But the danger of nuclear war still exists, so nuclear weapons must be retained as a deterrent.

By contrast, new thinkers believe that a nuclear war must not be contemplated. It can bring nothing but the annihilation of human life, so efforts to prepare for it are senseless. Moreover, they think that a protracted conventional war in the European theatre is also impossible, because, as the Chernobyl disaster shows, even the destruction of nuclear power plants by conventional weapons would bring about the same catastrophe as nuclear war.[30] The attitude of the military to the debate on conventional strategy tells us that they will not be able to accept this revision.

Regarding the principle of military build-up, predicators on future wars are reflected in decisions on the procurement of weapons. The army which tries to win a war at the conventional stage, avoiding nuclear escalation, naturally emphasizes efficient conventional weapons. This was the main point of Ogarkov's arguments. But the possibility of using nuclear weapons is not ruled out. In order to deter imperialist aggression, military capability should be retained. Thus, despite the shift in stress to conventional armaments, the military demand both conventional and nuclear weapons.

Gorbachev's emphasis is of course on conventional weapons. New thinkers argue for retaining only a small-scale but invulnerable second-strike capability until nuclear weapons are totally abolished. Their goal is not an unarmed, peace-loving state, however, but one with modern armed forces with high-tech weapons. At issue is the extent to which these forces are deployed.

The opposition between the military and the new thinkers is still sharper over the required scale of forces. The Soviets had pursued strategic superiority until Brezhnev's Tula speech in 1977, when they began to argue for strategic parity. But the basic principle of Soviet military policy towards the West at that time was the assurance of 'equality and identical security'. 'Identical security' means that the USSR has the right to hold the same number of missiles or warheads as not only the USA but also Europe, whose Euromissiles are targeted at Soviet territory; this implies Soviet superiority over the USA. In the early 1980s the Soviets began to show a new attitude towards military build-up; that their defence capability should be maintained only at the level necessary for defence;[31] nevertheless they put the first INF negotiation in jeopardy and finally in deadlock by adhering to the principle of identical security.

At this time, parity meant stability, and parity for the USSR meant quantitative equality with all other nuclear powers. The Soviets took every opportunity to assert that they would definitely resist any attempts by the imperialists to destroy parity.

However, under Gorbachev the formula 'parity equals stability equals quantitative equality' has been completely revised. Gorbachev first revealed his new formula at the twenty-seventh party congress: parity does not necessarily mean stability. That is, if the USSR constantly takes counter-measures in response to the imperialists' attempts to destroy parity, parity will be maintained but at such a high level that it might not work as a deterrent; thus parity can cease to be a condition for stability. In order for parity to mean stability, its level should be reduced as far as possible; that is, to the level of reasonable sufficiency.[32]

New thinkers then began to formulate arguments against the other equation: parity equals equality. Special emphasis was laid on the point that parity has a dynamic range, which was the idea put forward by the Committee of Soviet Scientists for Peace against the Nuclear Threat. They said that nuclear weapons have such huge destructive potential that a certain margin of difference in numbers of warheads and missiles does not matter;[33] parity does not necessarily require quantitative equality. If psychological and political stability is achieved, quantitative parity ceases to be necessary. This argument led to the decision to discard the principle of identical security; in practice, this meant that British and French nuclear weapons were not included in the INF negotiations. The principle of identical security had appeared reasonable to the Soviets but had proved unfortunate in political terms. It increased the West's distrust of the USSR, and also brought an escalation of US deterrence in that the deployment of Soviet SS-20s made the Europeans accept American INFs; also, the USSR had clearly stated that it would regard an attack by INFs in Europe against Soviet territory as a US strategic strike to which it would immediately respond by a counter-attack on US territory. The argument for qualitative parity has been used by new thinkers to propose unilateral restriction of military activities and unilateral cuts in conventional forces.[34]

How are the military reacting to these new arguments? The first new element, that parity at a low level (reasonable sufficiency) equals stability, has already been accepted by the military. For example, the *Military Encyclopedia* (1986) published after the twenty-seventh party congress, accepts this formula.[35] However, the military strongly resist the civilians' argument that qualitative parity can be enough for stability. While civilian new thinkers regard not only low-level but qualitatively stable parity as reasonable sufficiency, the military insist on quantitative equality and reciprocity. The debate over reasonable sufficiency has been going on since 1987, so far inconclusively. After Gorbachev's UN speech in December 1988, civilians began to argue more openly. For instance, Arbatov said that the level of sufficiency can be determined fairly independently of the enemy's military capability. He called for debate in the military based on his definition of sufficiency.[36] The military have, of course, counter-arguments.[37]

4   Military Strategy

Nuclear Strategy

Soviet military strategy was finally established in the latter part of the 1960s. It was a strategy for the weaker side, with damage limitation, retaliation and strategic defence as its main features. Therefore, in the European theatre the primary targets are the enemy's nuclear forces and related facilities. In the strategic rear industrial-economic areas are also given high priority in targeting. Their achievement of a second-strike capability in the late 1970s–early 1980s gave the Soviets what they saw as theoretical parity.[38] This also made them realize that the situation of 'mutually assured destruction' (MAD) had been achieved. But a perception of a reality does not necessarily imply a change in strategy. Nevertheless, as a result the Soviets began to focus on the development of an invulnerable second-strike capability, disarmament and the prevention of nuclear escalation in a conventional war in the European theatre.[39] The unilateral nuclear no-first-use announcement made by Brezhnev in 1982 can be regarded as a step towards these objectives.

Thus in the early 1980s the Soviets retained both the capability and the will to fight, while calling for the prevention of nuclear conflict. Here was the 'discrepancy' between the two aspects of military doctrine, which civilian new thinkers pointed to as an 'error of past diplomacy'. If both the opposite sides, the USA and the USSR, adopted this military policy, the result would be an arms race, but nothing more. Gorbachev's sharp criticism of deterrence strategy concentrates on this point. However, new thinkers are severely critical of 'nuclear deterrence strategy' which, on the pretext of securing parity, in fact pursues nuclear superiority. They even said that 'as long as nuclear weapons exist, strategic parity can be a stabilizing factor with all its negative aspects'.[40]

Asserting that security should be mutual in the nuclear age, even if mutual distrust cannot be eliminated completely, new thinkers see their goal as reducing the danger of nuclear war to the minimum by securing strategic stability through common strategic concepts and efforts at confidence building. For instance, Arbatov says that

> stability implies an overall balance of the forces of both powers and a symmetrical, mutual confidence in the reliability of their deterrent potentials at, incidentally, the lowest level of these deadly arsenals, with the reduction to the minimum reasonable sufficiency and, ultimately, the complete abolition of strategic potential and nuclear weapons.[41]

How to retain strategic stability at each stage of the nuclear reduction process is one of the major research subjects of the Committee of Soviet Scientists. Because even if parity is maintained, a radical reduction of nuclear weapons could cause destabilization by making the remaining strategic power and C^3 much more vulnerable. On this point Kokoshin made the proposal in his article in *Krasnaya Zvezda* that both the opposing sides should make joint efforts based upon the concept of stability, including having symmetrical C^3I and missile warning systems.[42]

With regard to strategy after nuclear forces have been reduced to the minimum level, they assume a simple deterrence strategy based on retaliatory strikes. Arbatov calls for both sides to adopt the strategic concept with the most simple and restricted meaning, that of counter-attacking only when suffering a nuclear strike.[43]

In contrast, the discussion on nuclear strategy among the military has only just started. Following the adoption of the defensive military doctrine in May 1987 and the resolution of the nineteenth party congress in June 1988 on the principle of quality over quantity in military build-up, the military have assumed responsibility for developing weapons technology in line with those decisions. The newly appointed Chief of the General Staff Moiseev mentions that at present almost all elements of strategy, operational methods and tactics, need to be revised.[44] But since civilian and military spokesmen disagreed even about the doctrines as outlined above, to change strategies will still take time.

Deterrence through parity has been much discussed, and some attempt to define the concept of reasonable sufficiency has been made by the military. The problem is, however, that the military have no interest in reducing the level of parity or revising its operational strategy; their interest is in criticizing the United States for having tried to destroy parity. Colonel Skorodenko has said that NATO's nuclear deterrence strategy aims at superiority over the USSR; this forces the USSR to take every measure to recover parity.[45]

On the reduction of nuclear arsenals and strategic stability, the military are taking a more realistic stand than the civilians' conceptual analysis. But this might simply show the meagreness of their conceptual analysis on these issues. For example, V. Slipchenko's article, 'Strategic parity' published in *Krasnaya Zvezda* in June 1988, consisted from beginning to end of criticism of the SDI programme as a destabilizing factor.[46] In their actual proposals, the military have laid great emphasis on the reconstruction of sea-deployed nuclear forces. They regard SLCM and ASW as serious obstructions to parity.[47] Without concessions from the United States in these areas, the military are unlikely to support the party leadership in any further unilateral issues.

Conventional Strategy

The resistance of the military is still stronger in the sphere of conventional strategy. The present conventional strategy, which was established in the latter half of the 1960s, is to destroy the enemy's nuclear forces in a preventive attack; that is, regardless of their intention or readiness to use nuclear weapons. From the late 1970s to the beginning of the 1980s the USSR, by updating this strategy and reorganizing the command system, prepared for wide-ranging and high-speed offensive operations in several military theatres. The objective was to win any war at the conventional stage, avoiding nuclear escalation. At the same time, however, the Soviets' increasing interest in defensive operations was also noted. According to one observer, this was because it was becoming increasingly difficult to determine the moment for a preventive attack due to the change in US military strategy, the growing number of military theatres and for other reasons.[48]

Gorbachev calls for a military posture in which neither side can make a surprise attack or launch offensive operations. This is the so-called non-offensive or non-provocative defence advocated by Western academics and ex-servicemen. It demands a 180-degree change in the Soviet theatre strategy in Europe which is based on offensive operations with forward deployment of troops and quantitative superiority of armaments.

Naturally the military are very cautious about Gorbachev's arguments. Military spokesmen emphasize the need to retain offensive capability in spite of Gorbachev's order to devise a military structure that 'is sufficient for defence, but insufficient for attack'. Their position is understandable in view of their present strategy. In practice, military leaders such as Yazov, Commander in Chief of Air Defence Forces Tretyak and First Deputy Chief of General Staff Gripkov still believe in the need to maintain an offensive capability. For instance, Yazov said, 'In the event of an attack, the armed forces of the Warsaw Pact countries will cooperate with exceptional resolve. While repulsing aggression, they will also conduct counter-offensive operations.'[49] Such views expressed by the military leadership gave rise to a wide-ranging debate in 1988. The reformist Serebryannikov wrote in an article that, in order to prevent a war, a complete defence strategy for repelling the enemy's attack is necessary; this strategy will be difficult to formulate but is the only acceptable choice; military techniques, planning, preparation and management will change emphasis accordingly. Nevertheless, he concludes his article by saying that the capacity to conduct offensive operations – that is, to counter-attack – is absolutely indispensable.[50] The conservative Skorodenko argues even more strongly for the necessity of offensive operations, saying that it is impossible to repel the enemy decisively with defensive operations alone: a combination of defensive and offensive military doctrine would be necessary, he maintains, because such offensive operations would be a response to the enemy's attack.[51]

After Gorbachev's UN speech, the Soviets began to discuss these matters more openly. In February 1988, Arbatov, questioning what it means 'to ensure the final rout of the enemy', given that the inevitable outcome, whether a world war or a war in major theatres, nuclear or conventional, is a global catastrophe, argued that clear distinction should be made between defensive and offensive strategy. Arbatov, arguing with surprising openness for a Soviet debate, proposed a nuclear strategy emphasizing countervalue and the protection of the second-strike capability, and a conventional strategy relying on frontline forces stationed as deep as possible in the rear. Responding to Arbatov's argument, Serebryannikov remarked that although action aimed at 'routing the enemy in its own territory' may indeed lead to the total destruction of life on earth, the unilateral renunciation of offensive capability would give the enemy a wholly unacceptable military advantage, since the United States and other NATO countries were continuing to build up offensive means.[52]

5 Arms Control and Disarmament

It has been shown that although the military leadership has been reshuffled effectively, it is not yet ready to accept Gorbachev's disarmament policy; no significant progress has been made in the intensification of military discipline or the revision of military strategy. Under these circumstances, we can imagine that there was a certain resistance among the military to Gorbachev's accelerated disarmament policy. From this point of view let us examine the reaction of the military to Gorbachev's arms control and disarmament measures in the following three fields: glasnost, nuclear disarmament and conventional disarmament.

Glasnost in the military sphere is concerned with on-site inspection of arms control and disarmament measures and with the publication of military information. Gorbachev's predecessors obstinately refused on-site inspections. Gorbachev's new, flexible approach to the matter broke the deadlock in the negotiations on conventional disarmament in Europe, which had been dragging on unsuccessfully for more than ten years. According to Primakov, Gorbachev directed his advisers to change the Soviet position on inspection, since by sticking to National Technical Means the Soviets would not be able to get the support of international public opinion.[53] Using the same reasoning, Gorbachev calls for the publication and comparison of defence expenditure and military forces, but according to Akhromeev, the process would probably take at least a year or eighteen months.[54] Fuller military budget data were released in summer 1989; and the scale of the Warsaw Pact forces in Europe had been made public in January 1989.

The extent of military opposition to this glasnost policy is not clear. However, the fact that even Soviet civilian specialists have had no access to information about force deployment, and can only rely on Western sources, and that military speakers frequently criticize civilian arguments as 'views of journalists without expertise'[55] indicates the existence of military dissatisfaction. In fact, Deputy Minister of Foreign Affairs Karpov has said that the publication of the Warsaw Pact military forces was delayed for a year because of resistance in the military.[56]

As regards nuclear disarmament, the strongest military opposition has been to the asymmetric cuts under the INF agreement. Gorbachev forced the military to revise their position on this matter during the INF negotiation. First, in the autumn of 1985 the Soviets announced that they were ready to negotiate on the nuclear forces of Britain and France on a bilateral basis, and at the Reykjavik meeting they agreed to exclude them from the negotiations. The Soviets then agreed to exclude the US INF deployed in Europe from the category of strategic forces, thus separating negotiations on them from the START talks. Furthermore, the Soviets approved the asymmetrical cuts by proposing the global zero option. Each of these moves was regarded as an unacceptable concession by Gorbachev's predecessors. Naturally, concern is frequently expressed by the military. For example, Maksimov, Commander in Chief of Strategic Rocket Forces, agreed that in political terms the dismantling of the INF had been the right decision; but as a professional soldier, he had mixed feelings about the dismantling of newly deployed weapons.[57] Concern about asymmetric cuts has frequently been expressed in readers' letters to newspapers.[58]

As mentioned above, civilian specialists have frequently advocated unilateral cuts in conventional forces, but the military have always insisted on reciprocity. In 1988 especially, it seems that heated arguments between the two sides took place behind the scenes. For instance, Tretyak severely criticized the high positive view taken by civilians of unilateral disarmament in the Khrushchev era, pointing to the damage it caused the military in terms of personnel and material resources.[59] Akhromeev made it clear that the USSR was ready for disarmament but only on a reciprocal basis, saying 'it will be a waste of time to demand unilateral moves from the USSR'.[60] Yazov, although making some attempts to define the concept of reasonable sufficiency, has avoided clarifying its specific level by saying that it depends on what the United States and NATO do.[61] Significantly, Yazov used the terms 'equality and identified security' quite frequently at this time.[62]

In July the unilateral withdrawal of Soviet troops from Hungary was rumoured but did not take place. It is reported that at the first session of the Ministry of Foreign Affairs conference on foreign relations entitled 'Soviet foreign policy priorities', held at the end of the month, the unilateral withdrawal of troops stationed in Eastern Europe was proposed as a political gesture. Some argued against it,[63] but finally Gorbachev seems to have regarded it as essential for its political effect.

Since the Soviet Union's conventional offensive superiority is considered by the military to counter-balance the nuclear and qualitative 'superiority' of the West, they must have viewed the unilateral cuts with serious concern. Nevertheless, Robov's comment on the cuts, 'Could the Soviet army remain frozen and unchanged in this age of new political thinking?',[64] seems to reflect the fact that the military have had to come to terms and cooperate with perestroika.

Conclusion

Gorbachev's perestroika in the military sphere is making sure but slow progress, though to varying degrees in different areas. In contrast, he has had to take hasty measures on the food issue in order to stay in power. But his plan to redeploy some sectors of military industry for the production of civilian goods, notably for equipment for the production of these goods and for food processing, has made little headway on account of strong resistance by the military industries. The only comparable measures available to him are to economize by reducing the size of the military forces or restricting military activities in peacetime. Gorbachev has good reasons for accelerating perestroika in the military sphere. However, the military are not yet ready to accept his policy; and although personnel changes have been carried out, we cannot hope for a rapid improvement in military discipline. Nevertheless, Gorbachev is demanding a radical change in military policy.

Gorbachev's military policy is based certainly on the demands of the time. While retaining the nuclear option, the military are aware that denuclearization has begun. But Gorbachev's hastiness might, by arousing too much alarm or confusion among the military, endanger his position. During the first period of change after World War II, when nuclear weapons were incorporated into Soviet military thinking, Khrushchev over-emphasized nuclear weapons to the detriment of other services and thus incurred criticisms from the military. Of course the present situation differs from Khrushchev's time since there are now civilian specialists. But if Gorbachev tries to implement his policy too fast, a coalition of military and non-military conservatives might develop. Consequently, he is expected to concentrate on reductions in US sea-based weapons in the near future; this will force Japan to define its position in the matter.

Notes

1. Stephen M. Meyer, 'Soviet theatre nuclear forces', Parts I and II, *Adelphi Paper*, 186 and 187, IISS, London, 1984.

2. According to Fitzgerald, Ogarkov has given the following periodization for Soviet military doctrine:

> throughout the 1950s, nuclear weapons were few and viewed only as a means of supplementing the firepower of troops. Doctrine in the 1960s had been dominated by Marshal Sokolovskii's classic *Military Strategy*, which apparently focused on viable nuclear options. But in the 1970s and 1980s, Ogarkov said, the rapid growth of nuclear weapons led to 'a break in previous views . . . even on the possibility of waging war at all with the use of nuclear weapons'. (Mary C. Fitzgerald, 'The strategic revolution behind Soviet arms control', *Arms Control Today* (June 1987): 16)

As for the argument that the Soviets have transferred to conventional warfare, see also James M. McConnell, 'Shifts in Soviet view on the proper focus of military development', *World Politics*, 31 (3) (1985): 317–43; and William E. Odom, 'Soviet force posture: dilemmas and directions', *Problems of Communism* (July–Aug. 1985): 1–14.

3. 'Na novom etape perestroiki', *Krasnaya Zvezda*, 23 Jan. 1988.

4. Moiseev, Robov and Arkhipov all have close relations with Yazov; Moiseev was first Deputy Commander of the Military District of the Far East under Yazov; while Yazov was Commander of the Central Asian Military District before being Commander of the Far Eastern Military District. Robov was his successor and Moiseev was first deputy under him.

5. 'Perestroika trebuet del', *Krasnaya Zvezda*, 13 Aug. 1988; M. Moiseev, 'Na strazhe mira i sotsializma', *Krasnaya Zvezda*, 23 Feb. 1989.

6. In early 1989, a frank argument on the difference between parity and sufficiency had already appeared in the military journal. See V. Strebkov, 'Kriterii voenno-strategicheskogo pariteta', *Kommunist vooruzhennykh sil*, 4 (Feb. 1989): 18–24.

7. E. Primakov, 'Vstrecha v verkhakh vzglyad v proshloe i budushchee', *Pravda*, 8 Jan. 1989.

8. Gorbachev's reports to the April 1985 plenum and the twenty-seventh party congress (1986), *Pravda*, 24 April 1985 and 25 Feb. 1986.

9. 'Tezisy Tsentral'nogo Komiteta KPSS k XIX Vsesoyuznoi partiinoi konferentsii', *Pravda*, 27 May 1988.

10. D. Yazov, '70 let na strazhe sotsializma i mira', *Pravda*, 23 Feb. 1988.

11. Ibid.

12. 'V politbyuro TsKa KPSS', *Pravda*, 14 Oct. 1988.

13. *Voennyi entsiklopedicheskii slovar'* (Moscow: Voennoe izdatel'stvo, 1986), p. 240.

14. *Disarmament and Security: IMEMO Yearbook 1987*, pp. 209–12. Also see V.V. Zagladin's statement in 'Vneshnyaya politika i perestroika', *Krasnaya Zvezda*, 26 July 1988.

15. Brezhnev's report to the twenty-sixth Party Congress, *Pravda*, 24 Feb. 1981.

16. Chernenko's report on the anniversary of Lenin's birthday, *Pravda*, 23 April 1981.

17. Gorbachev's speech at the Peace Forum, *Pravda*, 17 Feb. 1987.

18. G. Shakhnazarov, 'The moment of fear and revelation', *New Times*, 49 (Dec. 1987): 19. As an interpretive paper of the ongoing debate, see A. Pavlov and V. Lyashenko, 'Sootnoshenie voiny i politiki diskussii i problemy', *Kommunist vooruzhennykh sil*, 21 (Nov. 1988): 23–30.

19. D.T. Yazov, 'Podvig vo imya zhizhni', *Pravda*, 9 May 1988.

20. Pavlov and Lyashenko, 'Sootnoshenie voiny i politiki diskussii i problemy', pp. 23–4. This is also Volkogonov's argument. See Pavlov and Lyashenko, p. 24, and T. Hasegawa, 'Gorbachev, the new thinking of Soviet foreign security policy and the military: recent trends and implications', in P. Juviler and H. Kimura (eds), *Gorbachev's Reforms* (New York: Aldine de Gruyter, 1988), p. 138.

21. Yu. Krasin points to Finland, Austria and Switzerland as models of 'non-militarized capitalism'. Rosin says that Japan did not owe its economic growth to militarism, although he does not deny the danger of militarization. Yu. Krasin, 'Strategiya mira – imperativ epokhi', *MEiMO*, 1 (Jan. 1986): 7; V. Rosin, 'Militarizatsiya Yaponii: mnenie ekonomista', *MEiMO*, 1 (Jan. 1988): 17–24.

22. A. Savinkin, 'What kind of armed forces do we need?' *Moscow News*, 6 Nov. 1988, No. 45. See also 'Army and society', *XX Century and Peace*, 9 (1988): 18–20.

23. 'Poka sushchestvuet opasnost' agressii', *Kommunist vooruzhennykh sil*, 2 (Jan. 1989): 18–25.

24. S. Tyshkevich, 'Ob agressivnosti imperializma', *Kommunist vooruzhennykh sil*, 8 (April 1988): 85–6.

25. D. Volkogonov, 'Samaya spravedlivaya voina', *Kommunist*, 9 (June 1986): 121–2.

26. V. Serebryannikov, 'Sootnoshenie politicheskikh i voennykh sredstv v zashchite sotsializma', *Kommunist vooruzhennykh sil*, 19 (Sept. 1987).

27. Serebryannikov says that the Soviet perception of war has changed several times; while in the 1950s war was expected to disappear only when capitalism perishes, in the 1950–60s the Soviets began to think it possible to prevent a war

while capitalism exists as a social system by 'compelling peace from capitalism'. In the 1980s the theory was further developed to hold that a world without nuclear weapons, armaments or compulsion can be secured even if capitalism continues to exist. V. Serebryannikov, 'Bezopasnost' gosudarstva v yadernyi vek', *Kommunist vooruzhennykh sil*, 9 (May 1988): 35–5; 'Blokirovanie voin: politicheskii mekhanizm', *Kommunist vooruzhennykh sil*, 18 (Oct. 1988): 20–1.

28. P. Skorodenko, 'Voenno-strategicheskii paritet kak faktor nedopushcheniya voiny', *Kommunist vooruzhennykh sil*, 12 (June 1988): 41.

29. Meyer, 'Soviet theatre nuclear forces', Part I, *Adelphi Paper*, 186, p. 28.

30. Zagladin's statement in the interview by *Asahi Shinbun* (2 Oct. 1987).

31. K. Miyauchi, 'Changes in Soviet military doctrine: deterrence or crushing', *Soviet Studies* (Japanese), 7 (Oct. 1988): 20.

32. Gorbachev's political report to the twenty-seventh party congress, *Pravda*, Feb. 1986.

33. Committee of Soviet Scientists for Peace against the Nuclear Threat. *Strategic Stability under the Conditions of Radical Nuclear Arms Reductions*, Report on a study, abridged, Moscow, April 1987, p. 6.

34. V. Zhurkin, S. Karaganov and A. Kortunov, 'Reasonable sufficiency: or how to break the vicious circle', *New Times*, 40 (1987): 13–15; A.A. Kokoshin and A.V. Kortunov, 'Stability and changes in international relations', *S.Sh.A: Ekonomika, Politika, Ideoligiya* (English version) (July 1987): 13–15. O. Amirov, N. Kishikov, V. Makarevsky and Y. Usachev, 'Problems of reducing military confrontation', *Disarmament and Security: 1987* (1988), pp. 395–400, has produced a plan of asymmetric cuts.

35. *Voennyi entsiklopedicheskii slovar'*, 1986, p. 609.

36. A. Arbatov, 'Defence dilemmas', *New Times*, 6 (7–13 Feb. 1989): 20–1.

37. See Serebryannikov's counter-arguments to Arbatov's paper (Note 50).

38. G. Shakhnazarov, 'The moment of fear and revelation', *New Times*, 49 (Dec. 1987): 19. Valentin Falin's statement in 'V sluchae voiny nekomu budet dokazyvat' svoyu pravotu', *Moskovskie novosti*, 45 (8 Nov. 1987): 6.

39. Weikhardt says that the USSR has changed its force structure and tried to improve its capability to survive rather than its first-strike capability by decreasing the number of ICBMs deployed in large silos and by shifting the emphasis in force preparation to mobile ICBMs, SLBMs, bombers and cruise missiles.

40. *Pravda*, 10 July 1987.

41. A. Arbatov, 'The illusion of an impenetrable shield', *New Times*, 8 (Aug. 1987): 15. A. Bovin calls this shift in strategic concept the one from 'deterrence by threat', the threat of overall retaliation, to 'defensive deterrence', based on military parity maintained at every level of nuclear disarmament (A. Bovin, 'Novoe myshlenie – novaya politika', *Kommunist*, 9 (July 1988): 120).

42. A. Kokoshin, 'Tri [kita] stabil'nosti', *Krasnaya Zvezda*, 16 Sept. 1988.

43. 'What will happen to deterrence', *Asahi Shinbun*, 5 Jan. 1988.

44. M. Moiseev, 'Na strazhe mira i sotsializma', *Krasnaya Zvezda*, 23 Feb. 1988.

45. Skorodenko, 'Voenno-strategicheskii paritet', p. 43.

46. V. Slipchenko, *Krasnaya Zvezda*, 17 and 24 June 1988.

47. See V.N. Lobov, 'Ukreplyat' stabil'nost' i bezopasnost'', *Krasnaya Zvezda*, 29 Jan. 1988; and 'Kto stremitsya k prevoskhodstvu', *Krasnaya Zvezda*, 14 July 1988; S. Akhromeyev, 'Voenno-morskie sily i vseobshchaya bezopasnost'', *Krasnaya Zvezda*, 5 Sept. 1988.

48. Edward L. Warner III, 'New thinking and old realities in Soviet defence policy', *Survival*, IISS (Jan.–Feb. 1989), pp. 25–6.

49. General D.T. Yazov, *Na strazhe sotsializma i mira* (Moscow: Voenizdat, 1987), p. 34, quoted from Warner, 'New thinking', p. 23. As to Gripkov's and Trechak's statements, see Arbatov, 'Defence dilemmas', p. 19.

50. Serebryannikov, 'Bezopasnost' gosudarstva' pp. 38–9.

51. Skorodenko, 'Voenno-strategicheskii paritet', p. 46.

52. Arbatov, 'Defence dilemmas', p. 20; V. Serebryannikov, 'More on the defence doctrine dilemma', *New Times*, 12 (21–27 March 1989): 17.

53. Primakov, 'Vstrecha v verkhakh'.

54. 'General Staff – changes', *Moscow News*, 29 Jan. 1989.

55. Arbatov, 'Defence dilemmas', p. 21.

56. Viktor Karpov, 'Vienna: after and before', *New Times*, 17 (1989): 7.

57. 'Pod boevymi znamenami', *Krasnaya Zvezda*, 9 May 1988.

58. For example, see a letter to the editor of *Pravda* by N. Prozhogin, 'Dogovor po RSD-RMD: za ili protiv', *Pravda*, 20 Feb. 1988.

59. 'Reliable defence first and foremost', *Moscow News*, 8 (1986): 12.

60. S.F. Akhromeyev, 'Chto kroetsya za bryussel'skim zayavleniem NATO', *Krasnaya Zvezda*, 20 March 1988.

61. D.T. Yazov, 'O voennom balanse sil i raketno-yadernom paritete', *Krasnaya Zvezda*, 23 Feb. 1988.

62. Ibid. See also D.T. Yazov, 'Kachestvennye parametry oboronnogo stroitel'-stva', *Krasnaya Zvezda*, 9 Aug. 1989.

63. A. Kovalev, 'First section: Soviet foreign policy priorities', *International Affairs* (Oct. 1988): 37.

64. 'Unilateral Soviet armed forces cuts', *Moscow News*, 8 Dec. 1988, p. 5.

9

De-Stalinization and Soviet Foreign Policy: The Roots of 'New Thinking'

Neil Malcolm

Gorbachev's foreign policy innovations fit into a cycle of alternations in the style and content of Soviet behaviour in the world which have occurred at intervals ever since the 1917 Revolution.[1] Yet they are also part of a deeper, transforming process which embraces radical changes in Soviet internal affairs.

It has long been predicted that with time, as revolutionary militancy waned, generation succeeded generation, and the imperatives of economic and social development worked their way out, radical changes would come about in the Soviet policy which would moderate, and perhaps eliminate, its distinctive 'communist' features. After 1968, when authoritarian tendencies reasserted themselves in Eastern Europe, over-ambitious 'convergence' and 'political development' theorizing came in for criticism, but there was a persisting sense that the neo-Stalinist system was losing momentum. During the 1970s a number of Western scholars pointed to the essential conservatism of the Soviet regime.[2] Lately hopes have emerged that an epochal change may at last be under way. In 1987 Alexander Yanov, who has described Russian history up to the present in terms of an inexorable sequence of reform and absolutist counter-reform, interspersed with periods of stabilization, expressed the hope that the current reformist push might 'succeed in breaking the vicious circle of autocracy and become irreversible'.[3] Evidence to support this proposition can be found in the pattern of change in internal politics and foreign policy since World War II. This pattern, it will be argued, is one in which a reform-reaction cycle is superimposed on, and distorted by, a longer-term tendency to decay of the system, which by the 1980s had reached a point where profound change was unavoidable.

Four major turning points, which relate simultaneously to home and foreign policy, can be identified. They were not sharply defined in time: on each occasion a period of wavering and uncertainty preceded the more or less decisive adoption of a new line at home and abroad. The first of these turns, which took place in 1945–7, was the only one not associated with the death of a leader. The factors at work seem to have been predominantly external ones. Nevertheless, when the wartime alliance finally fell apart and the sides began to dig in to their cold war positions, a parallel 'hardening' in internal affairs could be observed: consumption levels were kept down, purges and arrests returned in leadership politics, and a sharp crackdown was imposed in the cultural sphere. This tightening of control was supervised by the same Andrei Zhdanov who announced the founding of Cominform and the division of the world into two irreconcilable camps in September 1947.[4]

In 1953–7 the struggle for power in Moscow blurred the outlines of Soviet politics, but there took place a determined shift away from Stalin's dictatorial rule and his 'coercive isolationism' in foreign policy in the direction of some loosening up at home and a strategy of competitive engagement and peaceful coexistence abroad.[5] After Khrushchev's departure in 1964 internal policy was ill-defined at first, especially in ideology and culture, and in the economy. The new administration also kept a low profile in international relations. At the end of the decade, however, a clear trend emerged towards combining authoritarianism and centralism in internal affairs with renewed East–West dialogue. Finally, in the early 1980s, there began the comprehensive reappraisal of all spheres of policy which culminated in Gorbachev's reforms.

The first problem which arises when we attempt to map these changes in internal politics and foreign policy is one of terminology. Can the concepts 'reformism' and 'conservatism', for example, be applied in a consistent enough way to the history of the last four decades of Soviet politics to be usable? 'Reform', after all, is a relative concept, and the policy agenda changes: the 'conservatives' of the 1970s were content to defend certain positions which would have been regarded as innovative in the 1950s. The analysis which follows is based on the view that, in contrast to West European politics during the same period, there is an adequate degree of continuity. Stephen Cohen comments that by the 1960s 'something akin to two distinct parties took shape within Soviet officialdom and within the Communist Party itself', each largely defined by their attitude to the heritage of the Stalin era. Each had 'a characteristic cluster of policies, historical perspectives and ideological perceptions'. Typical reformist goals, in this definition, were democratization, decentralization of economic management, a switch of priorities to increased production of consumer goods, internationalism and a relaxation of relations with the West. Conservatives, by contrast, emphasized the authoritarian strands in Marxism-Leninism, traditional approaches to investment and management, nationalism, and conflict between East and West.[6] These very issues formed the content of political debate not just in the 1970s but also in the 1980s.

Similar clusters of ideas lie behind the phenomenon, identified by Alexander Dallin, of 'rational linkage' in official policy. He defines this as 'a congruence between the political and ideological content of the decision makers' domestic priorities and preferences and their foreign policy priorities and preferences; at times, these may be operationalized in budget terms'. During the period from 1917 to 1956, he notes, there occurred a series of shifts between confrontation and relaxation at home and abroad. In each instance 'there was a similar dominant political mood and/or strategy that created predispositions to pursue policies congruent with it in each of the two environments'. The argument is convincingly made that this kind of linkage is both a matter of economics *and* a matter of contrasting world views and mind-sets.[7]

Dallin used the words 'left' (authoritarian) and 'right' (reformist) to identify the two sides, making connections with the history of the first decade of Soviet power. Although this draws attention to suggestive precedents and parallels, many would consider that it carries risks of distortion. After all, many of the terms of the debate have changed, and the labels 'left' and 'right' are no longer used in their original Soviet sense in Moscow in the late 1980s. It is, of course, possible to go even further back, and to see the roots of the cleavage in the conflict between the autocratic and isolationist policies of tsarist officialdom and the Westernizing aspirations of the educated strata.[8] In a broad sense, this is quite justified. But the starting-point chosen here is the clash between Stalinist centralism and xenophobia on the one hand and the liberalizing, internationalist reaction which it provoked along elements of the Soviet intelligentsia on the other. The remarkably consistent configuration of the debate over recent decades is a tribute to the powerful impact which Stalin made on political consciousness in his own country and in Eastern Europe, and to the tenacity of the system which he created. During the long period of its decline, the agents of the process of change have continued to speak to each other in the categories which he established.

The challenge posed to the orthodox Soviet world view by 'new thinking' is not as recent as might be supposed. Innovative conceptions of capitalism which implicitly threw doubt on Stalin's foreign policy line were already being aired as early as 1946. It took forty years, however, for them to penetrate into official discourse. What we are principally interested in are the political processes governing the evolution of official doctrine and policy during that period.

Alexander Dallin remarks that after 1956 no single over-arching political orientation, no clear-cut general line embodying an ideologically harmonious, 'rationally linked' set of policies was sustained by any of the successive Soviet leaderships. He proposes as a reason for this that society had become too complex to sustain sudden and across-the-board shifts: change when it came had to be of an incremental kind.[9]

Another way of explaining this loss of consistency, however, is to see it as an effect of deepening stresses and strains as the established heavily centralized system came up against economic and social pressures for modernization. In the economy the differentiation of production and accelerating technological change appeared to demand a loosening of central control, greater local initiative, and some concessions to the universal tendency to internationalization. In society the education drive, recognized as essential to build and maintain Soviet competitiveness, was gradually increasing the proportional weight of elements which tended to a scientific, efficiency-oriented view of the world. Such people were attuned more to Western values than to those upheld by party 'dogmatists'. They came more and more to resent the political dominance of established elites, and in some cases in their own specialist writing helped to provide the doctrinal building blocks for an alternative, more congenial version of the ideology.

In such a situation institutions like the economic planning bodies, the armed forces and the party ideology agencies faced a direct threat to their prerogatives and to the assumptions which sustained them. They fought back using a variety of methods. They engaged in political manoeuvring, took ruthless direct action against their critics, and attempted to foster a continuing atmosphere of emergency and struggle of the kinds which had attended their establishment and growth in the 1920s and 1930s.[10] Thus, while the vagaries of official policy during the Khrushchev years expressed, from one point of view, the interplay of 'conservative' and 'reformist' tendencies, from another point of view they reflected a clash between the institutional interests of a majority of party and state officials on the one hand, and on the other the interest of the First Secretary in pursuing the kind of changes which he sensed were necessary to ensure the long-term viability of the Soviet system. Khrushchev was always able to find a number of bureaucratic allies, but in the end his coalition-building skills proved inadequate.

Under Brezhnev's consensus style of leadership policy was more consistent over time, but it was less internally consistent. The absence of political congruence between home policy (predominantly 'conservative') and foreign policy (predominantly 'reformist') was matched by incoherence inside each of these spheres. As external pressures increased and the performance of the system deteriorated, the oligarchical elements which enjoyed political dominance had themselves begun to understand that the traditional remedies no longer worked, but they were unable, or rather unwilling, to put together a coordinated and effective package of innovations. They clearly had no intention of presiding over the abolition of their own empire.

When Gorbachev came to power it became apparent that an influential section of the political leadership had grasped the need for a comprehensive effort at reform. It had reached the conclusion that powerful institutions in what came to be known as 'the administrative-command system' were blocking the way to vitally necessary changes. A strategy was therefore adopted in which economic reform, political democratization, a rise in the status of the intelligentsia, a downgrading of heavy-industrial and military priorities and the agencies associated with them, a discrediting of 'dogma', a broadening of international contacts and a drive for a political settlement with the Western powers went hand in hand, each element reinforcing the others. In the terms used above, the rationality of the linkage between the political, economic and foreign-policy demands of reformism had at last won acceptance at the top.

Thus it now seems conceivable that the time of anti-Stalinist reformism has come at last. It is important, therefore, to form a clear idea of the conditions which have permitted it to achieve its current ascendancy. The brief survey which follows concentrates on the foreign policy dimension.

Khrushchev and the Politicization of Soviet Foreign Policy

The relatively open political conflicts of the Khrushchev era demonstrated vividly the obstacles faced at that time by the advocates of new policies. This was not because of the total novelty of their ideas. The foundations for a new foreign policy doctrine had been laid seven years before Stalin's death, by his senior international affairs expert, the Director of the Institute of the World Economy and World Politics, Evgeny Varga. During the years of the alliance against Hitler the idea had gained ground that there was an important distinction to be made between 'democratic' capitalist regimes and fascist ones. Building on this, and pointing to the evidence of Roosevelt's New Deal and of the successes of wartime planning by the Allies, Varga argued that the capitalist state had acquired more power and autonomy from big business than had previously been thought. It was therefore capable of acting with prudence and long-term judgement in foreign affairs and of regulating internal economic and social processes in such a way as to ensure a new phase of prosperity and relative political calm. The director and his colleagues were no doubt acting as the mouthpiece of moderate elements in the leadership, at a time when many considered that the United States might agree to acceptable terms for prolonging collaboration with the USSR into the postwar years. In 1947, when policy swung firmly in the opposite direction, Varga's institute was condemned for 'reformist', 'apolitical', 'bourgeois objectivist' tendencies, and closed down. The militant rhetoric of party officials like Zhdanov and Suslov prevailed.[11]

By the beginning of the following decade the counterproductiveness of Soviet intransigence in foreign affairs was becoming increasingly obvious. In Germany, the 1948 Berlin blockade had succeeded only in creating favourable conditions for setting up the Federal Republic and establishing the NATO alliance. In Korea the offensive launched by the communist North had led to a dangerous confrontation with the United States and a military stalemate. Doctrinal adjustments in the direction of moderation began to emerge. In his *Economic Problems of Socialism in the USSR* Stalin declared that war between East and West was now unlikely. As was to happen thirty years later, Moscow threw itself into peace campaigning, and tried to stir up anti-American feeling in Western Europe. At the nineteenth party congress in 1952 Malenkov offered 'peaceful coexistence' with the West, and cooperation on the basis of equality and non-interference.

In his memoirs Khrushchev later wrote that coping with Stalin's legacy in foreign policy was 'an interesting challenge'.[12] He tackled it with characteristic energy, picking up the threads of postwar revisionism in order to elaborate his own doctrine of peaceful coexistence. He maintained that there were powerful 'realistic' elements in Western ruling circles and that there were prospects for demilitarizing the capitalist economies. Backed up by international relations specialists at the resurrected IMEMO institute, he moved to apply flexible tactics in order to exploit the possibilities which the new analysis opened up.[13] This meant adopting a more imaginative, 'political' approach, cultivating allies in Europe and in the developing world, and making small concessions for the sake of large benefits.

The budgetary case for relaxing East–West tensions was exhaustively debated. Khrushchev repeatedly criticized the 'metal eaters' and called for a readjustment of priorities to meet popular demand for food and consumer goods. Selective cooperation with the West – in trade and arms control – would make it possible, so the new line ran, for the USSR to succeed in the real competition, which was essentially no longer a military one, but an economic one.

Yet economic pressures were not yet seen as compelling enough to force a radical change of policy. The Soviet leadership still appeared to share a deep confidence in the underlying superiority and competitiveness of their own system. While they no longer declared that capitalism was on the point of collapse and while they could not ignore the socialist world's persisting military and economic disadvantages, the First Secretary and his colleagues apparently believed quite genuinely that the USSR would outpace its rivals in the foreseeable future, and that imperialist aspirations were already being tamed by the 'changing balance of world forces'. They were aware of their country's relative weakness, in other words, but saw it as a temporary phenomenon. In such circumstances a certain amount of world-revolutionary rhetoric and missile-rattling (over Suez, Berlin, Cuba) was permissible. There was a congruence based on 'political mood' between what was later criticized as adventurism in Khrushchev's foreign policy and the Utopian aspects of his domestic programme, which envisaged enhanced mass participation as a significant step towards the withering away of the state, and promised that communism itself could be built 'in the main' in the coming decades.[14]

Because the system appeared still to be successful and dynamic, its central institutions confidently defended traditional values and resisted the kind of reforms which might reduce their powers. In 1953 and 1954 Khrushchev himself was only able to defeat Malenkov and establish his authority as national leader by playing on the fears aroused by his rival's reformist-tending 'new course' in 1953 and 1954 and gaining the backing of military and heavy industry spokesmen. Even after 1957 he was obliged to continue to manoeuvre for support, pitting one section of officialdom against another.

In foreign affairs this occasionally created an appearance of indecisiveness. Indeed, as Khrushchev's period in office proceeded, there was an increasingly obvious tug-of-war over various aspects of policy between two fairly clearly defined tendencies, which fit well into Cohen's reformist-conservative categories. They had various code names – 'politics-first' and 'economics-first', 'dogmatist' and 'revisionist', 'Chinese' and 'Yugoslav'. As the battle between the two sides fluctuated, so they found opportunities to forward their preferences in home and foreign affairs. Policy shifts in these two areas form a coherent pattern.[15]

In 1959, for example, Khrushchev used the twenty-first party congress to launch a drive for reform at home and detente abroad. He lifted the deadline which he had set two months earlier for an agreement with the Western powers on the future of Berlin, and began preparations for the Camp David summit with Eisenhower later in the year. Subsequently he adopted a neutral position in the Sino-Indian border dispute and announced a one-third cut in Soviet ground forces. In May of the following year, however, mounting opposition at home was encouraged by the shooting down of an American U-2 spy plane over Soviet territory. This incident exposed the riskiness of the current strategy of 'nuclear bluff' (pretending that Soviet long-range rocket forces were larger than they were), and its consequences demonstrated the fragility of recent improvements in East–West relations. Soon radical changes in the composition of the Party Secretariat were forced through, seriously weakening Khrushchev's position and strengthening that of his conservative rivals. The Paris summit meeting which followed was a failure. By 1961 Soviet spokesmen were announcing a one-third *increase* in the military budget, a suspension of troop reductions and the resumption of nuclear tests.

Later in the year, at the time of the twenty-second party congress, Khrushchev took the offensive again. He invited Kennedy to a meeting in the USSR, cut nuclear testing and reduced the pressure on Berlin. In 1962 Brezhnev was sent to Yugoslavia to prepare top-level talks with Tito. Meanwhile at home the campaign against neo-Stalinism was renewed, and a radical reform of the party's structure was announced. Then, after the Cuban missile crisis in October, another retreat began. Unorthodoxy in the arts and the media came under violent attack, and there was official criticism of 'revisionist splitters and opportunists of every brand',[16] in Yugoslavia and elsewhere. In the economy heavy industry and defence priorities were reaffirmed, and management was recentralized in a new Supreme Economic Council, headed by the arms industrialist Ustinov. This last move ran directly counter to Khrushchev's entire strategy of economic reform. Although further conciliatory initiatives were made in foreign policy in 1963, the domestic scene was set for a change of administration. The Supreme Council foreshadowed the re-establishing of the system of industrial ministries by Khrushchev's successors, and the partial rehabilitation of traditional priorities and values, as the core institutions of the administrative-command system reasserted themselves.

Expertise and Foreign Policy

Stalin's successors in the leadership have had a complicated relationship with the most highly educated part of Soviet society. Although Khrushchev enlisted them in his campaigning against 'dogmatism', he was capable of riding roughshod over their preferences and ignoring their advice, most notoriously in the arts and the natural sciences. Yet the government and the party became inexorably more dependent on their cooperation. As the web of relations with the outside world became denser in the years following 1953, for example, officials began to express concern about the scantiness of the expertise which was available in Moscow in the field of foreign affairs. The Minister of Foreign Trade, Anastas Mikoyan, complained openly in a speech at the twentieth party congress in 1956 about the closing down of Varga's research institute after the war. 'We are lagging seriously behind', he declared, 'in the study of contemporary capitalism; we do not study facts and figures deeply.' In the following year a new Institute of the World Economy and International Relations (IMEMO) was established in the Academy of Sciences, and it grew rapidly in size and influence.[17]

This created a new set of problems. To adopt the language of theorists of modernization, communist regimes which wish to achieve a level of technical rationality adequate to the post-mobilization phase of social development are obliged to make substantial changes in the working conditions of specialists, broadly speaking in order to allow them wider access to information and greater freedom of expression. Such changes are likely to generate uncomfortable tensions in the political system as a whole, however, and are therefore not easy to bring about.[18] From 1956 onwards, for instance, leader like Mikoyan complained that international affairs briefings submitted by diplomats and academics who felt obliged to describe reality in agitprop terms – class struggle, the vanguard role played by foreign Communist Parties, the heroic activism of the workers' movement – were of limited practical use. But until very recently social scientists in the USSR have been subject to cramping restrictions and, when they have escaped them, they have frequently become entangled in political disputes.[19]

The specialist journals characteristically provided a semi-public outlet for policy debates for which there were no other legitimate means of expression. IMEMO scholars soon began to provide ingenious revisions of theory to justify Khrushchev's new policies towards the West and in the Third World. A group of young radical-minded experts were brought into the Central Committee apparatus to form a 'consultant' group, which by the end of Khrushchev's period in power was reporting to the head of the party's Department for Relations with the Socialist Countries, Yury Andropov. Its members included the international affairs specialists Georgy Arbatov and Aleksandr Bovin, the political scientists Georgy Shakhnazarov and Fedor Burlatsky, and the economist Oleg Bogomolov.[20] But in some of the other Academy research institutes, and in IMEMO itself, there were passionate supporters of more traditional positions. Officials soon began to express concern about unseemly squabbling among the academics. The problem was that allowing the kind of atmosphere of unfettered debate which was required to produce the best advice risked a 'degeneration' into pluralism, and threatened the party's authority and its leading role. From the early 1960s ideological managers made a concerted attempt to overcome what was described as a 'tendency to departmental dissociation' and to find ways of reaching 'integrated solutions' to foreign policy problems.[21]

After 1964 this trend intensified, with the new administration's emphasis on 'businesslike', 'scientific' decision making. Coordinating procedures were refined and the research institute system was enlarged: by 1974 well over 1,000 international affairs specialists were employed in the Academy of Sciences. Their brief was to refrain from adventurous generalizations and to concentrate on providing accurate empirical surveys and prognoses. IMEMO and its sister institutes (for the USA and Canada, the Far East, Latin America and so on) reported to the Central Committee International Department, the Foreign Ministry and other government agencies, and provided them with highly trained staff on secondment or transfer.[22]

The growth of the foreign policy research network resulted from a conscious effort on the part of Khrushchev's successors to modernize the policy-making system. Intolerant of dissent and even of mild innovation in so many other areas, the Brezhnev leadership allowed a remarkable amount of leeway to its international affairs experts. This inconsistency reflected disarray in the face of increasingly powerful forces pushing for a reconstruction of the Soviet Union's external relations. The specialists exploited their relative freedom to describe the outside world in new ways in order to develop further the postwar revisionist tradition of thinking about international relations. Thus they helped to lay the foundations for the official 'new thinking' of the Gorbachev administration.

This activity did not go unchallenged. In 1969 professional ideologists in the party's Academy of Social Sciences felt that the time was right to launch a comprehensive attack on Varga and the whole tradition which he had founded. However, the director of IMEMO, Inozemtsev, confidently rebutted the criticisms, declaring that life 'again and again' had demonstrated the truth of his predecessor's 1946 thesis about the powers of capitalism to survive. Varga's underlying conception of the active role of the capitalist state, and implicitly the recommendation of greater flexibility in East–West relations, were endorsed by other institute directors and officials (Arbatov, by now head of the new USA Institute, Aleksandr Yakovlev, First Deputy Head of the CPSU Propaganda Department).[23]

In the years that followed, as detente got under way, the readers of Soviet specialist journals tended to be presented with a more rational, cooperative picture of the West – no longer automatically militaristic and predatory, but capable of restraint and genuine compromise. The implication was clear that the USSR should be ready to respond in kind. In 1973, for instance, Arbatov restated Khrushchev's view that many Americans realized the destructive effect on their economies of large defence budgets. As a result, he claimed, they were now turning away from the futilities of the arms race and looking for far-reaching agreements with the USSR. Transparently addressing his own side, Arbatov warned that 'propagandizing war and hatred for other countries' could damage the prospects for detente. Aleksandr Bovin was more explicit: 'We must agree not to fight and not to threaten each other. We can and must "win peace".'[24]

So far as policy in the Third World was concerned, the debates of the Khrushchev period continued, but successive failures encouraged a less optimistic tone. Specialists like Evgeny Primakov (then *Pravda* correspondent in Cairo) argued against sacrificing detente and East–West understanding in order to gain short-term local victories for unreliable client regimes. Other writers repeatedly suggested that the superpowers should work together to defuse regional conflicts before they escalated into a larger confrontation. A growing number of experts began to argue that backing revolutionary nationalist and Marxist-Leninist vanguard party regimes was in general likely to bring miserly returns. This view was supported by second-rank officials in the International Department like Karen Brutents, who proposed that the USSR should concentrate on building ties with the larger newly industrializing states.[25]

Another common theme among specialists which prefigured official doctrine in the 1980s was that international cooperation, in a variety of spheres, was essential if the human race was to survive. As the director of IMEMO wrote in 1977:

> When the productive forces, science and technology are developing with unprecedented rapidity, the interconnection and interdependence of countries and people increases sharply . . . Mankind is increasingly contending with problems truly global in scale, the solution of which requires collective effort on the part of different states.[26]

This was part of an internationalist current of thinking which was particularly strong in IMEMO, and which stretched back to the 1950s. It emphasized the increasing technologically driven unity of the global economy. Autarky, it was argued, had become 'an impermissible luxury'. From at least the beginning of the Brezhnev period economists like Oleg Bogomolov were making proposals for liberalizing foreign trade procedures. While such ideas led to nothing at the time, they had backing from powerful officials, such as Dzhermen Gvishiani, Kosygin's son-in-law and Deputy Chairman of the State Committee for Science and Technology.[27]

Despite the leeway they enjoyed, the foreign affairs experts were for the time being relatively unimportant as a political force. The official world continued to manipulate traditional doctrinal stereotypes, the rhetoric of class struggle and national *grandeur*. With rare exceptions, decision-making practices continued to favour established institutions like the military. Obsessive security-mindedness and compartmentalization of debate restricted the flow of information and discussion. As a result, civilian experts trying to analyze arms control issues, for example, were obliged to go to American sources for data on Soviet weaponry.[28]

The frustration felt by foreign affairs specialists during the later Brezhnev period was, however, part of a wider *malaise* among a whole new generation of intelligentsia close to the centre of power, but excluded from it by an older, less well-informed official caste, which wrapped itself in increasingly ill-fitting militant phraseology. Inside the official world itself there was a discontinuity in outlooks between generations, intensified by the age gap left by the purges, World War II and the years of intellectual stagnation which followed. The top layers of the leadership had built their careers in the 1930s, when conformity and doctrinal correctness were the first consideration. Immediately behind them, in many cases, came men in their fifties, whose early years at work had been passed in the quite different atmosphere created by Khrushchev's de-Stalinization drive. This generation of officials were independent-minded enough in private – Moshe Lewin has described the informal networks formed between them and intellectuals as part of a nascent 'civil society operating in the very fortress of statism' – and they were receptive to new ideas about foreign policy.[29]

There were also formal channels of communication. We can assume that men like Arbatov, who had worked in the central party apparatus and who was a member of the Central Committee, established a wide network of contacts with his contemporaries in the official world. Numerous roundtables, conferences and symposia regularly brought together middle-ranking members of the research institutes, ministries and party departments. Institute briefing papers were circulated on a confidential basis, and the specialist foreign affairs journals, printed in tens of thousands of copies, steadily eroded stereotyped views of the rest of the world among broader groups of the elite.

Obliged to take the first essential steps towards rendering foreign policy-making more effective, the Brezhnev administration thus gave impetus to a process which was to contribute to the displacement of its own scale of priorities and its own methods. There were other, deeper-running factors at work, however.

The Brezhnev Era: Towards 'Pre-Crisis'

The pattern of political debate in the Brezhnev period was far less well-defined than under Khrushchev. The leadership were more careful to preserve an appearance of unity, and there were fewer zig-zags and reversals of policy. Sovietologists commented on the absence of a clear 'left–right' cleavage, and focused their attention on processes of coalition-building and bureaucratic politics. In Alexander Dallin's analysis, the 1970s exemplified what he called 'reciprocal linkage' in Soviet policy. By this he meant a combination of 'the search for increased interaction with the outside world *and* increased efforts to minimize the domestic political costs of such a foreign policy (for instance by stifling political deviance)'. At first glance this outcome might be taken as a compromise between powerful groups supporting and opposing detente and associated relaxation at home. But it is difficult to see where the supporters of reform would come from in sufficient numbers and with sufficient bureaucratic clout. More convincing is Breslauer's explanation, that the top leadership itself, temperamentally conservative as it was, was being forced along the path necessary if it was to 'deliver' – growth, welfare, and ultimately national security. Like a number of its pre-revolutionary predecessors, it complied with no great enthusiasm, and in the end the contradictions inherent in reciprocal linkage fatally undermined the whole programme. Reality enforced more 'rational', direct links between home and foreign policy and between different aspects of foreign policy.[30]

Slowing economic growth was already provoking discussion and giving rise to experiments with reform in the Soviet Union in the 1960s. The deceleration was uneven, but apparently unstoppable. Official annual GNP increases fell from double figures in the 1950s to 3 per cent or 3.5 per cent in the 1980s. Some foreign reinterpretations put Soviet GNP growth per head of the population as low as 0.5 per cent per annum in 1984–5. The rate of return on capital was particularly low by world standards. Far from catching up with US levels of production, the USSR had been falling further behind.[31]

It was military strength which made the USSR a superpower, but that military strength depended on a huge productive infrastructure and large inputs of skills and resources. The Soviet leaders were determined to continue to provide whatever inputs were necessary to maintain what they perceived as the necessary level of defensive capacity. The military effort continued, however, to be a heavy burden on the economy. As weapons technology became more diverse and sophisticated, the old strategies of technological specialization and the substitution of quantity for quality had become less reliable. Ready access to a wide spectrum of know-how (home-grown or imported) had become a more and more pressing necessity.

The confident spirit of rivalry with the capitalist economies in which Khrushchev extended offers of help to the developing countries was proving unjustified. As it turned out, the USSR never managed to compete effectively with the West in supplying high-quality products to client states. Buying their loyalty by offering more comprehensive support proved prohibitively expensive – Cuba is said to cost the USSR $9 million per day – and by the time Brezhnev came to power Moscow had resolved to build its commercial dealings with the Third World strictly on the principle of 'mutual advantage'. Radical regimes which embraced the classic Soviet model of development produced depressing results. All this contributed to a substantial drop in the prestige of Soviet socialism around the world.[32]

By the late 1970s ominous signs were accumulating. Up to 40 per cent of hard currency for imports was being spent on food, industrial investment growth rates were falling, and even military expenditure began to flag.[33] As events in Poland and elsewhere in Eastern Europe were beginning to show, regimes which attempted to justify their existence by claiming to possess a unique 'scientific' insight into the laws of economic development and by guaranteeing security and rising living standards were especially politically vulnerable to setbacks in the sphere of consumption.

The two most promising strategies which specialists proposed for revitalizing the Soviet economy were to decentralize decision-making, to use market levers, and to participate on a more equal basis in the accelerating internationalization of economic life. The problem was that both these approaches threatened the power of the administrative-command bureaucracies. They also fitted badly with the assumptions which justified that power. As a result, market-type reforms were repeatedly blocked and underminded, and insertion into the world economy proceeded haltingly, with numerous restrictions. When Brezhnev finally authorized a large expansion of commercial contacts with the capitalist world (Soviet machinery imports from the OECD countries increased five times between 1970 and 1975), this measure seemed to be conceived of not as a catalyst for radical changes in the domestic economy, but rather as an alternative to them. The results were predictably disappointing. It is difficult to sell Soviet manufactured goods abroad, and the best use was not always made of advanced imported equipment. Western politicians, the Americans in particular, were eager to exploit the opportunities which trade offered for political leverage. For their part, Soviet leaders were clearly reluctant to accept the limitation on national sovereignty which closer international economic ties implied. This and other factors, such as balance of payments problems, meant that the rate of growth of trade slowed markedly after 1976.[34]

Since Gorbachev's accession, Soviet writers have been acknowledging with remarkable frankness the processes of social 'stagnation' which accompanied, and contributed to, the economic problems of the later Brezhnev years. The population as a whole, and especially the intelligentsia, now proportionally four times more numerous than in the 1960s,[35] had come increasingly to feel alienated from a regime which they perceived as cynical and incompetent, as well as autocratic and repressive. It had exhausted its

revolutionary credit but seemed uninterested in renewing the democratic basis of its legitimacy. Demoralization and corruption, and
a 'crisis of confidence' of the people in the leadership, had reached
a stage where the futility of successive partial reforms was becoming
more and more widely recognized.

There were successes on the plane of East–West political
relations, especially in Europe. The Helsinki agreement, for
instance, embodied a long-sought-after recognition of the postwar territorial settlement, and set in train a continuous process of
cooperation and consultation on the continent. Yet in this sphere
as well the partial nature of Soviet readjustments turned out to be
crippling.

The contradictory nature of Brezhnev's policy towards the West
can be summed up by saying that he attempted to superimpose
political dialogue on the pre-existing (and indeed intensified) ideological struggle and strategic competition. As in several other policy
areas, internal political dilemmas were not resolved but were
instead reproduced in incoherent doctrines and an unworkable
compromise policy.[36] In 1974, for instance, when the General Secretary of the CPSU attended his third summit with President Nixon
in as many years, his Defence Minister was announcing that the
Soviet state 'supports the national liberation struggle, and resolutely resists imperialist aggression in whatever distant region of our
planet it may appear'. Leading ideologists like Konstantin Zarodov
were belabouring Western Communist Parties for failing to understand the need 'to smash the burgeoisie's resistance by force'.[37] The
war of ideas was stepped up, military budgets continued to grow,
and the global reach of the armed forces was exploited in new
forms of intervention in the Third World. Moscow's ruthless determination, demonstrated by the 1968 invasion of Czechoslovakia,
to enforce its political preferences in Eastern Europe set tight limits
on the scope for detente on the continent. There seemed no reason
for foreign publics to take successive 'peace offensives' much more
seriously than their predecessors.

The United States, for its part, resolved to enforce the 'linkages'
wilfully ignored by the Soviet leadership. It deliberately stepped
up political confrontation and put obstacles in the way of East–West
trade and technology transfer. It launched its own 'ideological
offensive' and pushed the arms race onto a new level of technological sophistication (SDI, new conventional weapons and so on). It
intervened actively in a whole string of regional conflicts in order
to deny victories to Soviet clients.

Already in the early 1980s and especially after the death of Suslov in 1981 the old postures began to crumble in Moscow. There were no new interventions in the Caribbean, Asia or Africa. Support was directed less to radical regimes, more to countries like Syria, India and Iraq. In his new role as director of the Institute of Oriental Studies and semi-official spokesman, Primakov declared that his government no longer saw Middle East diplomacy as a zero-sum game against the USA. A searching review of national security policy was instituted, and Brezhnev and his Defence Minister began to describe ideas of obtaining victory in a nuclear war as 'dangerous madness'.[38]

Gorbachev's Strategy

For the new generation of leaders who came to power in the mid-1980s the lesson of the previous two decades was that the time for half-measures had passed: a more thoroughgoing reformist programme in home and foreign affairs was essential.

In the sphere of foreign trade, for example, the direct gains even from a substantial increase in the flow of trade, technology and credits from abroad would be relatively small for such a huge and resource-rich economy as the Soviet one (except perhaps for freeing bottlenecks). An all-round political and economic *rapprochement* with the capitalist world, on the other hand, could have wide-ranging beneficial consequences, if it was accompanied by a determined programme of economic decentralization at home. Most directly, domestic producers could acquire experience in operating in world markets without intermediaries, and could be exposed to the stimulus of foreign competition. Imported consumer goods could be used to make cash incentives to managers, skilled workers and entrepreneurs more meaningful than they had turned out to be in an insulated, shortage economy. A proportion of the valuable resources tied up in military research, development and production could be released to the civilian economy. Most important of all, by breaking down fearful zero-sum perceptions of relations with the West, an atmosphere could be created inside the country in which the administrative-command system and its ideology – now seen as the primary obstacles to progress – could be more easily dismantled.

In regard to East–West relations as such, the underlying connections between political, military and ideological elements had to be acknowledged and observed. This demanded a wholesale revision of doctrine, a sharp change in emphasis from rivalry to cooperation in international affairs.

Much of the groundwork had already been laid: as we have seen, many new concepts endorsed in the Gorbachev period were thoroughly rehearsed years, and sometimes decades, earlier, albeit less forthrightly: economic and ecological interdependence, the prospect of a demilitarized imperialism, the possibility of universal cooperation to settle regional conflicts and to solve 'global problems'. Specialists had even found ways of advocating more or less openly a number of the policy changes which came to be introduced – modifying hostile ideological stereotypes, withdrawing from dangerous alliances with radical nationalist regimes, removing barriers to East–West trade. In the years following Gorbachev's appointment as General Secretary these ideas were systematically developed, and they and their authors emerged into the limelight of approval by the leadership.

With remarkable swiftness there came about a substantial change in the official Soviet position regarding first the political content of international relations, second, ways of guaranteeing national security, and third, modes of participation in international economic life. In each of these areas new policies were adopted and important agreements reached with foreign partners.

The traditional image of international affairs primarily as an arena of class struggle, conflict between the forces of socialism and progress and the forces of imperialism and reaction, was substantially modified. It was acknowledged that there are important areas in which collaboration and compromise can benefit both sides. Indeed, in the face of a number of global threats to civilization, of which the most pressing is the danger of nuclear war, it was stated to be essential that 'all-human interests' prevail over 'class interests'. As part of this adjustment of doctrine, Gorbachev deliberately cast doubt on the Leninist conception of imperialism: in November 1987 he raised the possibility that in the world system of the late twentieth century advanced capitalism would no longer be synonymous with militarism, aggressiveness and ruthless exploitation of poorer societies. There has been a further shift away from Stalin's conception of 'two camps' in international relations. The Soviet leadership emphasized growing multipolarity in world politics, and declared its refusal to view events solely 'through the prism of superpower relations'. It proclaimed a more tolerant stance towards its bloc allies, welcoming diversity and declaring that 'the days of Comintern, Cominform, and even binding international conferences are over'.

In practical terms Moscow adopted a considerably more forthcoming position in a number of regional disputes. In South-east

Asia, the Middle East and Southern Africa progress towards solutions is being made, and relations with China, Israel, and the Western powers have improved. In Afghanistan Soviet forces made an unprecedented retreat from territory which had been regarded as potentially socialist. Old allies were not abandoned, and the leadership continues to express support for nations suffering from exploitation and oppression, but the tone adopted is more moralizing than militant.

At the twenty-seventh CPSU congress in 1986 Gorbachev dissociated himself from his party's traditional overwhelming reliance on military strength, when he declared that in the nuclear age the only reliable guarantees of national security are political ones. An obsessive search for exact strategic parity (or, worse, superiority) was now stated to be counterproductive: it aroused feelings of insecurity on the other side, and stimulated it to make new efforts in the arms race, which in the current state of military technology was capable of generating extremely dangerous and destabilizing configurations of forces. Ways should be found, therefore, of preparing for the possibility of war without making war more likely in the process. Leading officials and specialists openly criticized the large-scale deployment of SS-20s and the invasion of Afghanistan because of their provocative effect. It was suggested that strategic equilibrium is broadly enough based not to be upset by moderate quantitative changes. Apparently serious proposals were put forward to rely on a 'reasonable sufficiency' of weapons for defence, and to move to non-threatening deployment patterns.

In accordance with these ideas, the USSR has acted swiftly to remove long-standing obstacles to progress in disarmament and arms control. It has shown greater readiness to make unilateral concessions in order to keep up the momentum of negotiations, and it has adopted a strikingly more forthcoming position on verification. One result was unexpectedly rapid and successful outcomes at the Conference on Disarmament in Europe at Helsinki, and at the talks on Intermediate-Range Nuclear Forces in Geneva. It is considered likely that important agreements will be reached on reducing the level of conventional armaments in Europe and on cutting strategic missile forces.

The increasing 'interdependence' of the contemporary world to which Gorbachev refers is most obvious in economic relations. Here Soviet leaders speak less of the prospect of defeating the crisis-ridden West in economic competition and more of drawing the leading powers into a new system of international regulation capable of ensuring universal economic stability and security. They have made new approaches for collaboration to international bodies such as GATT and the European Community, and have set about dismantling long-established barriers to trade and economic cooperation, encouraging direct commercial contacts with Soviet enterprises and joint ventures with foreign capital, and making plans for double convertibility.[39]

What is the broader political context of these changes? With reform under way across the board, in politics, law, culture and the economy as well as foreign policy, 'rational linkage' appears to have returned with full vigour. There is a congruence between the various measures which are being taken, not only on a practical plane, but also in terms of political mood. In all spheres the emphasis on conflict, unity and authority is being replaced by an emphasis on compromise, on the toleration of diversity and on a patient search for answers through rational debate. Just as it is officially maintained that the aspirations of different social groups inside the USSR should be respected and deferred to, so it is proposed that international problems should be settled by negotiating a balance between competing, equally legitimate national interests. At home pressure groups and political movements are treated as useful sources of new ideas and as acceptable allies in the process of perestroika. Abroad the Soviet leaders declare that they are ready to learn from the experience of all political parties, notably social democratic ones, and they adopt a much more flexible approach than before in their choice of diplomatic partners.[40]

Changes in the content of policy have been accompanied by changes in policy-making which in turn reflect internal political changes. At a conference held at the Soviet Ministry of Foreign Affairs in the summer of 1988, Eduard Shevardnadze spent some time analysing the shortcomings of his country's foreign policy in the postwar period:

> Serious damage was inflicted on it and, by implication, to the country, by administrative-command methods, disregard of special, professional knowledge, and an undemocratic secretive wilful style of taking decisions affecting millions of people, the priority of military over political means of countering imperialism.[41]

If Shevardnadze's criticism of 'subjectivism' in decision-making and of neglecting expertise echoes the attacks made on Khrushchev by his successors, the general tendency, the hostility to bureaucratic and especially military vested interests is strongly reminiscent of Khrushchev himself. In policy itself there are some obvious continuities with the 1960s. Yet the new leadership is operating in a different internal political environment from the one which existed twenty-five years ago, and Gorbachev and his colleagues' view of the world is undoubtedly quite different from that of his reforming predecessor.

In both these respects a crucial role has been played by the economic, social and foreign-policy failures of the Brezhnev era. They served to discredit central features of the neo-Stalinist system – its legitimating doctrines, its institutions and its decision-making procedures. The dominance of military leaders, central planners and ideologists in determining priorities was called into question. This put Gorbachev in a much stronger position in his fight for greater autonomy from the apparatus. He and his supporters can argue convincingly that there is no alternative: 'In principle the matter is as follows – either we decline to the status of a second-rank or even a third-rank power, or we commit ourselves to a radical process of renewal and move forwards.'[42]

In comparison with the immediate postwar decades, Soviet leaders in the 1980s can afford to feel much more secure from a military point of view, but they are likely to see the *tendency of development* of the international balance of forces in a far less optimistic light than Khrushchev did. This is partly because illusions about their own system have been undermined,[43] and partly because a much clearer understanding has been achieved of the strengths and weaknesses of the West. A key contribution to creating this more sober view of the world has been made over the years by the growing Soviet community of social scientists, and especially the foreign policy specialists. In Franklyn Griffiths' words, the foreign affairs institutes have acted as an essential component of a new 'goal-changing feedback mechanism' which has enabled the Soviet system as a whole to respond more effectively to changes in the environment.[44]

Civilian intellectuals specializing in foreign policy were just one particularly visible part of a new generation of Westernizing elites which were challenging the existing distribution of authority. After Gorbachev came to power there was evidence that the political fortunes of this group as a whole had improved dramatically. Most striking has been the decline in the status of the military which has accompanied the decline of military priorities. Their monopoly on data relevant to security has been broken. Arms-control departments have been established in the Central Committee apparatus, in IMEMO and in the Foreign Ministry, where a new 'Coordination Centre' has the task of applying the findings of civilian research to policy in this sphere. Secondly, Suslovite ideologues who had retired from senior party posts have been replaced not by men of their own kind, but by standard-bearers of reform. Those newly promoted to key positions have in a large number of cases either worked in Academy of Sciences research institutes or have been associated with the specialists in one way or another: Yakovlev (ex-Director of IMEMO), Shakhnazarov, Brutents, Chernyaev, Bogomolov, Aganbegyan, I.D. Ivanov, V.F. Petrovsky. Reformist academics and journalists with interests in foreign affairs like Arbatov, Primakov (now Director of IMEMO), Burlatsky and Bovin have begun to speak with a new freedom and authority, as their own formulations become incorporated in official documents.[45]

The alternative posed by Shevardnadze to the earlier style of foreign policy making, where decisions were taken by a small clique was, in his words, 'democratization, full primacy of the law and elective bodies expressing the will of the people, greater openness, and better interactions with the public'.[46] 'The public' in such a context, implies the informed public, that part of the intelligentsia whose status and political influence has expanded so much since 1984, at the expense of traditionally dominant elites. The 'elective bodies' themselves look likely to provide a channel for exerting such influence. Whereas the old Supreme Soviet had seven journalists out of 1,500 deputies, the Congress of People's Deputies formed in 1989 had sixty out of 2,250.[47] No secret is made of where the Gorbachev administration looks to for support in society. Asked during an interview published in the reformist periodical *Ogonek*, who would be the guarantors of a radical perestroika, the Director of the Institute of Economics, Leonid Abalkin, pointed to 'an alliance of the top political leadership, progressively thinking scholars and cultural figures, and . . . the mass media'. The masses would have to be won over if a final victory was to be won, but in the meantime the crucial part was to be played by 'this tripartite alliance – I do not know what concept to use to describe it'.[48]

Indeed, when reform reaches a certain stage, we have to look again at our overall conception of the regime. Some of Gorbachev's changes are beginning to affect basic features of the Soviet neo-Stalinist system. For instance, there is a long tradition of explaining Soviet expansionism as an effect of Soviet totalitarianism. As Simes expressed it, 'A totalitarian country like the USSR must be committed to international change in order to maintain stability at home.'[49] Admitting that policy discussion had become 'secularized' in many respects, other authors nevertheless argued that leaders' choices were limited by the need to maintain a monopolistic, militant ideology as an essential justification of their rule. Now, however, in a way which corresponds uncannily to the predictions of 'political development' theorists, Gorbachev seems to be making a deliberate attempt to break down established stereotypes and styles of thought, and to encourage public discussion even to the extent of questioning what had been regarded as some of the most fundamental propositions of Leninism. Glasnost has admitted the entire educated public into the arena of policy debate. It is made clear that in these discussions expertise and good judgement will count for more than *ex cathedra* assertions by 'dogmatists'.[50] Transparent attempts are being made to tap new sources of legitimacy. General Secretary Gorbachev, the latest in the apostolic succession from Lenin, will be replaced by President Gorbachev, the world statesman and peacemaker, the successful revitalizer of the economy, the choice of a democratized election process.

In a longer historical perspective, it is clear that yet another attempt is being made to break free from Russian authoritarianism and isolationism. As before, the forces of Westernization and of liberalization appear to advance in step with each other. In the past, reaction has invariably followed reform. What will happen this time? Although it would be foolhardy to put forward firm predictions, a number of points can be made.

From a development point of view, the internal logic of 'modernizing' processes, internationalization, gradual 'de-Utopianization' of perceptions and increasing efficiency of processing information, the cumulative nature of the learning about the outside world and about the workings of the Soviet system which has taken place, all suggest a kind of inevitability. Clearly, many of the changes in Soviet internal and external policy which have taken place in the mid-1980s had to come, and are unlikely to be reversed. But this is not true of all of them. The 'political development' hypothesis offers only broad-brush, long-term predictions. Special circumstances have played their part. Not the least of these is the Westernizing reaction of key parts of the postwar generation of Soviet intelligentsia to Stalin's isolationism, one consequence of which was that they absorbed many of the assumptions of mainstream American theorists – in economics, in management and in political science.[51] Another is the pattern of generational turnover and personal contacts among the elite. Another is the way events in international affairs in the later Brezhnev years seemed to conspire to break down optimistic illusions.

Although several variants of reform could have been envisaged, these circumstances ensured that a fairly radical one came to be adopted. Whether a switch back to some less ambitious and less attractive version is to occur or not may depend to some extent on the behaviour of Moscow's international partners, and in particular on whether their actions justify the dismantling of hostile stereotypes which is now being undertaken.

Notes

1. Most recently these cycles have been identified, in respect of Soviet policy in the Third World, by F. Fukuyama, 'Patterns of Soviet Third World policy', *Problems of Communism* (Sept.–Oct. 1987): 1–13.

2. S. White criticizes a simplistic 'political development' approach in his 'Communist systems and the "iron law of pluralism"', *British Journal of Political Science*, 8 (1978). On the slackening dynamism of the system, see, for example, Z. Brzezinski, *Between Two Ages* (New York: Viking Press, 1970), p. 165.

3. A. Yanov, *The Russian Challenge and the Year 2000* (Oxford: Basil Blackwell, 1987), p. 276.

4. As Werner Hahn points out, Zhdanov himself took a relatively moderate line in the immediate postwar period, but subsequently moved rapidly to adjust to the cooling of the political climate. W. Hahn, *Postwar Soviet Politics: The Fall of Zhdanov and the Defeat of Moderation, 1946–53* (London: Cornell University Press, 1982), pp. 21, 93.

5. The phrase 'coercive isolationism' comes from Franklyn Griffiths' 'The sources of American conduct: Soviet perspectives and their policy implications', *International Security*, 9 (2) (1984): 27–30. Griffiths uses this term to define one of four characteristic tendencies in Soviet policy towards the United States. The others are 'expansionist internationalism' and 'reformative internationalism' (both evident in the Khrushchev and Brezhnev periods at particular times), and 'democratic isolationism' (the Gorbachev administration, while 'democratic', in Griffiths' terms, has proved determinedly internationalist).

6. S. Cohen, 'The friends and foes of change: reformism and conservatism in the Soviet Union', *The Slavic Review*, 38 (1979): 193. Cohen conceives of 'reformism' as a universal political tendency the content of which varies according to the status quo at any particular time and place, and he perceptively analyses its shifting content in Soviet politics. See too the responses to his article by Rigby, Starr, Barghoorn and Breslauer published on pp. 203–23.

7. A. Dallin, 'The domestic sources of Soviet foreign policy', in S. Bialer (ed.), *The Domestic Context of Soviet Foreign Policy* (London: Croom Helm, 1981), pp. 344–6.

8. See, for example, Yanov, *The Russian Idea*, and Hasegawa's contribution to this volume.

9. Dallin, (fn. 7), 'The domestic sources of Soviet foreign policy', p. 346.

10. In his illuminating analysis of the connections between Gorbachev's perestroika and his foreign policy changes, Jack Snyder uses Gerschenkron's term 'atavistic' to describe the role of the 'administrative-command' bureaucracies in the 1960s and 1970s. J. Snyder, 'The Gorbachev revolution: a waning of Soviet expansionism?', *International Security*, 12 (3) (1987–8): 94; A. Gerschenkron, *Economic Backwardness in Historical Perspective* (Cambridge, MA: Bellknap, 1962).

11. E. Varga, *Izmeneniya v ekonomike kapitalizma v itoge vtoroi mirovoi voiny*

(Moscow: Gospolitizdat, 1946); B. Parrott, *Politics and Technology in the Soviet Union* (London: MIT Press, 1985), pp. 81–7; Snyder, 'The Gorbachev revolution', (fn.10): 102–3; 'Diskussiya po knige E. Varga', *Mirovaya khozyaistvo i mirovoe politika*, 11 (1947), supplement.

12. N. Khrushchev, *Khrushchev Remembers* (Boston, MA: Little, Brown, 1970), p. 392.

13. W. Zimmermann, 'Soviet perceptions of the United States', in A. Dallin and T. Larson (eds), *Soviet Politics since Khrushchev* (Princeton, NJ: Princeton University Press, 1969), pp. 163–79; P. Marantz, 'Prelude to detente? Doctrinal change under Khrushchev', *International Studies Quarterly*, 19 (4): 510–16; F. Griffiths, 'Images, politics and learning in Soviet behavior towards the United States', Doctoral dissertation, Columbia University, 1972, pp. 418–22. By the end of Khrushchev's period in power it was even being stated in print that there was no substantial ground for conflict between the superpowers, that there was 'a community of national interest' between them (Zimmermann, 'Soviet perceptions': 174). For comprehensive reviews of the development of Soviet thinking about international relations, see M. Light, *The Soviet Theory of International Relations* (Brighton: Wheatsheaf, 1988); A. Lynch, *The Soviet Study of International Relations* (Cambridge: Cambridge University Press 1987).

14. Khrushchev is now being reassessed in the Soviet press. For a detached, reformist view, see A. Strelyanyi, 'The last romantic', *Moscow News*, 42 (1988). Khrushchev declared in 1958: 'The future is with our socialist system. Capitalism is at its ebb, heading for collapse'; M. Schwartz, *The Foreign Policy of the USSR. Domestic Factors* (Encino, CA: Dickenson, 1975), pp. 172–3, 143.

15. See the classic accounts by C. Linden, *Khrushchev and the Soviet Leadership* (Baltimore, MD: Johns Hopkins University Press, 1966); M. Tatu, *Power in the Kremlin from Khrushchev to Kosygin* (New York: Viking, 1968). Also R. Slusser, *The Berlin Crisis of 1961* (Baltimore, MD: Johns Hopkins University Press, 1973); C. Bluth, 'Defence and security', in M. McCauley (ed.), *Khrushchev and Khrushchevism* (London: Macmillan, 1987), pp. 198–207.

16. Linden, (fn.15), *Khrushchev and the Soviet Leadership*, p. 163.

17. *Pravda*, 18 Feb. 1956; O. Eran, *The Mezhdunarodniki* (Tel Aviv: Turtledove Press, 1979), pp. 70–2.

18. C. Johnson (ed.), *Change in Communist Systems* (Stanford, CA: Stanford University Press, 1970); R. Lowenthal, 'The ruling party in a mature society', in M.G. Field (ed.), *Social Consequences of Modernization in Communist Societies* (London: Johns Hopkins University Press, 1976), pp. 81–118.

19. On the development of the social sciences and of the foreign affairs research system since Stalin, see Eran, *The Mezhdunarodniki*, (fn. 17); A. Brown, 'Political science in the Soviet Union: a new stage of development', *Soviet Studies*, 36 (3): 317–44; N. Malcolm, *Soviet Political Scientists and American Politics* (London: Macmillan, 1984), pp. 4–18.

20. A. Brown, 'The foreign policy-making process', in C. Keeble (ed.), *The Soviet State* (Aldershot: Gower-RIIA, 1985), p. 211; J. Steele and E. Abraham, *Andropov in Power* (London: Martin Robertson, 1983), pp. 81–5.

21. O. Eran, *The Mezhdunarodniki*, (fn. 17), pp. 217–19; S. Bialer, 'Soviet Foreign Policy: Sources, Perceptions, Trends', in S. Bialer (ed.), *The Domestic Context of Soviet Foreign Policy*, (fn. 7), p. 414; W. Zimmermann, *Soviet Perspectives on International Relations* (Princeton, NJ: Princeton University Press, 1969),

pp. 62–3, 69; P. Cocks, 'The policy process and bureaucratic politics', in P. Cocks, R.V. Daniels and N.W. Heer (eds), *The Dynamics of Soviet Politics* (Cambridge, MA: Harvard University Press, 1976), p. 166; M. Schwartz, *The Foreign Policy of the USSR: Domestic Factors* (Encino, CA: Dickenson, 1975), pp. 172–3.

22. Eran, *The Mezhdunarodniki*, (fn. 17); Malcolm, *Soviet Political Scientists*, (fn. 19), pp. 12–18.

23. 'Tvorcheskoe nasledie E.S. Vargi', *Mirovaya ekonomika i mezhdunarodnye otnosheniya*, 1 (1970): 124; Griffiths, 'Images, Politics and Learning', (fn. 13), pp. 96–100; H. Gelman, *The Brezhnev Politburo, and the Decline of Detente* (London: Cornell University Press, 1984), pp. 89–92.

24. Khrushchev cited in Marantz, 'Prelude to detente?', (fn. 13), p. 512; G. Arbatov, 'O sovetsko-amerikanskikh otnosheniyakh', *Kommunist*, 3 (1973): 106; A. Bovin in *Izvestiya*, 11 July 1973 (Moscow evening edition only); J.P. Litherland, 'Soviet views of the arms race and disarmament', Doctoral dissertation, Bradford University, 1987, pp. 105–8.

25. V. Zhurkin and E. Primakov (eds), *Mezhdunarodnye konflikty* (Moscow: Mezhdunarodnye otnosheniya, 1972), p. 20 (Zhurkin is now Director of the Institute of Europe); J. Hough, *The Struggle for the Third World* (Washington, DC: Brookings Institute, 1986), p. 235 and *passim*; N. Malcolm, 'Soviet decision-making and the Middle East', in P. Shearman and P. Williams (eds), *The Superpowers, Central America and the Middle East* (London: Brasseys, 1988), p. 93; J. Hough, 'Soviet policymaking toward foreign communists', *Studies in Comparative Communism*, 15 (3): 179. Fukuyama ('Patterns of Soviet Third World policy', (fn. 1), p. 5) traces this last tendency from 1967.

26. N.N. Inozemtsev, 'Problemy sovremennogo mirovogo razvitiya', in *XXV s'ezd KPSS i razvitie marksistsko-leninskoi teorii* (Moscow: Politizdat, 1977), p. 93; Litherland, 'Soviet views of the arms race and disarmament', (fn. 24), pp. 162–75; E.P. Hoffmann and R.F. Laird, *'The Scientific-Technological Revolution' and Soviet Foreign Policy* (London: Pergamon, 1982), p. 69.

27. R.F. Laird and E.P. Hoffmann, '"The scientific-technological revolution", "Developed socialism", and Soviet international behavior', in E.P. Hoffmann and F.J. Fleron (eds), *The Conduct of Soviet Foreign Policy* (New York: Aldine, 1980), pp. 395–9; Parrott, *Politics and Technology in the Soviet Union*, (fn. 11), pp. 204–5, 268. Parrott (p. 268) cites Gvishiani's view that detente will lead inevitably to interdependence.

28. V. Petrov, 'Formation of Soviet foreign policy', *Orbis*, 17 (3): 848; Dallin, 'The domestic sources of Soviet foreign policy', (fn. 7), pp. 358–9; N. Malcolm, 'Foreign affairs specialists and decision makers', in D. Lane (ed.), *Elites and Political Power in the USSR* (Aldershot: Edward Elgar, 1988), pp. 215–16; D. Simes, 'National security under Andropov', *Problems of Communism* (Jan.–Feb. 1983): 37.

29. J.F. Hough, *The Soviet Leadership in Transition* (Washington, DC: Brookings Institution, 1980), pp. 109–30; F. Griffiths, 'Images, Politics and Learning', (fn. 13), pp. 273–5, 279–80; J. Hough, 'The evolving Soviet debate on Latin America', *Latin American Research Review*, 16 (1) (1981): 139; M. Lewin, *The Gorbachev Phenomenon: A Historical Interpretation* (London: Hutchinson, 1989), p. 80. Cohen notes that a strategy attempting to influence 'enlightened officialdom' was used by Russian reformists in the nineteenth century, and was openly recommended by Roy Medvedev and others under Brezhnev: 'The friends and foes of change', pp. 202–3.

30. On the complexities of foreign policy making under Brezhnev, see A. Dallin, 'The domestic sources of Soviet foreign policy', (fn. 7), p. 347; D.K. Simes, *Detente and Conflict: Soviet Foreign Policy 1972–1977* (Beverly Hills, CA: Sage, 1977), Part III; J. Valenta, 'The bureaucratic politics paradigm and the Soviet invasion of Czechoslovakia', *Political Science Quarterly*, 94 (1) (1979): 55–76; Gelman, (fn. 23), *The Brezhnev Politburo*; G. Breslauer, 'Political succession and the Soviet policy agenda', *Problems of Communism* (May–June 1980): 44–5.

31. P. Hanson, 'The Economy', in M. McCauley, *The Soviet Union under Gorbachev*, pp. 96–7; C.M. Friesen, *The Political Economy of East–West Trade* (New York: Praeger, 1976), p. 47; F.D. Holzman and R. Legvold, 'The economics and politics of East–West relations', in E.P. Hoffman and F.J. Fleron (eds), *The Conduct of Soviet Foreign Policy* (New York: Aldine, 1980), p. 431.

32. M. Bowker, 'The Soviet Union, the Third World and detente', in P. Shearman and P. Williams (eds), *The Superpowers, Central America and the Middle East*, pp. 195–6; E. Valkenier, *The Soviet Union and the Third World: An Economic Bind* (New York: Praeger, 1983), esp. pp. 3–20.

33. Hanson, 'The economy', p. 99; Gelman, *The Brezhnev Politburo*, (fn. 23), pp. 171–3.

34. *OECD Foreign Trade Statistics*, series C, SITC 7; B. Parrott, *Politics and Technology in the Soviet Union*, (fn. 11), pp. 231–94.

35. Lewin, *The Gorbachev Phenomenon*, (fn. 29), pp. 46–7.

36. K. Dyson (ed.), *European Detente* (London: Frances Pinter, 1986), pp. 256–7; Gelman, *The Brezhnev Politburo*, (fn. 23), pp. 112, 161. The memoirs published by the ex-diplomat Arkady Shevchenko reveal the frustration felt by Foreign Ministry officials at the way their advice was neglected because of pressure from the military and from the party apparatus. A. Shevchenko, *Breaking with Moscow* (New York: A. Knopf, 1985), pp. 135–6, 202. Shevchenko claims that because of arguments over SALT 1 Gromyko and Grechko refused to communicate directly with each other 'for some time'. On the way party documents were cobbled together under Brezhnev, see F. Griffiths, 'Ideological development and foreign policy', in S. Bialer (ed.), *The Domestic Context of Soviet Foreign Policy*, (fn. 7), pp. 16, 21.

37. Zarodov was the editor of the international Communist Party journal *Problems of Peace and Socialism*. His statement, which referred to the situation in Portugal, was given indirect public support by Brezhnev. Gelman, *The Brezhnev Politburo*, (fn. 23), pp. 47, 162–4.

38. K. Dawisha, 'The USSR in the Middle East: superpower in eclipse', *Foreign Affairs*, 3 (1982): 444; F. Fukuyama, 'The rise and fall of the Marxist-Leninist vanguard party', *Survey*, 29 (2): 134; D.L. Strode and R.V. Strode, 'Diplomacy and defense in Soviet national security policy', *International Security* 8 (3): 91–2; M. MccGwire, 'A mutual security regime for Europe?' *International Affairs*, 64 (3): 364–5.

39. On Gorbachev's 'new thinking' in foreign policy, see M. Gorbachev, *Perestroika* (London: Collins, 1987), Part 2; M.S. Gorbachev, *Politicheskii doklad Tsentral'nogo Komiteta XXVII s'ezdu KPSS* (Moscow: Politizdat, 1986), pp. 7–27, 80–98; M. Gorbachev in *Izvestiya*, 3 Nov. 1987; M. Gorbachev in *Literaturnaya gazeta*, 45 (1986); E. Shevardnadze in *Soviet News*, 15 June 1988; 'Diplomatiya novogo myshleniya', *Pravda*, 28 July 1988; C. Glickham, 'New directions for Soviet foreign policy', *Radio Liberty Research Supplement*, 2/86 (Sept. 1986); M. Light, 'Foreign policy', in M. McCauley (ed.), *The Soviet Union under Gorbachev* (London: Mac-

millan, 1987), pp. 210–30; S. Shenfield, *The Nuclear Predicament* (London, Routledge – RIIA, 1987).

40. For an example of the new approach to social democracy, see Yu. Krasin, 'Novoe myshlenie vo vzaimootnosheniyakh kommunistov i sotsial-demokratov', *Mirovaya ekonomika i mezhdunarodnye otnosheniya*, 4 (1988): 23–33. Similar attitudes are reflected in official speeches and in relations, for instance, with the West German SPD.

41. 'The 19th All-Union CPSU Conference: foreign policy and diplomacy', *International Affairs*, 10 (1988): 12.

42. Leonid Abalkin, Director of the Academy of Sciences Institute of Economics, cited in an interview. L. Pleshakov, 'Strategiya obnovleniya', *Ogonek* 13 (1989): 18.

43. For an extreme example of frankness about the Soviet experience, see Aleksandr Bovin's assessment in A. Bovin and V. Lukin, 'Na poroge novogo veka', *Mirovaya ekonomika i mezhdunarodnye otnosheniya*, 12 (1987): 51, where he suggests that in the twentieth century the Russians have fallen victim to Hegel's 'irony of history', which punishes those who try to evade its laws.

44. Griffiths, 'Images, Politics and Learning', (fn. 13), p. 6. The concept of 'social learning' is borrowed from Karl Deutsch.

45. A. Brown, 'Gorbachev and reform of the Soviet system', *The Political Quarterly*, 58 (2): 139–51; R.J. Hill and A. Rahr, 'The General Secretary, the Central Party Secretariat and the Apparat', in D. Lane (ed.), *Elites and Political Power in the USSR*, (fn. 28), pp. 49–95; C. Glickham, 'New directions for Soviet foreign policy', (fn. 39); J. Checkel, 'Gorbachev's "new political thinking" and the formation of Soviet foreign policy', *Radio Liberty Research Report*, RL 429/88 (23 Sept. 1988).

46. 'The 19th All-Union CPSU Conference: foreign policy and diplomacy', p. 4.

47. V. Marsov, 'Who'll sit in the Kremlin?', *Moscow News*, 16 (1989): 2.

48. Pleshakov, 'Strategiya obnovleniya', p. 18.

49. D. Simes, *Detente and Conflict* (London: Sage, 1977), p. 58.

50. Checkel, 'Gorbachev's "new political thinking" and the formation of Soviet foreign policy', (fn. 45); Snyder, 'The Gorbachev revolution', (fn. 10), pp. 110–11. For criticism of dogmatists, see G. Popov in *Pravda*, 20–21 Jan. 1987; E. Pozdnyakov, 'Natsional'nye, gosudarstvennye i klassovye interesy v mezhdunarodnykh otnosheniyakh', *Mirovaya ekonomika i mezhdunarodnye otnosheniya*, 5 (1988): 13.

51. See, for instance, Aleksandr Yakovlev's reference to the importance of political 'feedback' in *Pravda*, 13 Aug. 1988.

10

Soviet Foreign Policy: In Search of Critical Thinking

Marie Mendras

As soon as Mikhail Gorbachev came to power, he embarked on a resolutely active and productive foreign policy. The years 1985–8 saw a significant improvement in the USSR's standing and credibility and remarkable breakthroughs on a number of issues, in particular nuclear disarmament, Afghanistan, and diplomatic and economic detente with the West. Interestingly, although foreign policy went through an undefinable process of revision and improvement, the conduct of international affairs was not immediately submitted to a process of criticism and glasnost but, on the contrary, stayed in the closed spheres of top officialdom. The presentation of an official 'new political thinking' in 1986–7 did not itself involve criticism or open debate of past Soviet policies. It remained for some time a rather static body of principles that accompanied diplomatic overtures.

Foreign policy issues entered the sphere of official 'glasnost-permitted' debate in 1988. This debate, which proceeded along a sinuous path of remarkable openings and quick retreats, turned into a high-level polemic in the summer of 1988, a development not unconnected with the leadership reshuffle of the following autumn. After a few months latency, the debate started again in the spring of 1989.

This chapter seeks to give an account of the discussions on past foreign policy and to evaluate their effect on current policy orientations. In the course of the analysis, the difference in Gorbachev's handling of domestic and international affairs will be stressed. Foreign policy making has proved to be largely detached from the process of change in the economic and social spheres, and at the same time highly political – in other words, a decisive factor in Kremlin politics.

From the 'New Political Thinking' to Policy Criticism

As Mikhail Gorbachev proceeds in his fifth year at the helm, a kind of 'scissors crisis' drives a wedge between domestic reforms and foreign policy. The domestic process of perestroika has lost momentum and many economic problems have reached stalemate. The search for new institutions for political representation in 1988–9 may not conceal the lack of momentum in socio-economic affairs and the strains in nationalities-related issues. The Soviet leadership has had to reconcile itself to a slow pace of change along an erratic path.

In contrast to hesitant progress in the domestic sphere, foreign relations have improved steadily. The USSR has developed diplomatic and political contacts with most Western and Asian states. It has made substantial progress towards normalizing relations with old enemies, such as China, Japan, Israel and Pakistan. Disarmament negotiations are bearing fruit and have provided the momentum for East–West detente.

International and domestic affairs are regarded as closely intertwined – an interdependence that Mikhail Gorbachev himself has strongly emphasized in his declarations. As we take stock of the first four years of 'perestroika–glasnost–new political thinking', it becomes necessary to refine our approach. The interrelated character of the two domains of state activity, the boundaries of which are often difficult to define, is not in doubt. But the nature and the pace of evolution of the two spheres differ greatly. There is no automatic synchronization between disarmament and economic reform, between openings to the outside world and a rise in trade capacities, between undeniable progress on regional conflicts and a vague awareness of nationality issues in the USSR. It sometimes looks as if Gorbachev's diplomacy were moving along in an orbit separate from the Soviet internal scene. In the period 1985–7 it was commonly argued that the General Secretary's scope in foreign policy depended on his 'success in domestic perestroika'. The argument has proved less and less convincing as he makes progress in international relations in spite of a poor record in quantifiable economic results. A number of reasons may account for this: foreign relations by definition involve more than one actor and the dynamic does not come from the Soviet government alone; results in international affairs are readily attainable, sometimes spectacular (for example, the INF treaty), compared to changes in economic indicators; diplomacy and strategy belong to the 'reserved domain' of state and party ruling bodies and are less vulnerable to the built-in inertia in the Soviet system.

The purpose of this chapter is not to discuss the interaction between internal and external affairs. But it is important to clarify at the start that we do not accept as a working hypothesis the synergy and strict parallel between perestroika and changes in Soviet foreign policy, either in *approach* (which I prefer to 'thinking') or in *implementation*.

A Late Start in Policy Criticism
My initial observation is of a striking paradox in Gorbachev's political strategy. The party General Secretary has from the very beginning placed international affairs at the top of his personal agenda. He has deliberately assumed direct responsibility for foreign decisions and successfully imposed himself as a strong-willed and efficient representative of the Soviet Union abroad. This success played a major role in the steady consolidation of his authority at home. Surprisingly, Gorbachev has led an active East–West diplomacy and an innovative disarmament policy without criticizing past foreign policy in a style remotely comparable to his violent, often disproportionate, attacks against Brezhnev's domestic policies. The debate in the press came after, not before, policy choices were made. In domestic affairs the reverse phenomenon occurred. From the very start, Gorbachev encouraged an anti-Brezhnev public stance but policy implementation lagged seriously behind. He structured his reformist alternative on the basis of a steady denunciation of the Soviet predicament. The first three years, 1985–7, were a time of unprecedented criticism of past methods and lack of achievement in internal affairs. The blunter the criticism, the more formidable did the reformist projects sound.

In foreign policy, by contrast, little organized criticism was voiced but much was accomplished in improving the East–West climate and promoting a new Soviet image in the world. Concrete achievements crowned Soviet efforts, such as the INF treaty of December 1987 and the reactivated political dialogue and economic exchanges with the West. The political and ideological framework for Soviet overtures to the West and reinvigorated diplomacy on all fronts was the 'new thinking'. The 'new thinking' had a positive impact on foreign governments and public opinion because it sounded well-intentioned and non-confrontational. It claimed to be a 'universal' credo as opposed to a Marxist, voluntaristic, anti-capitalist ideology. In fact, it was essentially a set of very general notions, such as interdependence, mutual security, common interest, common danger, and necessary cooperation between all states. Such notions were not spectacular for Western politicians and experts who had proposed similar concepts in the 1950s and 1960s, but their adoption by the Soviet state seemed to augur new and promising developments in Soviet foreign behaviour.

The 'new thinking' in its 1986–7 form meant the timid emergence of critical views at an official level.[1] To call for a new departure and novel approaches implicitly amounted to a rejection of some of the underlying rules of past behaviour. The need for a fresh look at the concepts of security, balance of power, influence and political cooperation was slowly asserting itself. The scholarly reflections on war and peace, that appeared selectively in the early 1980s, had been the early expression of the new understanding of international affairs. But no explicit questioning of past policies had yet been phrased. Specific aspects of Soviet foreign policy were not discussed seriously and the Brezhnev legacy was neither endorsed nor strongly refuted until the beginning of 1988.

Stalinism and Foreign Policy
In 1988, the internal political dynamics changed significantly. The initial momentum of Gorbachev's politics of change showed signs of erosion. Major economic reforms were delayed and the implementation of the new legislation – for example, the Enterprise Law – encountered numerous difficulties. Most Soviet officials and social scientists recognized that perestroika was advancing slowly and that few results were to be expected in the near future, the year 2000 being the official deadline. The side-effects of all-out self-criticism and glasnost were unrest and violence in the Baltic and Caucasian republics, and general disarray in the population. Tensions grew as perestroika failed to deliver and as prospects for a rapid improvement in living standards receded. Soviet citizens began to feel more and more uncomfortable at watching the party ridiculing a socio-economic system which they had long had to accept as sacred and which they would have had to put up with for the foreseeable future whatever the party was saying now.

Official criticism shifted focus in the course of 1988. In intensity and emotional involvement, the debate on history and Stalinism replaced discussion of the ills of 'stagnation' under Brezhnev. Brezhnev himself has been the target of harsh press criticism[2] but this is much less damaging to the Soviet public's morale and much less dangerous to the regime than going deeper into self-introspection on the fallacies of socialism. The orientations of the public debate on history are essential to an understanding of the criticism of

Soviet foreign policy that developed in the Soviet media in the spring of 1988. The denunciations of Stalinism as a system, and not simply as the crimes of one man, opened up a Pandora's box. Policy decisions of the 1930s and 1940s came under attack, be it collectivization or the purges in the army in 1937–8. It became increasingly difficult to protect specific aspects of Stalin's policies from the general onslaught. Hence Stalin's policy of alliance with Nazi Germany on the eve of the war, the Ribbentrop–Molotov Non-Aggression Pact of 23 August 1939 and the subsequent occupation of Finland and the Baltic countries were questioned in various press articles, TV programmes and colloquia in 1988. As we will see below, even the establishment of a Soviet sphere of influence in Eastern Europe after the war was indirectly criticized. More generally, some historians and journalists spoke out against the mentality which pushed the Soviet leadership under Stalin and his successors into a confrontational relationship with the West.

Afghanistan

Before going into a more detailed reading of this attempted historical revision of Soviet international policy, I should stress another factor in the debate about foreign affairs in the spring of 1988: the Afghan question. The decision to withdraw troops from Afghanistan under the Geneva agreement of April 1988 served as a catalyst for a genuine reappraisal of Brezhnev's policies, although this would probably have taken place anyway sooner or later. As early as 1986, official Soviet spokesmen as well as Moscow experts began to prepare the diplomatic ground for a change of tactics in Afghanistan. Scholars of the Academy of Sciences started to distance themselves from the traditional writings on the socialist road to development and on the nature of revolutionary regimes. But the recognition of failure in Afghanistan has much broader implications than ideological revisions about the relevance of a socialist model.

It raises the crucial question – and one heretofore taboo – of the legitimacy of the *use of force* on foreign soil. In their diplomatic exchanges, the Soviet authorities have stopped giving the official justifications of the 1979 intervention; namely, the fulfilment of the USSR's 'internationalist duty' in a revolutionary country on the one hand,[3] and the direct threat to the security of the Soviet state on the other. What reasons, what potential dangers, can justify a military intervention? How should one define the security of the Soviet state? How to evaluate the threat? Within the general debate on history, the Afghan question has helped to raise such broad questions which touch on some fundamental aspects of Soviet foreign policy: for example, the predominance of the military factor in state policy; the definition of 'national security' and the role of East European countries as part of this security; the 'natural' alliance of Soviet socialism with the progressive regimes of the Third World.

The Burgeoning of the Debate

The key article in the foreign policy debate was an analysis by a historian of the Academy of Sciences, Viacheslav Dashichev, in *Literaturnaya gazeta*.[4] The article begins by quoting Eduard Shevardnadze. The Foreign Minister expresses regret that criticism has so far been limited to internal affairs when foreign affairs also need serious revision. This reference to Shevardnadze was one of many signs of his eminent role in the polemic of the following summer (see below). Dashichev recalls that security issues were a subject of discussion in 1918 before the Brest-Litovsk peace and that hesitations and mistakes can occur in foreign policy decisions.

Among the errors of the past, he underlines the non-aggression pact between Hitler and Stalin that left France and Great Britain isolated against Nazi Germany.[5] When he broke with the Western allies, Dashichev explains in substance, Stalin upset the balance of forces in Europe and weakened Western solidarity with the USSR at the time of the German invasion of Russia in June 1941. The emergence of socialist regimes in Eastern Europe after the war worsened this European rift. 'These results were very satisfactory for us', wrote Dashichev in reference to the establishment of 'the world system of socialism'. 'But the clear strengthening of Soviet influence in central and south-eastern Europe was understood by our former allies in the anti-Hitler coalition as a significant break in the European balance that endangered their interests.'

Dashichev analyses the Brezhnev years along the same lines. 'The build-up of our military forces', 'the extension of Soviet influence in Africa, the Middle East and in other regions' and the war in Afghanistan had reinforced the West's perception of a 'Soviet threat'. The USSR bears some responsibility for renewed East–West tension in the late 1970s as it does for the cold war of the 1950s. Dashichev does not stop short of direct criticism of the Brezhnev leadership and its 'errors' and 'inefficient approach in foreign policy'. When the weekly *Literaturnaya gazeta* published this article, it left no doubt that Andrei Gromyko, the primary target of criticism, would soon have to leave the political scene. Indeed, six weeks later, at the national party conference, a delegate publicly attacked Gromyko, together with Georgy Arbatov, head of the Institute of the USA and Canada and a long-standing spokesman for Soviet diplomacy abroad. By 1 October, Gromyko retired from all his party and state functions.

In an interview with *Komsomolskaya Pravda* on 19 June 1988, Dashichev continued his critique of foreign policy making. The decision-making process was 'elitist' and 'detached from the fundamental and vital interests of our country'. The historian stressed again the importance of perceptions. He called for 'an accurate image' of the adversary. In other words, the Soviet Union should not seek to justify its interventions, in particular in the Third World, by overestimating American imperialism.

Other similar comments were published in various papers in May–June 1988. Ambassador Israelyan criticized the aggressive character of Soviet diplomacy. He also gave a negative assessment of the 'elitist foreign policy' in which the population has no say.[6] Two weeks later, again in *Literaturnaya gazeta*, the Academician Oleg Bogomolov, the historian Nikolai Molchanov and Ambassador Mendelevich discussed the defects of the foreign policy making process. Mendelevich did not make a very strong case in defence of his own ministry but insisted that other state and party organs were involved in foreign policy and share responsibility for past mistakes.[7] Vadim Zagladin of the International Department of the Central Committee also took part in this campaign for pragmatism and glasnost in foreign policy.[8]

Izvestiya journalist Aleksandr Bovin was, with Dashichev, the most outspoken in his analysis of Soviet international behaviour. He went beyond the new boundaries of official, or authorized, criticism. In an interview he gave to *Moskovskii komsomolets* on 29 May 1988, he tackled the critical point: the closed borders of the Soviet state. 'We have been used for so long to living in a besieged fortress that it has impregnated our psychology. But I am convinced that it is time for us to become a civilized country where the individual can, when he wants to, . . . obtain a passport to travel abroad.' Bovin went further than the historians' revision of particular episodes of Soviet policy. He questioned the internal political mechanism that makes the Soviet system closed, taking up one of the main themes of the dissidents of the 1970s.[9]

However, the debate did not develop along those lines. It left the path of serious historical revision and deviated into an ideological polemic at the highest political level. In July and August 1988, Eduard Shevardnadze, Egor Ligachev, Aleksandr Yakovlev and other party figures engaged in a heated discussion over the nature of the international system, the role of 'class struggle' in East–West relations and the definition of peaceful coexistence.

Politicization of the Debate

On 'Class Policy'

A speech by Shevardnadze before the staff of his own ministry on 25 July 1988 started the polemic. The speech itself did not create much impression at first. Only excerpts appeared in *Pravda* the next day.[10] What attracted attention to it was Egor Ligachev's reply on 5 August in a speech in Gorkii. Ligachev, who at the time was still 'number two' of the party hierarchy, took issue with the Foreign Minister on the ideological revision of Soviet international policy, and in particular relations with the capitalist world.

According to the 26 July issue of *Pravda*, Shevardnadze said the following:

> The new political thinking understands peaceful coexistence in the context of the realities of the nuclear age. We are justified in not understanding it as a specific form of class struggle. Coexistence, which is based on such principles as non-aggression, non-interference in internal affairs, etc., cannot be identified with class struggle. The struggle between the two systems is no longer the prevailing trend of the present era.

The excerpts published in *Argumenty i fakty* were less ideological and more revealing in terms of policy orientations. Shevardnadze is reported to have said that 'it is in the general interest, and in our interest in particular, to strive to restrain the military activities of all states to their national borders'. And he explicitly referred to Afghanistan. He also spoke for disarmament and the INF treaty, adding, however, that the treaty was 'a major contribution to the strengthening of our security because, thanks to it, it is now possible to drive the American nuclear presence further away from our borders'. Strategic concerns were thus very present in this address on foreign policy making and the ideology of international relations.

Egor Ligachev would probably not disagree with Shevardnadze's strategic view. What he violently opposed in his 5 August speech was the ideological revision. He said in Gorkii: 'We proceed from the class nature of international relations. Any other way of posing the question only puts confusion into the minds of the Soviet people and our friends abroad. Taking an active part in the effort to solve common human problems by no means signifies any artificial slow down in the social and national-liberation struggle.'[11] In the same speech, Ligachev praised historical continuity and socialism, and spoke against market mechanisms and uncontrolled democratization.

A few days later, Aleksandr Yakovlev reaffirmed the 'de-ideologized' line exposed by Shevardnadze, dismissing class struggle as the determinant of state relations.[12] But hard-line views on foreign affairs continued to be published, in particular on historical questions. Lev Bezymenski and Valentin Falin, then head of Novosti Press Agency, stressed in *Pravda* the West's responsibility for initiating the cold war and the arms race.[13] Falin's position did not go unnoticed because he was also an active defender of Soviet policy towards Germany in 1938–9.

The polemic on the 'nature' of relations between capitalist and socialist states was closely intertwined with the debate on Soviet history, most notably the debate on World War II. Ligachev expressed the importance of this correlation in the following ways. If the Soviet Union destroys its own historical legacy, if it breaks down the ideological pillars of the state, how will it preserve its unity and power? This is in essence the 'conservative' argument.

The Tactics of Political Compromise
Mikhail Gorbachev has clearly understood the argument and taken it into consideration.

First, after his historical coup of 30 September–1 October 1988, when he took over Andrei Gromyko's position as head of state, a certain balance of forces in the party's leading institutions seems to have been respected. Yakovlev and Medvedev were promoted to head, respectively, the new International Commission and the new Ideological Commission of the Central Committee. Falin, not the most fervent de-ideologizer, succeeded Dobrynin at the head of the International Department of the Central Committee.[14]

Second, Gorbachev has defined a 'middle-of-the-road' line on the theoretical question of the 'class nature' of East–West relations. Already in September 1988, Vadim Zagladin reassured both the ideologues and pragmatists. He said that Shevardnadze's and Ligachev's divergence of views reflected the 'socialist pluralism of opinions' and that both positions were legitimate. He presented what he claimed to be Gorbachev's formulation in the following terms: 'the foreign policies of states have a *class nature*, but this does not mean that international relations could be reduced to a struggle between two systems'.[15]

Whatever the dialectical subtlety of this presentation, it is clearly an attempt to please all sides and calm down the polemic. In fact, the debate subsided after the 30 September 1988 plenum. And, indeed, Zagladin did give an accurate presentation of Gorbachev's discourse. In his book *Perestroika*, the General Secretary had already expressed this 'centrist', ideological, but not too doctrinal line. 'Ideological differences should not be translated into the sphere of international relations. . . . We no longer deem necessary to keep the definition of peaceful coexistence between states of different social systems as a specific form of class struggle.' But he added, 'ideological, economic and political competition between capitalist and socialist states is inevitable'.[16]

Since September 1988, Soviet diplomats and spokesmen have consistently repeated this line. In an informal conversation, a deputy director of IMEMO, the International Relations Institute of the Academy of Sciences in Moscow, has defined the de-ideologization of foreign relations in these terms:

> Because of the danger of war and of the need for cooperation, realism has prevailed. Relations between states must respond to pragmatic criteria (mutual security, respect of each other's interests, etc.) and not to ideological, class struggle notions that are confrontational. However, outside the strict domain of relations between governments, Soviet foreign policy is a class policy in the sense that it defends the interests of mankind and continues to defend socialist values.[17]

It is in the Soviet tradition to justify moves towards ideological and political compromises with the West in terms of *state* politics. 'States bear the heaviest responsibility in world affairs, they must act as rational actors and restrain from letting ideological beliefs lead them to confrontational policies.' In the same vein, a senior official of the Ministry of Foreign Affairs, the head of a department, replied to a French delegation in Moscow, on the subject of pan-European coexistence in the next ten to fifteen years: two systems of thought will continue to be at odds but will coexist in Europe in the year 2000.[18]

To sum up, the USSR's foreign policy remains a 'class policy' because relations with the Western world are by nature competitive and socialism by nature defends the interests of humanity. But class struggle is negative when negative trends in the world (ecological imbalances, nuclear proliferation, economic backwardness, human suffering and so on) jeopardize the universal values that all peoples and states seek to defend. This position is strikingly ambiguous and unsatisfactory if we try to use it as the political key to Soviet foreign strategy. Such discourse is essentially of a moral nature. The Soviet leadership hails a new morality of interstate relations that tends to blur the real stakes of economic, political and cultural exchanges and disarmament talks with the West. An article which appeared in April 1989, six months after the major Kremlin reshuffle of 30 September–1 October 1988, epitomizes this moral argumentation based on the notions of humanization and democratization of international life: 'Humanism is inseparable from morality. Faith in the possibility in principle of a humanization of international relations may only be guaranteed when morality defines policies.'[19]

As has often been the case in Soviet history, the substance of the debate on policy orientations has for a time given way under the weight of political considerations. Paradoxically, when the discussion of foreign policy entered the high sphere of ideology, it stepped aside from the path of historical revision and policy criticism.

Ideological Revision and Power Consolidation
We tend to assume that nothing will change in the Soviet Union unless ideology is revised. Doctrinal revision is supposedly the preliminary to serious political innovations. In fact, ideology has more often than not been an instrument in power struggles. Divergencies are exacerbated at crucial turning points in Kremlin politics and, in the end, one line wins over another. But as soon as power is secured, the victorious group may without much embarrassment adopt some of the language of the adversary. The Malenkov–Khrushchev struggle and Stalin's anti-right and anti-left strategy are well-known cases of policy debates which were closely intertwined with the succession process going on within the party elite.

In retrospect the ideological polemic of the summer of 1988 seems to have been used by Gorbachev in his strategy of personal authority building. Shevardnadze's provocative words on class struggle could not remain unanswered. At that time, Ligachev still had some pretensions to being the 'ideological secretary' and responded to Shevardnadze as the guardian of orthodoxy. He had been driven from his last position. But the real, immediate stake was the political balance of forces in the Kremlin, not policy choices. Indeed, just after the major reshuffle of the party leadership in the autumn of 1988, the leading team of international affairs and ideology – Gorbachev, Yakovlev, Medvedev, Shevardnadze – adopted a harder line on most issues. Medvedev's and Yakovlev's various speeches in October and November struck an uncompromising line. Moreover, the appointment of Valentin Falin at the head of the International Department of the Central Committee in October weakens the case for a simple interpretation of a victory of the pragmatists over the ideologues. Falin had defended the rationale of the Soviet policy of *entente* with Germany in 1939 and had refuted the critical revision of historians like Dashichev and Kulich. He had also reaffirmed the West's responsibility for the cold war in the late 1940s and 1950s.[20]

It is not possible to come to definite conclusions about the events that took place in the Kremlin in September and October. Did Gorbachev strike a deal with the more conservative elements of the leadership? Did he actually want to take a middle position so as to avoid being pushed too far in one direction? What can be said was that his motive force in 1988 was the consolidation of his position in the leadership and the restructuring of state institutions to further his own plans.

For a few months in the winter of 1988–9 the debate on foreign policy became dormant but awakened again in the early spring. Some historians, experts and journalists try to draw attention to the most sensitive and crucial issues. Current policy preoccupations emerge more and more clearly from the discussion on past foreign policy, and the limits of the debate reveal the intricacies of Soviet choices in a time of multifaceted challenge.

The Bottom Line: The Great Patriotic War and Eastern Europe

Not surprisingly, the sensitive issues include some of the themes that were stifled by the authorities in 1988. The Ribbentrop–Molotov Pact and secret protocol of August 1939, Soviet military command during the war and the postwar satellization of Eastern Europe undoubtedly constitute the crux of the ongoing interrogation about Soviet motives in a foreign policy which is slowly being recognized as a power strategy. Some authors are hinting at the expansionist tendencies of the Soviet government in the 1940s, even though they do not use the term. Their insistence on the error of composing a certain 'image of the enemy',[21] on the contradictions of a 'sphere of influence', and their stress on the constraints imposed by overstretching the USSR's commitments abroad leads to a criticism of the motivations underlying Soviet foreign policy in the 1940s. At stake clearly are the notion of a historical, universal *legitimacy* of Soviet socialism and definition of *power*; that is, both the basis of state power and the modes of projection of that power. The debate could of course be easily tolerated by the leadership if it did not inevitably lead to very specific and topical problems, namely the occupation of the Baltic states in 1940 and the imposition of communist rule in six countries of Europe after the war.

The 1939 pact with Germany is approached historically – was there an alternative for the USSR? – whereas developments in Eastern Europe in 1945–9 are mostly addressed indirectly in the course of general reflections on 'the image of the enemy' and 'correlation of forces'.

As mentioned above, the Soviet–German Non-Aggression Pact came to the forefront of the debate in the summer of 1986. Dash-ichev mentioned it as one of the 'errors of the past', and the Balts raised it as a current political matter by publishing the text of the secret protocol in a local newspaper in Lithuanian. Some authors like Dashichev criticized the pact and its secret protocol for the distrust if fomented between the USSR and its future allies in the war, and for the methods that were later used in occupying Finland and the Baltic states. Others, like Valentin Falin, then head of Novosti Press Agency, defended the policy of the Soviet govern-ment in 1938–9, justifying Stalin's decisions by the facts that the country needed time to prepare for the war and that Great Britain and France were guilty of the Munich compromise of 30 September 1938.[22]

In the winter of 1988–9, Moscow historians and publicists were wondering, in informal conversations, how far the party leadership would agree to go along with the 'search for truth' on prewar and war diplomacy. Some were strongly opposed to the publication of the secret protocol of August 1939, observing that it would only worsen the situation in the Baltic republics, to no avail since there was no reason to question the Soviet identity of the Balts after almost fifty years of socialism. Others saw the process of establish-ing truth in history as unsuppressible in the long term and criticized the repeated delays and hesitations on the part of the leadership. The media took the subject up again in the spring. Not only the press, in particular *Literaturnaya gazeta* which continued to act as the leading publication on 1939, but also Soviet television made room for further discussions.[23] At the time of writing, no Soviet political leader has endorsed a new interpretation of the USSR's war gains.

The status of Eastern Europe is certainly the bottom line of permitted debate on foreign policy. Many arguments stop short of a critical assessment of the postwar political division of Europe. Opinions remain either too broad or limited to military security aspects. In a polemic between Bovin and Lukin in the journal *MEiMO*, both international experts beat about the bush without quite spelling out their arguments on the building of a socialist camp in Europe.[24] In parallel, strategy specialists such as Aleksei Arbatov pursue their efforts at broadening the security dimension to political considerations (the concept of 'reasonable sufficiency' more or less explicitly incorporates national socio-economic and political criteria).[25]

As of the spring of 1989, the common denominator seems to be a cautious position which reads roughly as follows: the current epoch sees the disappearance of two military blocs or camps; nevertheless, two systems with different socio-economic structures continue to coexist; but ideological and political specificities should not interfere in the global domain of international life which may be managed in a de-ideologized fashion and geared towards common interests.

The Soviet Union is facing a complex challenge. On the one hand, it must accommodate internal diversity in Europe, a diversity that has exposed the irreparable fragility of the façade of political homogeneity, and that forces a serious re-examination of the cooperation/control tandem. On the other hand, the Gorbachev leadership has engaged in a decisive strategy of dialogue, multiple interaction and security reappraisal with the West. The two imperatives are in many respects contradictory. In the management of its 'sphere of influence', the USSR faces instability and unpredictability, two characteristics that the Soviets dislike profoundly. Although current developments in Poland and Hungary deserve reasonable coverage in the Soviet Union, the Soviet media have not issued much information on East European politics since World War II and party leaders are sparing of comments on decisive moments in Soviet–East European relations, such as 1956 and 1968. Ideology may officially cease to be sacred, but national security and power politics are still protected from open criticism. The evolution of the debate on foreign policy inside the USSR will continue to provide valuable hints as to the direction of Soviet policy.

Notes

1. An early official text was an article by Anatolii Dobrynin, then head of the International Department of the Central Committee, 'Za bez'yadernyi mir, navstrechu XXI veku', *Kommunist*, 9 (1986): 18–31.

2. See, for instance, Roy Medvedev, 'L'avantage d'être médiocre', *Les Nouvelles de Moscou*, 37 (11 Sept. 1988): 8–9.

3. For the international community, the Soviet authorities have given up this justification and have insisted on the fact that the military intervention was a mistake. Selected articles in the Soviet central press have also conveyed this message. But it should be pointed out that, in some sections of the press, propaganda about 'internationalist, fraternal aid' to the Afghan people and the heroism of Soviet soldiers continued in 1988. A collection of army songs on the Afghan battleground,

full of romanticism about the glorious future of Afghanistan and the 'international-ism' of Soviet heroes, was published in 1988 by 'Molodaya Gvardiya' under the title *Kogda poyut soldaty*.

4. V. Dashichev 'Vostok-Zapad: poisk novykh otnoshenii', *Literaturnaya gazeta*, 18 May 1988, p. 14.

5. The Ribbentrop–Molotov Pact of 23 August 1939 was one of the most heated subjects of discussion in the summer of 1988, and again in the spring of 1989 (see below).

6. V. Israelyan, 'Mir ne mozhet byt' zaklyuchen tol'ko sverkhu', *Literaturnaya gazeta*, 5 June 1988, p. 14. It is worth noting that the Moscow weekly *Novoe vremya* had opened the discussion on 'elitism' in foreign policy making in the autumn of 1987. See *Temps nouveaux* 44 (1987): 4–7.

7. 'Ot balansa sil – k balansu interesov', *Literaturnaya gazeta*, 29 June 1988, p. 14.

8. V. Zagladin, 'Kursom razuma i gumanizma', *Pravda*, 13 June 1988.

9. A. Bovin is also one of the most outspoken publicists on Soviet relations with East European countries. See his article 'Mirnoe sosushchestvovanie i mirovaya sistema sotsializma', *MEiMO*, 7 (1988): 5–15.

10. Another selected summary of Shevardnadze's speech was published in the weekly *Argumenty i fakty*, 10–16 Sept. 1988. Fuller versions appeared in *Vestnik MID*, 18 (1988) and in *Mezhdunarodnaya zhizn'*, 10 (Oct. 1988).

11. *Pravda*, 6 Aug. 1988, p. 2.

12. Speech in Vilnius, *Pravda*, 13 Aug. 1988.

13. V. Falin and L. Bezymenski, 'Kto razvyazal'kholodnuyu voinu . . . ?' *Pravda*, 29 Aug. 1988, p. 6.

14. This nomination came some time after Dobrynin's retirement after 11 September. It was announced by TASS on 20 Oct. 1988.

15. V. Zagladin at a Hungarian television interview on 11 Sept., BBC, *Summary of World Broadcasts*, SU/0256, 14 Sept. 1988 (emphasis mine).

16. M. Gorbachev, *Perestroika* (Paris: Flammarion, 1987), pp. 203 and 208.

17. Conversation with the author in Moscow, March 1989.

18. Moscow, March 1989.

19. E. Pozdnyakov and I. Shadrin, 'O gumanizatsii i demokratizatsii mezhduna-rodnykh otnoshenii', *MEiMO*, 4 (1988): 22.

20. V. Falin and L. Bezymenski, 'Kto razvyazal kholodnuyu voinu . . . ?', *Pravda*, p. 6.

21. See, for instance, Andrei Melville, 'L'image de l'ennemi et la nouvelle mental-ité politique', *Sciences sociales* (Moscow), 1 (1989): 151–66.

22. See V. Falin in *Pravda*, 20 Sept. 1988; Mikhail Semiryag, '23 avgusta 1939 goda'; Gennadii Bordyugov and Vladimir Kozlov, 'Revolyutsiya sverkhu i tragediya "cherzvychaishchiny" ', *Literaturnaya gazeta*, 12 Oct. 1988, p. 11; G. Bordyugov and V. Kozlov in *Pravda*, 30 Sept. and 3 Oct. 1988. See also Milan Hauner's analysis, 'From the Nazi–Soviet Pact to appeasement and back again', *Radio Liberty Research Bulletin*, RL 455/88, 5 Oct. 1988.

23. For example, under the general heading 'Eshche raz o dogovore 1939 goda' (Once more about the 1939 agreement), *Literaturnaya gazeta* published two articles and two readers' letters on 26 April 1989, p. 14; V. Granovskii, 'U istorii net variantov' and V. Ezhov, 'Antigitlerovskaya koalitsiya do voiny? Vozmozhnosti i

real'nosti', Soviet television broadcast programmes on the same issue on 12 and 14 May 1989.

24. After Lukin had published a response to an article by Bovin in *MEiMO*, the same journal printed a debate between the two protagonists in March 1989: 'Perestroika mezhdunarodnykh otonshenii – puti i podkhody', *MEiMO*, 3 (1989): 58–70.

25. A. Arbatov, 'Skol'ko oborony dostatochno?', *Mezhdunarodnaya zhizn'*, 3 (1989): 33–47.

11

Soviet Asian Policy in a New Perspective

Yutaka Akino

The changes in domestic and foreign policy under Gorbachev have been deep and significant rather than the incremental modifications we have traditionally come to expect from the Kremlin. Indeed, we can consider the perestroika reform as a kind of revolution. By 1987, this revolution had reached the making and implementation of Soviet foreign policy. This chapter will examine how the Soviet Union's Asian policies have been affected by the changes introduced under Gorbachev. We will first review changes in overall foreign policy and then turn to Asian policy. The chapter argues that changes in Soviet Asian policy have been concrete and substantive rather than rhetorical. To support this argument we will review changes in personnel and organization in the Soviet Foreign Ministry; Moscow's policies towards its Asian socialist allies; the Kampuchean problem; and policies towards China, the Korean peninsula and Japan. While such an exercise is necessarily preliminary, it seems clear that these changes have gone sufficiently far not to be ignored by either scholars or policy makers.

1986

It would be fair to say that there were hardly any new elements in Moscow's diplomacy in 1985. In that year Gorbachev reaffirmed that his government would carry out the foreign policy laid down by Andropov but sabotaged under Chernenko. However, 1986 witnessed at least some signs of new foreign policy directions although the implied changes were nuanced, subtle and sporadic. For instance, Gorbachev asserted at a closed meeting at the Soviet Foreign Ministry in May 1986 that Brezhnevian 'directive by which the USSR must be as strong as any potential coalition of states opposing it as absolutely untenable'.[1] This represents a clear departure from the past in so far as it recognizes that a policy aiming at matching the capabilities of any possible alliance is unworkable, since any Soviet effort, however great, could certainly be matched or exceeded by the total of lesser efforts from individual adversaries.

Another new departure in 1986 was Gorbachev's speech in Vladivostok in which he clearly defined the USA as a Pacific state and the USSR as belonging to the Asia-Pacific region. He thus implied that the two superpowers are first of all regional powers, and that Moscow should end its previous tendency to subordinate regional concerns to global competition with the USA.[2] Two months before this major address in Vladivostok, Gorbachev said at a closed meeting at the USSR's Foreign Ministry that 'our approach to the problem of the Asia-Pacific region should cease to be just the sum of political and economic ties with various countries there'.[3] This amounts to an admission that Soviet policy had not been guided by a coherent regional strategy.

1987

In 1987 Moscow's foreign policy began to reflect this less confrontational and more regionally oriented outlook. Moscow placed more emphasis on the United Nations, and began to advocate a multipolar world in which the five permanent members of the UN Security Council, plus Japan, would play a major role.[4] The Kremlin declared that its military doctrine was defensive, and that its armed forces and armaments should be cut to a 'reasonably sufficient' level. It was proclaimed that the concept of parity in strategic nuclear weapons might not have to be interpreted in the same way as parity in conventional weapons.[5]

In 1987 the emergence of these important new foreign policy concepts was matched by the disappearance of some more traditional concepts. For instance, 'balance of power' was replaced by the new concept of 'balance of interests', meaning that the interests of *all states concerned* should be taken into account. By the summer of 1987, this 'balance of interests' had become a guideline of Moscow's policy on regional conflicts. Gorbachev himself answered to *Merdeka* in late July 1987 that 'today we should not establish international relations without taking into account the interests of all states. Balance of interests is needed. In fact, this is the point I wanted to make in my speech in Vladivostok.'[6] The traditional Marxist-Leninist concept of 'capitalism in general crisis' also vanished from the official Soviet lexicon, and the term 'imperialism' has been used much less frequently in the Soviet press. Previously unheard-of concepts such as 'all-human interests' and 'all democratic interests' came into prominence. As regards Moscow's policy towards Eastern Europe, Gorbachev proclaimed in his speech commemorating the seventieth anniversary of the October Revolution that relationships between socialist states should be based on strict observance of the 'principles of peaceful coexistence', including non-interference in internal affairs. Moreover, he asserted that socialist internationalism is based on these principles.[7] This amounts to a clear departure from the old Soviet policy in this region of vital importance to Moscow.

More significantly, the Kremlin began to ask questions in public which had never been raised within official Soviet Marxist circles. Are 'class interests' more important than the 'all-human interests'? Is it true that capitalism inevitably evolves into imperialism and culminates in militarism?[8] Although Gorbachev did not attempt to find the *answers* in 1987, the fact that the Kremlin publicly questioned Marxist-Leninist axioms is quite significant. It was surely deliberate iconoclasm. The resulting debate in the world communist movement has not been negligible, as will be discussed later in this chapter.

1988

In 1988 it became clear that Moscow's foreign policy line should be based on 'all-human interests'. 'Class interest' has ceased to be a mandatory buzz-word in the rhetoric of Soviet foreign policy. Other class terminology, such as 'proletarian internationalism' is no longer ubiquitous in the Soviet mass media. The image of capitalism as enemy has also been toned down. Japan is often cited as an example of how capitalism can develop without degenerating into militarism. Aleksei Arbatov recently wrote that 'we see them [the main source of threat to Soviet security] not in the US or NATO and not in capitalism as such, but in militarism'.[9] Here is an explicit assertion that militarism is not a direct product of capitalism.

Soviet policy towards regional conflicts is taking a new shape. The USSR is withdrawing its armed forces from Afghanistan. Its formerly detached stance on the Kampuchean problem has become much more positive, with Moscow proclaiming that it is prepared to contribute to the *earliest solution*. The pace of Sino-Soviet *rapprochement* also seems to have accelerated. The Kremlin has even decided to 'take into account' South Korea's state interests which had previously been disregarded in deference to the Soviet Union's North Korean ally. For example, the Soviet government established trade relations with Seoul soon after the Olympic Games.

The communiqué of the summer 1988 Warsaw Pact summit suggested unmistakably that the East European bloc now perceived a reduced threat from the NATO countries, whose alliance had a strictly regional orientation. The summit communiqué did not mention 'imperialism' or 'revanchism', did not criticize the Western countries, and even avoided references to non-European issues.[10] All of this is of course unprecedented.

Soviet foreign policy seems to have entered a new era after late September 1988, when Ligachev was effectively removed from the number two position in the Kremlin. Since then the Soviet Foreign Ministry has become vanguard of perestroika in external relations. A strikingly progressive article by Andrei Kozyrev (Deputy Director of the International Organization Department of the Ministry) in the Ministry's monthly journal appears to have been an adamant declaration of the Ministry's new course.[11] In December Gorbachev made it clear in his UN speech that Moscow would cut its military forces by half a million. In this speech he even declared that the epoch made by the October Revolution and the days of the cold war were now over.[12] This speech amounted to a confession of Moscow's capitulation.

1989

In 1989 Moscow completed a partial withdrawal of its forces from Hungary, Poland, Czechoslovakia, East Germany and Mongolia. In May Gorbachev at last visited China and restored party-to-party relations. The normalization of Sino-Soviet relations certainly marked an important milestone in his struggle for a new Soviet Asian policy. In Europe Moscow endorsed the results of the Polish parliamentary elections in which Solidarity won a landslide victory over the Communist Party.[13] In so doing Moscow signalled that East European communist parties could share power with competing political organizations. This would have been unthinkable only half a year ago. In June Gorbachev paid a visit to West Germany and proclaimed that every nation has a right to choose its own political system.[14]

The Emergence of a Regional Policy

Hitherto, Moscow's only coherent regional strategy has been towards Europe. Since 1986, however, another integrated regional policy – towards Asia – has been developing. At a round-table discussion in the summer of 1988, Chizov, head of the Department of Pacific and South Asian Countries in the Soviet Foreign Ministry, made the following responses to the allegation that Moscow has so far had no concept of an Asia-Pacific policy:

> There is every reason to affirm that we have an elaborate and profound concept of an Asia-Pacific region (APR) policy. Indeed, it is probably more elaborate and comprehensive than our concepts regarding any other region of the globe, with the possible exception of Europe. But I fully agree with those who say we must work to carry forward this concept and lend it concrete substance.[15]

The remainder of this chapter will examine the 'concrete substance' that has been infused into Soviet Asian policy since Gorbachev's accession to power. While such an exercise is necessarily preliminary, it seems clear that the changes that are under way are significant and cannot be ignored.

Personnel and Organizational Changes in the Asian Section of the Soviet Foreign Ministry

Concerning the ministerial personnel changes, mention must be made of the reshuffling among the deputy ministers in charge of Asian affairs. L. Il'ichev and M. Kapitsa, both of whom served for a long time as Gromyko's right-hand men for Asian matters (especially for China), left the ministry to follow their master. The young and energetic I. Rogachev replaced them as deputy minister. Rogachev, an expert on China, visited Peking often in order to improve Sino-Soviet relations at a more rapid pace, as designed by the Kremlin. Rogachev's flexible and energetic diplomatic activities are symbolic of the new positive Soviet Asian policy. At the same time, his appointment as deputy minister shows Moscow's unchanging priority on China in its Asian policy.

There is another new deputy minister, B. Chaplin, former ambassador to Hanoi and now also a candidate-member of the Central Committee. Although he is now in charge of intra-ministerial affairs, he visited Hanoi twice in the last two years as a special envoy. Also, in July 1988 he met with three Indochinese ambassadors accredited to Moscow.[16] Shevardnadze would be unlikely to make any significant decisions regarding Indochinese affairs without consulting Chaplin.

Shevardnadze has also been reshuffling Soviet embassy staff in Asian countries, especially the socialist ones. As is well known, the Kremlin has traditionally sent ambassadors with full Central Committee membership to a mere dozen foreign countries, such as France, India and other non-socialist countries as well as to all Warsaw Pact member countries and Yugoslavia. These countries can be said to belong to a category of first importance to Moscow. A second category consists of countries to which the Kremlin sends ambassadors with Central Committee candidate-membership. The rest of the world is sent a third category: Soviet ambassadors with non-Central Committee membership. In this way the party status of Soviet ambassadors reflects the Kremlin's priorities as regards foreign countries. Although there are some exceptions, this status ordering can be regarded as a general rule.

Just before the Gorbachev era, none of the Soviet ambassadors accredited to countries in South-east Asia and the Far East (except Japan) had Central Committee membership, which means the region did not have any countries in the first category. Only Vietnam and Mongolia (CMEA full member countries), and North Korea (a country bordering on the USSR) has Soviet ambassadors with candidate-membership in the Central Committee. These three countries were in the second category; all other Asian countries fell into the third.

Since Gorbachev's coming to power, however, the status of these ambassadors has changed significantly. In 1986 the Soviet ambassador in Hanoi was replaced by a full Central Committee member. In late 1987, Bartoshevich, another full Central Committee member, was accredited to Pyongyang. In 1986 Moscow appointed as its new ambassador to China a candidate-member of the Central Committee, his predecessor not having been a member of this important party apparatus. The Soviet ambassador to Afghanistan is another interesting example: in 1986 Shevardnadze appointed Mozhaev, a Central Committee candidate-member, to Kabul in the place of Tabeev, a full member. In 1988 Mozhaev was replaced by Egorychev, who was not a member of the Central Committee. This clearly shows the sharp decline in the importance the Kremlin attaches to Afghanistan over the last four years and is certainly connected to the Kremlin's change in policy towards Najibullah and Kabul. (But in the autumn of 1988, Vorontsov, a full Central Committee member and the first Deputy Foreign Minister, suddenly replaced Egorychev. However, since Vorontsov remained deputy foreign minister, his posting as ambassador was probably temporary.)

Soviet ambassadors recently appointed to Asian countries have tended to be recruited from experts on the region rather than from non-experts with party credentials. Examples include the ambassadors to Japan, China and Laos. Another interesting choice is the new Soviet ambassador to Manila, Sokolov, a veteran diplomat who served at the Soviet Embassy in Washington under Dobrynin for many years. The Kremlin may have appointed him in the hope that he would prove influential in a country made strategically crucial by the presence of US military bases. In fact, Sokolov, who speaks fluent and even idiomatic American English, is extremely well received among intellectual society in Manila. The same is true of other high-ranking Soviet diplomats accredited to other Asian countries.

In July 1986 Shevardnadze made fundamental changes in his ministry's Asian section. Under Gromyko this section had been unable to function efficiently enough to keep up with the changing realities in this rapidly developing region. The largest organizational change, however, is that the Foreign Ministry set up a special bureau for relations with Asian socialist countries. The Asian section under Rogachev initially had one bureau and two departments; the South Asian department and the Pacific Asian department (which is even in charge of relations with Australia and New Zealand).[17] This change suggests that the ministry has finally decided to give due attention to Asia in its own right. In 1987, the two departments were elevated to the status of bureaux to match the Asia socialist bureau. It can be said that through these personnel and organizational changes, Shevardnadze has achieved a much more efficient basis for policy making and its implementation in Asia. Significantly, these changes seem to reflect the Kremlin's determination to formulate an Asian policy based upon a more integrated concept of the region.

Moscow's New Policy towards Socialism in Asia
One of the most prominent features of Gorbachev's new Asian policy in 1986 and 1987 was his strategy towards the Asian socialist countries.[18] Today the Kremlin has five pro-Soviet allies in Asia: Mongolia, North Korea, Vietnam, Laos and Kampuchea. The Kremlin seemed to be trying to forge an Asian socialist front. Important moves towards institutionalization (some would say regimentation) of this front were witnessed in Ulan Bator (Mongolia) in 1986 and 1987. The initial move in 1986 was the first-ever convention of the Asian socialist countries' parliamentary delegates, attended by representatives of the USSR, Mongolia, North Korea, Vietnam, Laos and Kampuchea (Heng Samrin government).[19] Seven months later Ulan Bator announced that it would host the first conference of the Asian communist and labour parties in the summer of 1987.[20] Two motives can be observed behind this decision: the first was to organize the Soviet Union's socialist allies, and the second was to enlist support of Asian opposition communist and labour parties in the struggle against a foreign 'nuclear threat'.

No less interesting was another unprecedented meeting of deputy foreign ministers from the Soviet Union's five Asian socialist allies, which took place in Moscow on 12 January 1987.[21] Similar meetings of deputy foreign ministers had been held in the past (in Vietnam in 1981 and in Ulan Bator in 1983), but always with a largely East European representation. In this sense, the January 1987 meeting can be described as the first comprised exclusively of Asian ministers. The Kremlin's objective was probably to establish a mechanism for policy coordination in Asia; it probably also wanted to build up a political platform from which to launch not just its own foreign policy initiatives but also those of the Asian division of the socialist commonwealth. This function is comparable to the Warsaw Pact's political (rather than military) role in the European theatre.

The first conference of Asian communist and labour parties took place from 7 to 9 July 1987 in Ulan Bator, and was attended by twenty-three party delegations from twenty-one countries.[22] But, as had been predicted by many observers, no delegations from China and Japan were present. Dobrynin led the Soviet delegation and made a speech at the conference. Moscow did not regard the conference as very successful, mainly because the North Korean party did not attend either, thus demonstrating that the Soviets had failed in their objective to organize their six Asian allies. This may be why the Soviet press did not give the conference much coverage.

All in all, however, the Kremlin seems to have been aware of the significance of the Ulan Bator conference, despite its limited success. According to Tass, Politburo members were told that 'participant countries expressed the strong wish for multilateral party contacts on a more regular basis and in a more diversified way'.[23] It is important to note that the expression 'more diversified way' indicates Moscow's wish to include social democrats along with its traditional allies.

As explained above, one of the main emphases of the Kremlin's Asian policy until the summer of 1987 was on strengthening the ranks of its Asian socialist allies and organizing the Asian communist movement. However, these efforts to strengthen socialism in Asia have undergone a significant change, which is probably related to the Kremlin's overall foreign policy changes of later that year. With the improvement in US–USSR relations since the middle of 1987, Moscow has become less vociferous in criticizing Washington's efforts to establish an Asian NATO to oppose the USSR and its Asian allies. In 1986 the Kremlin's sense of facing an Asian NATO must have made Gorbachev's leadership feel the need for an Asian Warsaw Pact. But the Kremlin finally came to realize that in the circumstances it would not be well advised to try to force the creation of an Asian socialist bloc.

For instance, at the Ulan Bator conference Dobrynin pointed out that some positive tendencies had recently been observed in the Asia-Pacific region; this perception has brought increased awareness of the need to avoid potentially dangerous conflicts in the region.[24] Of course, any mechanism of policy coordination will need a great deal of preparation, so the Soviets are likely to continue their efforts at collaboration with their allies in Asia. But their methods will probably become more subtle. As for the communist movement in Asia, in my opinion, it will not be based on 'class interests' or, more precisely, on 'proletarian internationalism'; instead, the movement seems to be becoming more broadly based, including both communists and social democrats. Especially since Ligachev was replaced by Medvedev as chief ideologist in September 1988, the Soviet emphasis on 'all-human interests' as its foreign policy guideline has become more clear-cut.[25] Accordingly, as was declared at the meeting of party secretaries for ideology of the socialist commonwealth in Ulan Bator in March 1988 and in Gorbachev's report to the nineteenth party conference, Moscow's policy orientation would be towards 'normal' relations even between socialist states.[26] This tendency, though still subtle, has been reflected in its policy in Asia.

The Kampuchean Problem and the Sino-Soviet Rapprochement

A New Stance on the Kampuchean Problem

There are several reasons why a solution of the Kampuchean problem is particularly important for Gorbachev. First, it has been poisoning both East–West relations and the political atmosphere of the region. Second, Moscow has been obliged to give enormous amounts of financial assistance to Vietnam. Finally, it has been the biggest hindrance to normalization of Sino-Soviet relations. For these reasons, Gorbachev's leadership has developed some new approaches to solving the problem.

At the beginning of the 1980s, the Soviets did not recognize the Kampuchean problem as such, instead referring vaguely to it as 'situations around Kampuchea'. But after Gorbachev's accession to power, Soviet policy has approached the problem through political means, 'taking into account the existing reality' (balance of interests). Vietnam, however, at first to accept this formula.[27] For, while 'the existing reality' could of course be interpreted to mean the existence of the Heng Samrin regime, it could also mean the regime's failure to gain international recognition and the question of whether it would be strong enough to survive without the direct backing of Moscow and Hanoi. When the Vietnamese party leader Nguen Van Linh visited Moscow in May 1987 Gorbachev succeeded in persuading him to accept this formula.

However, the Soviets and the Vietnamese could not agree on how to treat the Pol Pot group, one of the most intractable dimensions of the Kampuchean problem. During Nguen Van Linh's visit to Moscow, this discrepancy between Moscow's and Hanoi's positions loomed large. Before his departure, the Vietnamese press launched a campaign to stress the importance of the 'exclusion of the Pol Pot clique'. In Moscow Linh himself made efforts to emphasize this principle.[28] Gorbachev, however, did not follow suit. In fact, he mentioned the problem only once, in a speech at a banquet on 19 May, when he said that 'Kampuchea is steadily though gradually recovering from the terror of Pol Pot's genocide',[29] but he did not mention 'exclusion'.[30] Nor was this long-recognized principle referred to in the joint communiqué. Vietnamese dissatisfaction with Moscow's line was shown when Hanoi reiterated the importance of exclusion after Linh's return.[31]

After Nguen Van Linh, Heng Samrin, the Kampuchean party leader, visited Moscow towards the end of July. Soviet statements were not to Vietnam's liking. According to Tass, Gorbachev said that 'there is no place for those guilty of genocide in the process of national reconciliation and resolution';[32] this rather vague form of words fails to mention Pol Pot by name. A few weeks later, *Izvestiya* published a very interesting interview with Heng Samrin's former Foreign Minister, Kong Korm, in which he mentioned for the first time the 'exclusion of Pol Pot and his closest associates [blizhaishie podruchynye]'.[33] This formulates that Pol Pot and Ieng Sary should be excluded, but that Khieu Samphen is acceptable. A few weeks later, on 29 August, an official announcement by the Heng Samrin regime made a very similar reference to 'Pol Pot and closest accomplices [edinosheenniki]'. Once again we witness the long arm of the Kremlin, although its role in this episode was behind the scenes. The day before Heng Samrin's announcement, four representatives of the Kampuchean, Laotian, Soviet and Vietnamese foreign ministries began three days of consultation in Phnom Penh.[34] Shevardnadze sent Kiriev, the director of the Asian Socialist Countries Bureau, and an influential policy maker, to the meeting.[35] After this consultation, more explicit identification of 'the Pol Pot clique' was forthcoming; the stalemate over how to resolve the Kampuchean problem was thereby broken.

Recognizing that the Kampuchean problem was the biggest obstacle to improving Sino-Soviet relations, Gorbachev again altered Soviet policy. His previous stance was that, in so far as the USSR was not directly involved in the Kampuchean problem, it was not an appropriate topic for discussion between Moscow and Beijing.[36] But, since the tenth Sino-Soviet political consultation meeting of April 1987, the USSR has acceded to the Chinese demand that it should tackle the matter.[37] A month later, Gorbachev expressed the opinion that, 'although the Kampuchean problem has nothing to do with Sino-Soviet relations, the USSR and China are interested in resolving it'.[38] As implied by this statement, Moscow has reluctantly agreed to include Kampuchea in talks with the Chinese. In this context it is quite understandable that the eleventh political consultation meeting did not bring much progress, probably because of the Kampuchean impasse. The Kremlin was clearly unable to make any substantial concessions by bypassing Vietnam; Hanoi would probably have reacted rather stridently, perhaps even threatening to deny Soviet use of the naval base at Cam Rann Bay.

When Hun Sen met Prince Sihanouk in France in December 1987 and January 1988, he dutifully stopped over in Moscow on his way there and back for Soviet advice and instruction. Moscow's involvement became even more overt. On 30 May 1988, the Soviet government issued a statement welcoming Hanoi's decision to withdraw its military forces (approximately 50,000 troops) from Kampuchea and declaring that 'it is prepared to make contributions to searching for constructive solutions to the conflict-ridden situation in South-east Asia'.[39] Thus, the Soviet attitude appears to be becoming more positive. A few months before the Bogor cocktail party, Shevardnadze sent Rogachev to Phnom Penh to join a four-country consultation on the Kampuchean problem. Significantly, the level of the consultation was raised to deputy minister from bureau director a year before. After the Bogor meeting the Soviet Foreign Ministry issued a statement reiterating that the USSR was ready to contribute to the resolution of the Kampuchean problem.[40] Finally, Rogachev's visit to Beijing in the summer of 1988 was devoted solely to the problem and is alleged to have broken the ice between the two countries. The Soviet Union now claims it is prepared to contribute to the 'earliest' solution of the Kampuchean problem.[41] In any event, at about that time Kampuchea seemed to recede as an obstacle to normalization of Sino-Soviet relations.

In order to understand the Soviet approach to the Kampuchean problem, one must think of the difference between it and Afghanistan. Moscow's tenacious efforts to strengthen its relations with Heng Samrin's pro-Soviet regime are important here. The more flexible the Soviet stance has become on the Kampuchean problem, the more they have tried to strengthen their ties with the regime. There have been numerous clear examples of these Soviet cooperative efforts. When Hun Sen and Heng Samrin paid a visit to Moscow in 1987, Medvedev, then Central Committee secretary in charge of liaison with ruling communist parties, was present with Gorbachev and other top level leaders in their talks with the Kampuchean political representatives,[42] a sign that Moscow is now treating Heng Samrin's incipiently socialist regime as a fully fledged socialist country. At the same time the Soviets were trying to secure Kampuchean participation in various conferences and meetings, despite the opposition of other socialist countries to its presence. Relations with Kampuchea came to be handled by the Bureau of Asian Socialist Countries at the Soviet Foreign Ministry. Furthermore, a special edition of the journal *Novoe vremya* commemorating the seventieth anniversary of the October Revolution made it clear that Kampuchea is the latest entrant into the 'world socialist system'.[43] Finally, when Rogachev visited Phnom Penh in mid-March 1988, an agreement on exemption for mutual entry visas between Soviet and Kampuchean citizens was concluded.[44] Thus, despite Moscow's frequent statement to the contrary, Gorbachev's policy towards Kampuchea has been different from his approach to Afghanistan (which is now definitely recognized to have no basis for the construction of socialism).

Moscow's New Policy towards China
As is well known, the pace of Sino-Soviet *rapprochement* was not accelerated even after Gorbachev's Vladivostok address. The 'goodwill' shown by Moscow, such as the partial withdrawal of Soviet armed forces stationed in Mongolia, bilateral talks on the Sino-Soviet borders, and the 'global zero' decision which took account of Chinese apprehensions concerning the Soviets' SS-20 in Asia,[45] did not satisfy Beijing.

Apart from the Kampuchean problem, another obstacle to Sino-Soviet normalization is the definition of the principles by which relations between these two 'great' socialist countries are to be regulated. More specifically, the problem is whether Moscow is entitled to hegemony within the socialist camp (an extended form of the Brezhnev doctrine). A spring 1988 Soviet–Yugoslav joint communiqué proclaimed that intervention into the internal affairs of parties is not allowed 'under any pretext' (compare this with the language found in the 1955 Belgrade Declaration).[46] And since the autumn of 1988 Moscow very clearly declared that all the principles of 'peaceful coexistence' should be incorporated into relations among socialist states.

If relations between socialist states need no longer be exclusively governed by the obsolete doctrine of 'class interests', the Soviet hegemony need no longer pose a threat to other socialist states. In other words, the national interests of other socialist states could be more easily reconciled with the 'international interest' (as defined by the Soviet Union). If this interpretation of shifts in official Soviet rhetoric was perceived by Beijing as genuine, resumption of inter-party relations between the Soviet Union and China would be a question of time. And the time came in May 1989. Thus the first priority in Moscow's new Asian policy is now attained. The goals the Kremlin is going to target are perhaps the solution of the situation in the Korean peninsula and the normalization of Japanese–Soviet relations. This is clearly shown in Gorbachev's speeches in China.[47]

New Policy in the Korean Peninsula

After Kim Il Sung's visit to Moscow in 1984, Moscow–Pyongyang relations improved at a rather surprising pace. For instance, Moscow sent some of its most sophisticated systems (such as Mig 29s) to Pyongyang, and military cooperation between the USSR and North Korea is increasing. This should not be surprising, however, as helping its allies to modernize their armed forces is a normal and necessary measure for the Kremlin to take. But my own view is that the rate of overall improvement in Moscow–Pyongyang relations had already slowed down by 1988, despite Central Committee Secretary Medvedev's statement to the contrary.[48]

In this context several points can be made. First, Pyongyang rejects Soviet request to join the CMEA, the socialist commonwealth. This is clearly shown by the fact that Pyongyang continues to propose proletarian internationalism as the principle for regulation of Soviet–North Korean relations, while Moscow instead insists on the terminology of socialist internationalism (which always refers to relations within the socialist commonwealth).[49] Second, to Moscow's chagrin, Kim Il Sung (like Beijing) failed to send a party delegation to the Asian communist parties' conference in Ulan Bator. Third, Moscow's participation in the Seoul Olympics was extremely disappointing to Pyongyang. Fourth, Beijing–Pyongyang relations have improved since the resignation of Hu Yaobang, whose relations with Kim Il Sung were alleged to be bad. More interesting, however, is that Moscow apparently welcomes Chinese involvement in the Korean peninsula. A Soviet historian has commented that 'it is pleasant to see that China is closely cooperating with the Democratic People's Republic of Korea, and is supporting this country's attempts at the peaceful resolution of the Korean problem'.[50] This may imply that Moscow and Beijing should each have equal influence in Pyongyang instead of competing with each other there. Finally, judging from the general direction of Moscow's foreign policy, Soviet efforts to strengthen North Korea militarily might be plausibly described as a form of compensation for Soviet participation in the Seoul Olympic Games, in the face of Pyongyang's pleas for a socialist boycott. In any case, there is surely a limit beyond which military cooperation cannot develop without common goals and broad mutual understanding in the political, economic, cultural and ideological spheres.

Some of these points may require further explanation. Since Gorbachev's 'new thinking' has been on the ascendant, the two countries' relations have become more and more contentious. First, Pyongyang and Moscow clearly do not see eye to eye on the world situation, especially in Asia. North Korea has been talking desperately of further international tensions caused by the 'wicked policy of imperialism'; of the ever-increasing danger of a 'Washington–Tokyo–Seoul military triangle'; and of the socialist countries' need to close ranks on the sacred matters of 'class solidarity' or 'proletarian internationalism', while Moscow has been very reticent about this terminology. The contrast was illustrated by the exchange of speeches between Kim Il Sung and Chebrikov, who visited Pyongyang in September 1988. This conservative Soviet leader, a close associate of Ligachev, looked like a dove in Pyongyang.[51]

Second, the Soviet Union's recent overtures to South Korea must be traumatic to Kim Il Sung. Just after the Seoul Olympics, Moscow rubbed salt into the wound already caused by Soviet participation in the games by his telegram to Kim Il Sung on the fortieth anniversary of the founding of the North Korean state (9 September 1988). The Kremlin failed to mention 'internationalism', and instead referred to 'balance of interests' as a principle for solving the situation in the Korean peninsula.[52] As already mentioned, 'balance of interests' is a buzz-word for the 'new thinking', meaning that the state interests of South Korea should no longer be disregarded. About a week later Gorbachev declared in Krasnoyarsk that 'in the context of the improvement of the situation on the Korean peninsula the possibility of establishing economic relations with South Korea could be considered'.[53] And soon afterwards Gorbachev acted on his words: a formal trade relationship between the USSR and South Korea was established.

Third, although there can as yet be no certainty, Moscow appears to have been moving towards 'cross recognition' of both Koreas. In October 1988 Bovin said that he was personally not against 'cross recognition'. More significantly, before making any move, the Kremlin tried to consult East Germany on the matter. Rogachev visited East Berlin for bilateral consultations on the 'Asian situation', and an East German delegation reciprocated in July. In Tokyo in November 1988, an important adviser to Honecker, when asked what advice he would like to give to his North Korean friends, answered: 'I would be very happy if North Korea could learn invaluable lessons from what happened in Central Europe. We have already had some discussions with them on this problem.'[54]

North Korea's rejection of 'cross recognition' has nevertheless remained categorical, as was graphically illustrated by its explosive response to Hungary's recent establishment of diplomatic ties with South Korea. *Naewoetongsin* regarded Budapest's action as a 'betrayal of the cause of socialism'. Pyongyang is in fact attacking Moscow when it blames Budapest for the 'exaggerated illusion that Hungary has become a hero leading the "new way of thinking", or "new thinking" '.[55] Not satisfied with this statement, a month later a spokesman for the North Korean Foreign Ministry publicly criticized Hungary. Referring to Hungarian claims that 'an ally expressed its understanding and support' for the establishment of a diplomatic partnership with Seoul, the spokesman did not miss his main target. He said that (1) 'as far as North Korea knows this is such a fact'; and (2) 'supposing it is true, then it means that Hungary undertook factional activity within the socialist ranks, in collaboration with another ally, without consulting us beforehand'.

Under these circumstances it is possible that Moscow–Pyongyang relations may become more distant, especially if Beijing tries to exploit the dispute between them, although this is not likely. For now Moscow can only hope that China will not do so. In this context, Primakov wrote in *Pravda* that: (1) reality must be taken into account; (2) the reality is that South Korea is a rapidly growing economic organism; (3) this reality is now taken into account by other countries in the world including China. Besides the Chinese factor, Moscow also faces the danger of a rift among the socialist countries in which Pyongyang and Havana may play a leading role.

A network of 'friendship treaties' is already emerging among such 'pariah states' as Cuba, Nicaragua, Najibullah's Afghanistan and North Korea. These countries (possibly plus Vietnam) may form a group which puts unchanging emphasis on 'class interest' in the communist movement. This may be simply because they feel threatened by the common enemy of 'US imperialism', or because they need a foreign bogey man in order that they may maintain control of their regimes. Their sense of being abandoned by their Soviet and East European allies will become even stronger if the Warsaw Pact is further Europeanized.

The Approach to Japan

In 1986 and 1987, when Moscow was trying hard to organize its Asian socialist allies, the alleged revival of Japanese militarism must have seemed a good way to rally the socialist forces and to strengthen 'class solidarity' in the Asia-Pacific region. In 1988, however, there have been virtually no such criticisms of Japan as an independent centre of imperialism. In Krasnoyarsk, Gorbachev pointed out that 'Japan seems to prove that it is possible for a nation to attain the status of a major power without relying on militarism'. But he reminded his audience that Japan could, of course, revert to being militaristic. The Kremlin now seems to understand that what it previously termed 'Japan's tendency to be militaristic' has been at least partly a product of those Soviet policies which have posed a threat to Japan.

This is the background against which Moscow's new approach to Japan should be assessed. Also in this context we should take note of the possible impact on Japanese–Soviet relations of Gorbachev's visits to China and West Germany. First, in his trip to China he accomplished his long-standing desire for the full normalization of Sino-Soviet relations. Naturally, Japan is looming as the next goal in his dynamic foreign policy. Second, Gorbachev's visit to West Germany, an arch-enemy in World War II and a country of revanchism, may possibly give stimulus to the normalization process between the USSR and Japan, taking account of the parallel circumstances of West Germany and Japan.

As for the deadlock with Japan over the problem of northern territories, we have been witnessing a new approach by Moscow. Although Moscow has never acknowledged the existence of a territorial dispute, it now seems ready to give two of the islands (Habomai and Shikotan) back to Japan.[56] Shevardnadze's recent endorsement of the US–Japanese security treaty is a clear sign of his desire to tackle the most difficult problems from new angles.[57]

Concluding Remarks

It cannot be denied that Gorbachev's foreign policy differs considerably from that of his predecessors. But it is important to ask what in his policy is actually 'new'. It has certainly been much more dynamic and positive. More specifically, the Kremlin under Gorbachev, Yakovlev and Medvedev has been trying to escape from the old Marxist-Leninist dogmas which have hitherto forced the USSR's hand, constrained its diplomacy and hampered its state interests.

For instance, its perception of capitalism has changed dramatically. Moscow's recent approach to the West has been based upon the recognition that world capitalism is not about to collapse; it follows then that the East must coexist and even cooperate with it. The image of the West as its historic enemy has been relaxed. As Gorbachev tries to carry through his political perestroika, his supporters have come to realize that there is much to learn from the political system of the West. A high-ranking official at the Soviet Foreign Ministry wrote that 'bourgeois democracy' is a most valuable part of human culture, which the Soviets should study and understand.[58] Also important is Moscow's new policy towards its socialist allies (as well as towards countries of socialist orientation).

Then comes the question of the content of Gorbachev's diplomacy. This diplomacy is a mixture of very uncompromising statements and some new policies. It has successfully forged a good image of the new USSR in Western society. In consequence, most Western critics of the USSR warn that, since the new elements in Gorbachev's policy have so far been confined to rhetoric, the West should be careful not to be deceived by his 'low cost' overtures. This is a legitimate caution, but we should not dismiss out of hand the potentially significant changes Gorbachev has signalled.

I would suggest that Soviet Asian policy since 1986 reflects the following significant changes. First, through organizational and personnel changes in the Foreign Ministry, Moscow has become better equipped for policy making and implementation. The Kremlin has been trying to pursue an Asian policy based upon its practical, non-ideological interests in the region. Second, Moscow's policy towards communist movements in the region has changed substantially. Its former, heavily dogmatic approach to these countries has been replaced by a 'new thinking' based upon more sober calculations of reality. Third, while Moscow's stance on capitalist countries in the Asia-Pacific region looks new, in fact its policy has not so far changed very much (except towards South Korea) despite some significant changes in rhetoric or in assessment. Perhaps this is because Moscow's previous policies towards Japan and ASEAN countries were never as ideological in character as its other regional policies.

But this is not to say that nothing substantially new is in the offing. As already mentioned, since autumn 1987, Moscow has revised its long-standing dogma that the transition from advanced capitalism to imperialist militarism is inevitable. It has come to acknowledge that such a transition would not result from any iron rule of economic imperatives. Japan is the principal case in point: whether or not Japan becomes militaristic depends upon its political choice and its perception of external threats.

For the last decade the main priority of Soviet Asian policy has been the improvement of Sino-Soviet relations. And this goal is likely to be accomplished in the not too distant future. The next objective in the Asia-Pacific region will no doubt be to improve relations with Japan, the NIEs and ASEAN countries. Asian politics may change as a result of the Kremlin's new style; in particular, policy changes towards relations with Asian socialist countries are bound to have some favourable repercussions on the region's political and military situation. But that is not enough. Moscow has to do something substantial. The biggest question is whether the USSR will be able to make the most of its geographical position, sandwiched between the economically prosperous Asian and European regions.

Notes

1. *Mezhdunarodnaya zhizn'*, 9 (1988): p. 18. But his assertion seemed so unpalatable to other Soviet leaders that it took more than two years before it was finally made public. This part of his speech is not included in *Vestnik ministerstva insotrannykh del SSSR*, 1 (5 Aug. 1987).
2. *Pravda*, 29 July 1986.
3. *Vestnik ministerstva inostrannykh del SSSR*, 1 (5 Aug. 1987).
4. E. Agaev and B. Prokof'ev, 'OON: za ob'edinenie usilii i demokraticheskii dialog', *Mezhdunarodnaya zhizn'*, 11 (1987): 59.
5. *Pravda*, 30 May 1987.
6. *Pravda*, 23 July 1987.
7. *Pravda*, 4 Nov. 1987.
8. Ibid.
9. *Moskovskie novosti*, 39 (25 Sept. 1988).
10. *Pravda*, 16 July 1988.

11. A. Kozyrev, 'Doverie i balans interesov', *Mezhdunarodnaya zhizn'*, 10 (1988): 3–12.

12. *Pravda*, 8 Dec. 1988.

13. *Pravda*, 9 June 1989.

14. *Pravda*, 14 June 1989.

15. 'Vladisvostokskie initsiativy; dva goda spustya', *Mezhdunarodnaya zhizn'*, 7 (1988): 147–8.

16. *Radio Press: Vietnam News*, 14 Nov. 1988.

17. This is well illustrated by the fact that the second European department of Gromyko's ministry dealt directly with Australia and New Zealand despite their Asian location, ostensibly because of their membership of the British Commonwealth. But since Great Britain's entry into the EEC, these two countries have become politically and economically, as well as geographically, genuine Asia-Pacific countries.

18. The need to strengthen ties among the Asian socialist countries was clearly expressed when Gorbachev and Kaison, the Laotian Party General Secretary, agreed 'to intensify further coordinated action of Asian socialist countries' on the occasion of Kaison's visit to Moscow in October 1986 (*Pravda*, 16 Oct. 1986).

19. *Rude Pravo*, 27 March 1986.

20. *Pravda*, 26 Oct. 1986.

21. *Pravda*, 13 Jan. 1987. Similar kinds of deputy foreign ministers' meetings were held in the past (in Vietnam in 1981 and in Ulan Bator in 1983) in which, however, most of the East European deputy foreign ministers participated. In this sense, the January 1987 meeting in Moscow can be described as the first meeting and was composed exclusively of Asian socialist deputy foreign ministers.

22. Dobrynin, then Central Committee secretary in charge of world communist movement of the Soviet delegation, made a speech at the conference (*Pravda*, 10 July 1987).

23. *Pravda*, 18 July 1987.

24. *Pravda*, 10 July 1987.

25. *Pravda*, 5 Oct. 1988.

26. *Pravda*, 17 March 1986 and 29 June 1988.

27. D. Pike, *Vietnam and the Soviet Union: Anatomy of an Alliance* (Boulder, CO: 1987), p. 208.

28. *Radio Press, Vietnam News*, 9 June 1987.

29. *Pravda*, 25 May 1987.

30. *Radio Press*, 27 May 1987.

31. *Pravda*, 29 July 1987.

32. *Izvestiya*, 11 Aug. 1987.

33. *Radio Press*, 31 Aug. 1987.

34. *UPI*, 26 April 1987.

35. *Sankei Shimbun*, 31 Oct. 1987.

36. *Pravda*, 20 May 1987.

37. *Pravda*, 31 May 1988.

38. *Pravda*, 4 Aug. 1988.

39. *Pravda*, 18 Sept. 1988.

40. *Pravda*, 23 June 1988.

41. *Novoe vremya*, 1987 (special issue commemorating the seventieth anniversary of the October Revolution).

42. *Izvestiya*, 18 March 1988.

43. *Radio Press (Soviet News)*, 23 July 1987.

44. *Pravda*, 19 March 1988.

45. V. Medvedev, 'Sotsialisticka spoluprace: nova etapa', *Otazky miru a socialism*, 5 (1988): 17.

46. Y. Akino, 'Soren no azia shakaishugi doumeikoku seisaku [Soviet policy towards its Asian allies]', *Sorenkenkyu*, 3 (Oct. 1986): 79–80.

47. *Pravda*, 18 May 1989.

48. *APN*, 24 Sept. 1987.

49. *Izvestiya*, 11 Sept. 1988.

50. *Pravda*, 9 Sept. 1988.

51. *Pravda*, 18 Sept. 1988.

52. Max Schmidt, Director of the Institute for International Politics and Economy, expressed this opinion at a meeting in Tokyo on 2 Nov. 1988.

53. *Radio Press (Korean News)*, 20 Sept. 1988.

54. *Chosenjiho*, 31 Oct. 1988.

55. *Pravda*, 8 Oct. 1988.

56. G. Kunadze and K. Sarkisov, 'Razmyshlyaya o sovetsko–yaponskikh otnosheniyakh', *Mirovaya ekonomika i mezhdunarodnye otnosheniya*, 5 (1989): 83–93.

57. *Mainichi Shimbun*, 5 May 1989.

58. A. Kozyrev, 'Doverie i balans interesov', *Mezhdunarodnaya zhizn'*, 10 (1988): 12.

12

The Impact of Perestroika on Soviet European Policy

Hannes Adomeit

'History and life itself' is full of paradoxes. One of them concerns perestroika and Soviet–Western European relations: the 'restructuring' has significantly affected Soviet internal affairs, including politics, ideology, economics, nationality affairs, history and the legal system. It has led to significant changes in approach towards the United States, China and other countries, socialist or non-socialist, contributed to the solution of regional conflicts and evoked a new interest in international political and economic organizations. It has also transformed Soviet–Eastern European relations and influenced governments and public opinion in Western Europe. However – at least until autumn 1988 – it only marginally affected Soviet policy *towards* Western Europe. Until that time traditional elements of that policy were more pronounced than the new directions.

From Gorbachev's assumption of power in March 1985 until October of the same year it may have seemed that the new Soviet leader was going to give top priority to the improvement of relations with Western Europe. In fact, it appeared as if he was aiming at the encouragement of a common European identity, curtailment of American political influence and removal of the US military presence on the Continent. Such aims, however, failed to turn into corresponding practical policy. In the period from autumn 1985 to autumn 1988 it was the restructuring of relations with the *United States* that took precedence over relations with Western Europe.

The visit by West German chancellor Helmut Kohl to the Soviet Union in October 1988 and other high-level contacts between Gorbachev and West European leaders in that month, however, may signify a change of tack. Not least because of the election of a new American president and the uncertainty as to his foreign policy course, but also because of certain objective requirements, Soviet relations with Western Europe are likely to become more substantial and lively. This change of tack will not establish a 'Europe first' approach. But it is likely to lead to a more equal treatment of these two regions in Soviet policy.

This is all the more likely because of the fact that, since the end of World War II, there has never been a separate Soviet–West European policy. There has only been a comprehensive approach *vis-à-vis* the West – a Soviet Westpolitik – in which policies towards both the United States and Western Europe have formed a unified whole.

How, then, did Gorbachev's approach towards (Western) Europe evolve? What role did the US angle play in its evolution, and what influence was exerted by Moscow's traditional objective of safeguarding its pre-eminence in East-central Europe? Are current Soviet policies a direct extension of requirements generated by internal perestroika or, if not, what are the 'driving forces' (dvizhu-shchie sily)?

The 'Common European House': Initial Promises, 1984–5

In Gorbachev's approach to Western Europe several themes can be discerned. The first was raised during his visit to London in December 1984. Speaking before the House of Commons, he referred to Europe as 'our common house' (nash obshchii dom),[1] at that time clearly implying that the United States, as a trans-atlantic power, really had no business in that house. As a *Pravda* editorial put it, 'Washington is a stranger to that house.'[2] Another implication of this slogan – this implication being valid then and today – is the idea that the European countries have common interests which needed to be safeguarded. Such interests, Gorbachev and other spokesmen have asserted, existed above all in the sphere of European security.[3]

A second theme which supplements the first is the assertion that, in addition to geography, 'Europe' is bound together by 'historical ties' and a 'common foundation of European culture', including a common 'political culture'.[4] In 1985 Gorbachev supporters were still to claim that 'European political standards are superior to those in the United States'. They asserted that it was in Europe that 'the norms of peaceful coexistence were worked out', and that the 'cowboy attitude to the problems of war and peace currently preva-lent in the United States is not typical of present-day Europe. People on this side of the Atlantic approach detente and the nature and prospects of East–West contacts more seriously and more responsibly.'[5]

A third theme was first put forward by Gorbachev in his speech before the elections to the Supreme Soviet in February 1985. The Soviet Union considered a normalization of relations with the United States to be important. 'However', he continued, 'we are not for a single moment forgetting that the world is not limited to that country alone.'[6] Similarly, a few weeks later in an interview in *Pravda*, he acknowledged: 'The relations between the USSR and the USA are an extremely important part of international politics.' But he then added that 'we are far from seeing the world through the prism of these relations. We understand the weight which other countries have in international affairs and take this into account in our assessment of the overall situation in the world.'[7] Such statements have been interpreted to mean that if relations with the United States were to develop unsatisfactorily, the Soviet Union had other options which it could pursue.

A fourth theme was sounded by Gorbachev in May 1985. Both in talks with Gianni Cervetti, the head of the communist section of the European parliament and member of the presidium of the Italian Communist Party, and Bettino Craxi, the then Italian prime minister, Gorbachev advocated the expansion of economic contacts between the Council for Mutual Economic Assistance (CMEA) and the European Community (EC) as well as the establishment of official relations between these two organizations. This position taken by Moscow was not new. But Gorbachev continued by saying that, 'to the extent to which the states of the EEC were acting as one single unit', the Soviet Union would be prepared 'to search for a common language with them on specific international problems'.[8] This was unprecedented. Whereas previously Soviet interest had extended only to regulating economic relations between the two organizations, Gorbachev for the first time signalled a Soviet interest in coming to some arrangement with the EC at the political level.

Fifth, in his talks with Cervetti and Craxi, Gorbachev seemed to view the attempts made by major Western European countries to increase technological cooperation (the Eureka programme) as positive and even to express interest in Soviet participation as long as this programme remained confined to civilian research and development. Such an interest would fit well with his emphasis on speeding up the 'scientific-technological revolution' in the Soviet Union.

As if to demonstrate the priority of Soviet–Western European relations, Gorbachev's first visit abroad as party leader was not to Washington but to Paris in October 1985. However, the promise of preferential treatment of Western Europe remained unfulfilled.

The Promises Unfulfilled: Autumn 1985 to Autumn 1988

In the period from autumn 1985 until autumn 1988 the 'common house of Europe' turned out to be more of a slogan than a clearly defined concept, and more rhetoric than substance. Both new and traditional elements characterized Soviet policy towards Western Europe. But, on balance, the traditional elements were still dominant.

In *trade and economic relations* 'objective' factors continued to limit change. In fact, the overall volume of trade with the EC (despite the addition of Portugal and Spain to the trade statistics) fell from US$28 billion in 1981 to US$23 billion in 1986.[9] This was probably the combined result of (1) the substantial lowering of the world market price for oil and gas; (2) the decrease in the demand for energy imports in Western industrialized countries; (3) the significant reduction in the value of the US dollar (the currency in which oil purchases and holdings are denominated); (4) the continued need for the Soviet Union to import large quantities of grain; and (5) the inability of the USSR effectively to compete with industrial products on the Western European market. Especially dramatic was the deterioration in the export performance of the Soviet Union: in the period from 1981 to 1986 Soviet exports to the EC declined by approximately one-fourth.[10]

As a result of the contraction of Soviet–Western European trade and gains made by more efficient competitors of the USSR (notably by the countries of the Asian-Pacific region), the share of the Soviet Union and the other CMEA countries in overall EC trade by the end of 1987 amounted to only approximately 3 per cent. Direct investments by Western European countries in CMEA remained practically non-existent (0.1 per cent of overall extra-EC investments) and, relative to Community investments in other countries and areas, have been declining.

'Subjective' factors also played a role in limiting Soviet–Western European trade and economic relations. Notwithstanding the greater interest which the Soviet leaders expressed in the 'international economic division of labour', they remained reluctant, at least until 1988, to increase the level of indebtedness to the West.

At the *political level*, Soviet diplomats were busy chiefly with playing the traditional game of utilizing 'irreconcilable contradictions' both among the Western European countries and within these countries. It was quite noticeable, for instance, that although four Soviet–American summit conferences had taken place (Geneva, Reykjavik, Washington and Moscow), and Gorbachev found the time to visit, in addition to all the Warsaw Pact capitals, New Delhi (November 1986 and November 1988) and Belgrade (March 1988), he considered it expedient to delay time and again a visit to the country that, due to its economic potential and political influence in the Western alliance, is perhaps the most important building block for a 'European house': the Federal Republic of Germany. This neglect persisted despite the fact that a succession of West German visitors had been to Moscow: President Richard von Weizsäcker in July 1987; Chancellor Kohl three times consecutively (July 1983, March 1985 and October 1988); Foreign Minister Genscher five times; the Bavarian prime minister, Franz-Josef Strauss, in December 1987; and the prime minister of Baden-Württemberg, Lothar Späth, in February 1988.

Soviet Foreign Minister Shevardnadze's visit to Bonn in mid-January 1988 only produced a vague commitment that the question of a potential visit by Gorbachev to West Germany would 'be decided' in autumn 1988. Only in March 1988 was this vague commitment revised because Chancellor Kohl agreed to visit Moscow for a third time; and only then did the Soviet leadership relent and consent to a Gorbachev visit to Bonn, which took place in June 1989.

Shortly after having assumed power in the USSR it became obvious that France and Great Britain were treated more favourably and with more respect than West Germany. Thus, during Gorbachev's visit to France in October 1985, the Soviet Union offered to negotiate separately with France and Britain on nuclear weapons. This may have been conceived in Moscow as a skilful gesture to support inclinations towards greater independence in the two countries outside the NATO framework and to take one more step in the direction of eroding nuclear deterrence in Europe. At least it was interpreted in this fashion in Paris and London, and quickly brushed aside in these two capitals.

Utilization of 'imperialist contradictions' at the Western European domestic level was evident, particularly in the preferential treatment accorded to the social democrats, notably those in West Germany.

The limitations inherent in Gorbachev's approach to Western Europe were conspicuous on a number of political issues. The Soviet political leadership continued to view with unease the processes of vertical and horizontal integration in Western Europe, and it vehemently opposed any semblance of military integration, including efforts at French–West German defence cooperation and the strengthening of the role of the Western European Union (WEU).

Nothing came of Gorbachev's hint to establish political links with the European community. Due to Soviet recalcitrance on the West Berlin problem, it seemed for quite some time – until spring 1988 – that even the establishment of legal and organizational ties between CMEA and the EC would not be achieved. As the October 1988 visit by Austrian Chancellor Vranitzky in Moscow showed, the Soviet Union has continued to oppose Austrian inclinations to become a member of the EC.

Western European officials and international relations experts quite unsuccessfully attempted to receive clarification from Moscow as to the substance of the 'European house'. Clearly, in the context of Soviet Westpolitik it was the reordering of relations with the United States, rather than with Western Europe, that received top priority in Moscow until autumn 1988.

Priority for the Soviet–American Relationship: October 1985–October 1988

This priority is apparent, at the Soviet domestic political level, in the pre-eminence of the Amerikanisty (Soviet specialists on American affairs) in the central decision-making apparatus. At the international level, it manifested itself in the complete reversal of the anti-American positions and rhetoric to which Brezhnev, Andropov and Chernenko had tenaciously clung. It is demonstrated by the four Soviet–American summit meetings and approximately thirty working sessions held between foreign ministers Shultz and Shevardnadze in the period from March 1985 (Gorbachev's assumption of power) and January 1989 (the end of the Reagan administration's second term). Finally, it is visible in a new network of treaties and agreements, including the December 1987 Washington agreement on the abolition of intermediate-range nuclear missiles.

The Soviet approach of priority development of relations with the United States was maintained even though, as late as 1986, the Reagan administration adopted a number of policies that domestic critics in the Soviet Union could, and some actually did, characterize as provocative.[11] Such policies included the following:

– Continuation of strategic modernization programmes and the announcement by the Reagan administration, in May 1986, that it no longer felt bound by the SALT II treaty.
– The apparently unshakeable commitment of the Reagan adminis-

tration not only to research, development and testing as part of the Strategic Defence Initiative (SDI) but also to the *deployment* of space-based defensive weapons.
- The refusal, connected with SDI, to agree to a comprehensive nuclear weapons test ban.
- Procrastination or lack of interest in the conclusion of an agreement concerning limitation of anti-satellite systems.
- Adoption of a more assertive, militarily oriented policy of countering Soviet advances in the Third World.
- Persistent demands for the curtailment of Soviet embassy, consular and United Nations personnel.
- Continued adherence to the policy of restrictions on West–East technology transfer; pressure on Western allies to curtail their credit relations with Eastern European countries; and opposition to most-favoured nation status for the USSR and to Soviet membership in GATT while agreeing to support the Chinese application.

In 1987 and 1988 Gorbachev's perseverance continued – and yielded some results. The INF agreement was concluded. A number of regional conflicts were defused, above all the war in Afghanistan. The Reagan administration adopted a less strident ideological stance. It acknowledged that important changes were taking place in the Soviet Union, showed renewed interest in arms control agreements, and held out the prospect for an increase in Soviet–American economic cooperation.

But was the improvement of relations with the United States the main rationale for the priority accorded to the United States in the period under review? If not, what was the main rationale? And is the priority accorded to Washington likely to remain a constant feature of Gorbachev's Westpolitik?

The Rationale of Soviet Policy

The first and foremost reason for the priority accorded to the United States in Gorbachev's foreign policy until autumn 1988 is most likely connected with a re-evaluation of the apparent strength of 'antagonist contradictions' in the West. It probably has much to do with Moscow's experience that it proved *impossible to separate the United States from Western Europe (and Japan)*, and that the 'objective forces' which bind together these 'power centres of imperialism' are stronger than those which put them at odds with each other.[12] In fact, many of the issues which had been particularly divisive in the Western alliance – East–West sanctions over Afghanistan and Poland, the gas, credit and pipeline deal with Moscow, the sanctions over this issue, the stationing of medium-range missiles in Western Europe, and doubts about the reliability and loyalty of various allies – had after 1984 receded in importance or disappeared altogether.

In such circumstances, any attempt by Gorbachev to embark on a European 'peace offensive' would have been regarded by the Reagan administration as a continuation of previous endeavours to drive a wedge between the USA and Western Europe. It would have brought to nothing the approach of reordering the relationship with the West.

The second rationale for the priority of the United States in Gorbachev's foreign policy probably lies in Moscow's *claim to superpower status and political equality with the United States*. Negotiations with lesser powers at the periphery of the Soviet Union may be useful for a variety of reasons. But only by being seen internationally as being engaged in negotiations with the opposed world power do the assertions of the Soviet leaders that the two countries have 'a special responsibility for the destinies of mankind' appear somewhat more credible. Since the claim to equal political status is derived from military parity, this very fact also helps explain why nuclear arms control in 1985–8 was the driving edge of Soviet policy toward the West.

A third reason is connected with the significant *international isolation which the Soviet Union suffered in the period between autumn 1983 and summer 1984*. When taking office, Gorbachev saw himself confronted with increasing security cooperation not only between the USA, Western Europe and Japan but also between these 'power centres of imperialism' and China. Any attempt to prevent this development from gaining momentum had to take Washington as its primary focus. Only the United States was (and is) able to influence the character of relations at every angle of this quadrangle.

Fourth, *costs, benefits and risks of expansionism in the Third World* appeared in a different light to the Soviet leadership in the 1980s than they had in the 1970s. Whereas in the previous period, the despatch of military advisers and arms, as well as the cooperation with 'proxies', such as Cuba and Vietnam, seemed to have brought about substantial gains at little risk of confrontation with the United States, the subsequent years began to look different. The adversary superpower gave the impression that it had overcome the Vietnam and Watergate syndromes and was ready more vigorously to oppose the USSR worldwide.

In order to reduce the economic 'costs of empire', to contain the global political repercussions of military overcommitment and to lessen the risk of counter-intervention by the Reagan administration, Gorbachev had to turn directly to the United States. Western Europe was and would have been of little help in that endeavour.

A sixth element in Gorbachev's policy toward the West in 1985–8 derived from a reassessment of the *utility of the arms competition*. In the 1970s and early 1980s, it may have appeared to Soviet political leaders and analysts that NATO was no longer able successfully to compete with the Warsaw Pact in the arms competition. They seemed to have concluded that the West, and above all the Western European countries, were increasingly putting faith in arms control negotiations to redress a deteriorating military balance. But in the 1980s such trends could no longer be regarded as unbroken. Defence outlays in the United States had risen sharply. New challenges were issued to the Warsaw Pact in the form of the stationing of intermediate-range nuclear missiles in Western Europe, the strategic defence initiative (SDI) and the development and deployment of more sophisticated conventional weapons.

Efforts to lessen the arms competition became necessary, and these too had to be directed primarily to the United States, rather than to Western Europe, since the former rather than the latter was setting (or attempting to set) the pace.

A seventh factor is closely connected with the preceding one. It lay in the necessity, so often and emphatically expressed by Gorbachev, *for the Soviet Union to give priority to the development of the economy*. In order to improve Soviet economic performance, Gorbachev came to realize that what is required is the successful interplay of a number of factors, including major structural economic, social and political reform (perestroika); exposure of the economy to competition with the Western industrialized countries; improved access to Western technology, know-how, and credit; and a reduction in the pace of the arms competition. For this combination of factors to become effective it was (and is), as Gorbachev has repeatedly stated, necessary to create the right international political climate. The United States was needed in order to achieve this.

In the final analysis, then, the flashing of the 'European card' in the first three years of Gorbachev's rule may have had a much more modest purpose than is often assumed. This limited purpose was hinted at by Bovin as early as September 1985. He was 'not revealing any secrets by saying', he wrote, that

> Soviet policy takes into account the differences of view between Western Europe and the United States. But it does so by no means in order to squeeze the United States out of Europe and gain political control of the continent. . . . Our objective is much more modest. We would like to utilize Western Europe's potential to make good, via the trans-atlantic channel, the obvious shortage of common sense in the incumbent US administration.[13]

In other words, the flashing of the 'European card' was to serve the purpose of changing the direction of American foreign policy.

It can be argued that this purpose has successfully been achieved. The relations with the United States are indeed on a new footing. Are conditions ripe for Moscow now to give substance to its concept, previously so nebulous, of the 'European house'?

Relations with Western Europe: New Promises and Prospects

To some extent this is the case. Since October 1988 political contacts with Western European governments have become more frequent. Moscow has concluded new trade, scientific, technological and credit agreements with Western European governments and private institutions. There has been some movement in cultural affairs. However, there are still stringent limitations to a rebuilding of the European security framework. Furthermore, it is doubtful that the movement at the European angle of the triangular relationship will be at the expense or neglect of the United States.

Broadening of Political Contacts
Indicative of Gorbachev's revised approach towards Europe is, among other developments, the higher frequency of political contacts with Western European leaders. In mid-October 1988 Shevardnadze went to Paris for the first official visit of a Soviet foreign minister to France since 1980![14] In the same month Italian Prime Minister de Mita, Austrian Chancellor Vranitzky and West German Chancellor Helmut Kohl held talks with Gorbachev in Moscow. French President Mitterrand went to the Soviet capital at the end of November. Return visits took place in June and July 1989.[15].

Harbingers of an increased interest by Gorbachev in mending Soviet–Western European relations could be noticed in spring 1988: in June the two economic organizations, the EC and CMEA, finally succeeded in concluding an agreement on mutual diplomatic recognition and trade relations. This step was overdue. Brezhnev, in 1970, had acknowledged the EC to be a 'reality'. It took almost two decades of precedence of politics over economics for the Soviet leadership finally to revise its stand on the Berlin problem and to agree to treat that city as part of the EC.

Probably the most significant development of Soviet–Western European relations in early 1988 was the visit by Federal Chancellor Kohl, who went to Moscow with a large delegation of officials and businessmen. The event was claimed by the German chancellor to have 'broken the ice' in Soviet–West German relations.[16] A number of agreements were concluded, including those on cooperation in environmental protection, peaceful uses of space, nuclear energy, prevention of accidents at sea and food production. A first two-year programme of cultural exchanges was arranged.[17] Projects on the training of Soviet managers in West Germany are to be set up. German enterprises are to build a high-temperature nuclear reactor in the USSR. They are to participate in the expansion of the Soviet food and light industry. For that very purpose a West German banking consortium, led by the Deutsche Bank, has agreed with the Soviet foreign trade bank to provide a credit facility of 3 billion German marks. German businessmen accompanying Kohl concluded a number of joint ventures with Soviet enterprises, the total value of the contracts signed by German businessmen reportedly amounting to 2.7 billion German marks (US$1.5 billion at the exchange rate at time of publication).[18]

Economic Affairs

As these results may serve to show, Soviet–Western European economic relations are likely to become somewhat more lively. At the very least it would seem that the low point in Soviet–Western European trade has been reached. West German exports to the USSR in the first nine months of 1988, for instance, increased by 17.4 per cent.[19] This increase, however, is far from compensating for the decline of exports that occurred in 1985–7.

As for credit relations, a compilation of data from European bank sources shows that the Soviet Union intends to borrow approximately US$10 billion in Western industrialized countries.[20] That amount is being sought primarily in Western Europe and Japan. So far US$6 billion has been made available in so-called framework credit arrangements (of which US $1.7 billion has been granted by West German banks); for the rest of the amount negotiations are continuing.

Human Rights, Scientific and Cultural Affairs

Gorbachev has made significant moves to alter the facts and the corresponding image of a country dealing with political dissent in labour camps and mental asylums. In contrast to Brezhnev's adamant rejection of any discussion of human rights in the USSR as 'inadmissible interference in the internal affairs of the socialist countries', the new party leader is no longer averse to discussing these matters. In line with his activism in other spheres of international relations he has called for the holding of a human rights conference in Moscow. The USSR has not only increased the number of exit visas granted to Jewish 'refuseniks' but has also allowed more ethnic Germans to emigrate. In accordance with his revision of nationality policy, he has promised (for example, during Kohl's visit) to grant a greater measure of cultural autonomy to ethnic Germans who wish to remain in the USSR.

There has been a significant increase also in scientific contacts between Soviet and Western European scholars. New channels of communication and cooperation are being opened. These include the agreement concluded between the Deutsche Gesellschaft für Auswartige Politik (DGAP) in Bonn and the newly (in January 1988) founded Institute of Europe in Moscow to establish a mixed academic and government forum on Soviet–West German relations.[21]

As mentioned, a first programme of cultural exchanges was agreed between the Federal Republic and the Soviet Union, and Gorbachev's visit to Bonn and Paris in summer 1989 saw that the USSR has finally given consent to the opening of cultural institutes of Western European countries on Soviet soil.

Ideology and Political Theory

The reform process in the Soviet Union has now become comprehensive, embracing the spheres of politics, ideology, society, the economy and law. Part and parcel of this process is the search for workable models that may help transform the orthodox Marxist-Leninist, centralized, one-party state into a more modern, pragmatically oriented, democratic and pluralist system. In the course of this process the transformation in the nineteen and early twentieth centuries of the ideologically radical West European Marxist workers' parties to mass-based social democratic parties has provided a model that may be relevant for Gorbachev's efforts to reform the CPSU. Similarly, the mixture of elements of state planning, market economy and social welfare, so characteristic of many West European countries, has much to recommend itself as a model to Soviet reformers. The new interest in Moscow to learn from abroad may well enhance the quality of contacts between the Soviet Union and Western Europe.

Similar considerations apply to reformist trends in Eastern Europe and the Soviet attitude towards them. Even more so than in the Soviet Union, the intellectual and cultural elite in countries such as East Germany, Hungary, Czechoslovakia and Poland very much shares the Western values embodied in the Renaissance, the Enlightenment and the Reformation. Furthermore, they were part and parcel of the European-wide movement, in the nineteenth century and first decades of the twentieth century, of the establishment of diverse political parties. To revert to this tradition is easier there than in the USSR. Whether or not Moscow can, or will, look with equanimity on the restoration of a multi-party system in all of the countries in Eastern Europe, not just in Hungary, remains to be seen. (See also the last section below.)

European Security Affairs
Conditions for an improvement in European security have also become more favourable. This observation is warranted because of the 'new thinking' ordained by Gorbachev and new concepts of Soviet security that are being discussed. The latter include ideas such as the pre-eminence of political rather than military factors of security; 'reasonable sufficiency' (razumnaya dostatochnost') of armed forces; the achievement of security at 'lower levels of armament'; and the removal of imbalances in some categories of weapons through reductions by the side that is ahead rather than increases in the level of armament by the side that is behind.

An amelioration of European security may result also from Soviet criticism of traditional perceptions of threat and images of the enemy (obrazy vraga). Such revision ranges from general observations about the changing nature of threats to the Soviet Union[22] to very specific claims about the reduced danger from West German revanchism and militarism.[23] In conjunction with other reinterpretation, the revision of threat perceptions can serve to create the right kind of conditions for changes in Soviet military doctrine and deployments.

Some changes in Moscow's European security policy have already occurred. They are reflected in the two East–West agreements concluded since Gorbachev's ascendancy to power: the September 1986 Stockholm accord, negotiated under the auspices of the Conference on Security and Cooperation in Europe (CSCE), on Confidence-building and Disarmament in Europe (CDE), and

the December 1987 Washington treaty on the abolition of intermediate-range nuclear forces (INF). Even though the INF treaty was
signed by the superpowers, it has direct implications for Western
Europe. Its noteworthy favourable features are the exclusion of the
British and French nuclear forces from the scope of the treaty; the
scrapping of an entire category of modern weapons; the acceptance
of significant asymmetrical cuts; and a comprehensive regime of
on-site verification. It seems that the Soviet political leadership has
accepted the view, expressed by civilian analysts, that Brezhnev's
decision to station the SS-20 missiles was motivated by an erroneous
definition of security interests; by military-technological considerations rather than by political analysis;[24] and by over-insurance and
unwarranted reliance on numerical superiority ('the more missiles,
the more stable Soviet security').[25]

However, in 1987 and 1988 one could legitimately ask whether
the Washington agreement was just a different tack on the very
same road which Brezhnev had travelled; namely towards the
achievement of the de-nuclearization of Europe, the erosion of
NATO's doctrine of 'flexible response' and the separation of Western Europe from the United States, or whether Gorbachev would
indeed move towards greater balance and stability of armed forces
and armaments in Europe and follow suit with significant concessions in the *conventional* sphere.

Gorbachev's announcement of 7 December 1988, at the United
Nations, concerning unilateral troop cuts is an important step in
the latter direction. Reducing the more than 5 million officers
and men of the Soviet armed forces by 500,000 is relatively easy,
considering that some 3 million of the total, according to Western
estimates, are conscripts. Effective cuts can be made simply by
shortening the length of compulsory service, currently two years in
the army and three in the navy. That corresponding measures
may be under discussion is indicated, for instance, by statements
Gorbachev made to the Soviet youth organization. He believed,
the party secretary said, 'that the length of military service will be
reconsidered'.[26]

The most important aspect of Gorbachev's announcement of
December 1988, however, concerns the issues of surprise attack
and invasion capability. From Czechoslovakia, Hungary and the
GDR, 5,000 tanks are to be withdrawn with 50,000 troops, includ-
ing assault landing formations and river-crossing units which, in the
NATO perspective, have been designed for offensive operations in
West Germany. Six tank divisions, of the twenty-eight Soviet tank
and motorized rifle divisions which Western intelligence says are

based in those countries, are to be disbanded, and a further 5,000 tanks pulled out of the western Soviet Union.

As for the modalities of the cuts, according to later clarification provided by Gorbachev and information provided by the Soviet defence ministry and civilian arms control experts, not 5,000 but 5,300 tanks are to be withdrawn from Eastern Europe. They are to replace older models in the western parts of the Soviet Union; in this region a total of 10,000 tanks are to be dismantled. As for the withdrawal and dissolution of Soviet tank divisions in Eastern Europe, four of the six divisions are to be withdrawn from the GDR, one from Czechoslovakia and one from Hungary. The four tank divisions in East Germany and the one in Czechoslovakia are all so-called Operational Manoeuvre Groups (OMGs), consisting of troops with special training, having the best commanders and the most modern equipment to enable them to conduct surprise offensive operations in the depth of enemy territory. Also to be withdrawn unilaterally are one in four of Soviet artillery pieces in Europe and one in eight combat aircraft, according to Western estimates of current deployments.[27]

The announcement has already served to enhance the credibility of Gorbachev's professed readiness to change from an offensive to a defensive military posture in Europe. The unilateral decrease in Soviet conventional forces makes the task easier for the scheduled talks on armed forces reductions in Europe (CFE) in Vienna since the asymmetrical cuts by the USSR put the Soviet potential closer to the levels of the Western alliance. The extent to which the cuts can be verified will be important since the Vienna talks will have to deal with a 'moving target' of constantly changing Soviet force levels.

The announced cuts, if properly implemented, would most likely significantly constrain the possibility for suprise attack but not yet eliminate the Soviet High Command's military option to conduct major offensive operations in Europe. However, definite progress would have been made towards a reduction in the offensive potential. Prospects for a comprehensive reordering of security relations in Europe would improve also if the Soviet Union were to provide realistic data for the CFE talks and continue the process of asymmetrical cuts.

Chances for such a development do exist. They flow from the redefinition of the Soviet role in international affairs and pressures for the transfer of resources from the military to the civilian sector. But many hurdles in the 'reconstruction' of Soviet security policy are still to be taken. There remain also considerable uncertainties and obstacles to further changes in Soviet–West European relations.

Relations with Western Europe: Obstacles and Limitations

It is becoming increasingly obvious that the 'European house' to be built according to Soviet designs does not really deviate very much from the foundations and framework established in the early 1970s, notably the Final Act of the CSCE.[28] In fact, the very term 'common house' originated not with Gorbachev but with Brezhnev.[29] It would, of course, be foolish to assert that there is no difference between Brezhnev's and Gorbachev's policies in Europe. Yet it would be equally erroneous to neglect some parallels and the persistence of constraints on fundamental and lasting change. The foremost objective difficulty with which the Soviet Union finds itself faced are processes of integration in Western Europe and processes of disintegration in Eastern Europe.

Indeed, it is the processes that count. For that very reason, one of the major disadvantages in using the term of 'common house' is its static connotation, the impression it conveys is that an entirely new structure were needed, perhaps with new external (and internal?) walls.

Western European Integration, Eastern European Disintegration

No matter whether current perceptions and expectations will correspond with the future course of events, talk about 'Eurosclerosis' seems to be a thing of the past. A new dynamism is in evidence. The creation of a truly common market by 1992 is no longer a dim vision but a matter of practical policy. Portugal, Spain and Greece have become members; other countries, including member states of the European Free Trade Association (EFTA), are either planning to join the EC or attempting to limit the damage of not being part of it. New programmes of technology cooperation are being launched. Attempts are being made to deepen political coordination and military integration. Soviet and Eastern European observers are fully conscious of this trend.[30]

The new dynamism in Western Europe contrasts sharply with the 'pre-crisis' conditions of stagnation and decline in Eastern Europe. These internal conditions coincide with a blatant inability to develop effective forms of cooperation in the CMEA. 'Direct links' and 'joint enterprises' are largely artificial undertakings that have little to do with the real needs of the participants and bring little benefit. Scientific and technical advancement along the lines of the December 1985 CMEA plan has turned out to be unrealizable. The CMEA bureaucracy certainly cannot pass any cost-benefit test: it is vast, expensive, often simply for show and, on practical matters, geared primarily to supervising the relatively simple exchange of Soviet raw materials for Eastern European manufactures. As for manufactures, Gorbachev has lamented that up to now 'the practice was often as follows: products were specially selected for exports to the West – to earn hard currency. And to each other we sold the worst.'[31] Whatever the CMEA does, or most of it, could be done without that organization – if economic relations within the bloc were properly commercialized.

Perestroika is apparently meant to achieve just that. But Eastern Europe is far from having agreed on a coordinated, let alone uni- fied, reform effort. The responses to perestroika have been diverse. So far, only Hungary and Poland have embarked on a reform effort as comprehensive as the one envisaged by Gorbachev. But Poland is still ideologically, socially and politically so polarized that the implementation of a coherent programme is difficult. The GDR and Czechoslovakia are potentially the two most important countries for a successful modernization of the Eastern bloc as a whole. But they show no enthusiasm for the kind of market-orientation and social and political pluralism characteristic of the Soviet, Hungarian and Polish efforts. Bulgaria only tampers with reform ideas. And Romania even continues to practise Stalinism in its pure form.

In order to improve economic performance, it would seem that the Eastern European countries would *jointly* have to embark on comprehensive reform of their own economies and of the CMEA on market principles, including the convertibility of currency. But so far their instinctive tendency has been the principle of *sauve qui peut*. In their external trade this has meant rushing to secure the most favourable terms in bilateral relations with the EC.

Gorbachev's assumption for the next five to ten years of Soviet– Eastern European relations appears to be that a lessening of central control and the introduction of pluralist structures will enhance the legitimacy of party rule in Eastern Europe and ameliorate economic performance. He may be wrong. Perestroika and glasnost may fail to improve the economic situation, lead to social and political instability, threaten even further the weak legitimacy of the party and hence threaten Soviet control in Eastern Europe. It is doubtful whether this would be tolerated by conservative forces in the Soviet leadership.

On the other hand, relative success of perestroika in Eastern Europe is possible only on the basis of closer integration of this area with Western Europe. But this could mean that the reforming Eastern European countries would drift away from the USSR and become the outer rim of an expanding EC. This, too, would most likely arouse opposition by Soviet party officials faithful to the principles of Stalinism and the Brezhnev doctrine.

The optimal development, from Gorbachev's point of view, would be coordinated, gradual and successful perestroika in the whole Eastern bloc. But what are the chances of this occurring within a relatively short time? Probably very slim.

Thus, Gorbachev sees himself faced with a dilemma in his European policy. Any loosening of the reigns and consent to broader East–West European cooperation is likely to lead to a loss of Soviet influence at the expense of the EC, and notably West Germany. But any reimposition of Soviet control is likely to defeat the purposes of perestroika in Eastern Europe – and potentially in the USSR itself. This fundamental dilemma explains the reluctance with which Gorbachev, in the period from March 1985 until October 1988, has responded to persistent West German attempts to embark on a broadening of contacts and exchanges between East and West in Europe.

The German Problem

It is therefore highly unlikely that, as some West German conservatives and neutralists believe, Gorbachev will launch a new initiative on the German problem and perhaps even make an offer for a confederation or reunification of the two parts of Germany. If this needed any further proof it was unambiguously provided during the Kohl visit in Moscow. On that occasion Gorbachev stated angrily that he had already 'spoken several times about the so-called "German problem" ' but that the matter apparently still needed clarification. 'The current situation', he said, 'is the result of history. Attempts at overturning what has been created by it or to force things by an unrealistic policy are an incalculable and even dangerous endeavour.'[32]

The Soviet leadership has adopted a similarly restrictive approach towards West Berlin. This is the case despite the fact that, as mentioned, the city was included in the June 1988 EC–CMEA agreement as part of the EC. But practical problems thereafter remained. They surfaced in bilateral negotiations between Bonn and Moscow on the inclusion of experts from West Berlin in Soviet–West German economic projects and scientific-cultural events. In those negotiations the pettiness of the 'house rules' for the 'common house' have shown up on such issues as whether it would be a violation of the city's status under four-power control if the West Berlin postal code were added to the name of the invitees from that city; or whether the West German embassy in Moscow would be allowed to extend invitations to conference participants from West Berlin to lists which did not explicitly distinguish them from Federal German participants. The solutions found in October 1988 are not exactly to be considered examples of far-reaching change. They also do not deviate from previous Soviet legal positions.[33]

The reply given by the Soviet government, in mid-September 1988, to an initiative by the three Western allies concerning a possible transformation of Berlin to a focal point of contacts between East and West in Europe fits the restrictive pattern. According to (unofficial) West German government interpretation, the reply was resounding rejection.[34] The Soviet government has also voiced its opposition to the new flight connection between the Federal Republic and West Berlin operated by EuroBerlin France. Fifty-one per cent of the company shares are owned by Air France and 49 per cent by Lufthansa. The Soviet foreign ministry spokesman called the new connection an 'obvious violation' of the four-power agreement on Berlin by the French authorities.[35]

It does seem, then, that the concessions, so far limited, made by the Soviet Union on issues such as EC–CMEA diplomatic recognition, bilateral relations and the Berlin problem are motivated primarily by economic interests. The financial and economic position of the Soviet Union (and even more so of Eastern Europe) is such that it cannot offer much profitable trade and investment opportunities to Western European firms. The Soviet leadership therefore seems to have concluded that Western firms need a 'push' from government and, perhaps, public opinion to make an expansion of East–West trade and economic cooperation feasible. It may also have become aware of the need, in order to create such a push, to make concessions in political and security matters. But how far, really, can these be expected to extend?

Security and Conventional Arms Control in Europe

As mentioned, politically the December 1987 INF agreement may have had benefits for Western Europe. Militarily its merits are more dubious. The agreement, at least to some extent, has eroded NATO's doctrine of 'flexible response'. The abolition of the long-range nuclear weapons category runs counter to agreed NATO policy of cutting battlefield nuclear weapons but leaving intact an unbroken 'escalation ladder' with short and (before the INF agreement) medium-range nuclear weapons for purposes of deterrence. If nuclear deterrence in Europe is thought to be vitally important for complicating the task of Soviet war planning and compensating for NATO's inferiority in conventional weapons, the retention and, where technically necessary, modernization of some land-based systems in Western Europe would be desirable.

Some would argue that this would be the case even in conditions of conventional stability when both sides would have primarily defensively oriented armed forces. It certainly would be true for a period of transition to an entirely new security system in Europe.

Thus, the levels of deployment or, depending on political developments, the abolition of land-based nuclear system in Europe ('de-nuclearization' of Europe in this sense) depend on the progress and outcome of the conventional arms control negotiations. What, then, are their chances of success?

From the perspective of early 1989 they are mixed. There are still a number of uncertainties. Given their wide geographical scope, the large number of participants and the complexity of the matter, the Vienna CFE talks are certainly the most ambitious ever undertaken in the history of arms control. This is a problem that is vexing, even assuming determination by all sides to reach agreement. But, on the Soviet side, there are special problems. On security matters, there is still a considerable gap between 'new thinking' and practice; between the newly proclaimed doctrine of 'defensive defence' and the existing force structure; and between the principle of 'reasonable sufficiency' and actual military capabilities. In detail, as far as one is able to establish from available information, the gap manifests itself in the following dimensions.

- Some of the programmes designed by the previous chief of general staff, Marshal Ogarkov, for the modernization of the conventional forces are continuing.
- Production rates of hardware, notably in tanks (estimated by US and other Western intelligence to be at about 3,000 tanks per year) have not declined.
- The overall size and potential of the Soviet armed forces after the cuts announced by Gorbachev would still be impressive. The Soviet Union would retain – after substantial cuts in the strength of the Chinese armed forces (estimated at about 1.5 million in the last few years) – the largest military force in the world.
- The degree of glasnost in military affairs is still limited: this

concerns the size and composition of the military budget; the strength, organization and deployment of the Soviet armed forces; the priorities in military research and development; the scope and rates of weapons production; and the volume, composition and geographical distribution of arms exports and military assistance. Notably concerning the budget, Soviet officials have promised, since summer 1987, to provide reliable and comparable data. But so far the information has not been provided and, as it is now being said in Moscow, will not be provided prior to the implementation of a wide-ranging price reform in the Soviet economy.

- Thus far it does not seem that the growth rates of military expenditures have declined from the pre-Gorbachev levels.
- As a result of the INF agreement, conversion of some military production capacity to civilian use seems to have taken place. There are also a number of government decrees concerning the expansion of the civilian portion of the output of military-industrial plants.[36] However, implementation of the decrees so far appears to be painfully slow. A comprehensive approach towards conversion is lacking.

In the force comparisons provided by the Soviet defence minister in February 1988 it was claimed that, overall, 'violations of the military balance exist neither world-wide nor in Europe'.[37] Since then such claims have been toned down or abandoned altogether. But the first ever Warsaw Pact force comparisons, published in January 1989, in several weapons categories still deviate considerably from the ones used by NATO.[38]

Other problems are that the Soviet military may aim at making cuts from their large stocks of older equipment while modernizing the remaining stock and ending up with smaller, reorganized but still effective forces capable of offensive operations. In Vienna, at the CFE talks, the Soviet Union wants to include tactical air forces in the negotiations, and at the same time is reorganizing its air forces and transferring numbers of tactical aircraft to the air defence forces. Cuts in tactical air forces would reinforce Soviet advantages in attack helicopters and medium bombers for which there is no NATO equivalent. They would also increase the effectiveness of the Soviet air defence network which includes a large number of fixed SAM sites as well as aircraft. And of course the Soviet approach is also governed by an awareness that much of NATO's tactical nuclear delivery capability rests on dual-capable aircraft, whereas for their part, the Soviets have a superiority of dual-capable missile systems. Similar problems result from the Soviet aim of including naval forces.[39]

Important as these technical military details may be, the central question concerning the conventional balance in Europe is whether Gorbachev, at this stage of perestroika, can be interested at all in having the Soviet Union make a transition in military doctrine, strategy and 'operational art' to conventional defence with all the corresponding adjustments in its European force posture. Should he be interested?

Prospects

There may be three major reasons why he should be. The first would be the bankruptcy of the policy from positions of military strength, notably the inability of the Soviet leadership from Brezhnev to Chernenko to transform military superiority into political influence. The gradual drawing of Western Europe into the Soviet orbit through a gradual accommodation to Soviet military preponderance (the 'Finlandization' of Western Europe, as this potential danger was called in the 1970s) did not take place and, through another acceleration of the arms race, is not likely to occur.

The second possible reason would be that the logic of perestroika would be seen by Gorbachev to require a fundamental change in the relationship between military and civilian industry which is discussed by Julian Cooper in Chapter 7. In fact, because of the concentration of expenditure (approximately 80 per cent) on conventional forces and armaments it is cuts in the conventional sphere that are likely to yield considerable savings. It is correct that beneficial effects on the economy may only become visible in the long run. But starting the conversion process may be seen in Moscow to be required very shortly.

The third reason would be that the Soviet leadership may regard it as expedient to reduce, through conventional arms control, Western European threat perceptions so as to create a political climate that would be more conducive to the desired broad expansion of East–West economic and scientific-technological exchanges.

These interests may be counteracted by other factors. First, if the military instrument has thus far been the main device with which Moscow has been able to exert some degree of influence in world affairs, including in Europe, the question poses itself as to what will remain of the superpower once the 'power' is gone?

Second, given an essentially volatile situation in Eastern Europe, the Soviet Union may not wish to give rise to illusions about its ultimate resolution to intervene militarily if 'socialism' were threatened by 'counter-revolution'.[40]

Finally, it is doubtful that the major part of the Soviet military, foremost the ground forces, show much support for smaller defence budgets and the new concepts of numerically reduced, defensively oriented armed forces.[41] Thus, in order not to undermine his domestic position and endanger the course of perestroika, Gorbachev may want to proceed with much more caution and a longer time horizon than may be desirable from his own foreign policy perspectives.

Notes

1. *Pravda*, 19 Dec. 1984.

2. Literally, for Washington it is a 'chuzhoi dom', i.e., a house that belongs to others; 'Evropa – nash obshchii don', *Pravda*, 13 Nov. 1985.

3. Thus, in veiled criticism of the discussion during Reagan's first term, he added that Europe was, indeed, to be regarded as a home and not simply 'a theatre of military operations', *Pravda*, 19 Dec. 1984; similarly, the above-mentioned *Pravda* editorial claims that, to Washington, Europe is 'a battlefield on the maps of [its] strategists', *Pravda*, 13 Nov. 1985.

4. Aleksandr Bovin, 'Evropeiskoe napravlenie', *Izvestiya*, 25 Sep. 1985. The term 'political culture' he used *expressis verbis* in another article entitled 'Evropeiskoe napravlenie', *Izvestiya*, 20 July 1986.

5. *Izvestiya*, 25 Sept. 1985.

6. *Pravda*, 20 Feb. 1985.

7. *Pravda*, 8 April 1985. Similar formulations were used by Gorbachev in his speech to the twenty-seventh CPSU congress in February 1986.

8. In his talks with Craxi, *Pravda*, 30 May 1985; see also the report on his discussions with Cervetti, *l'Unità*, 22 May 1985.

9. Statistisches Bundesamt of the Federal Republic of Germany (ed.), *Länderbericht Sowjeturnion*, 1988 (Stuttgart: Kohlhammer, 1988), p. 97.

10. Ibid, p. 98.

11. Gorbachev himself, in his closing address to the twenty-seventh CPSU congress voiced such suspicions (*Izvestiya*, 3 March 1987); he did so again in a speech in Krasnodar, in reply to questions from Soviet citizens whether or not the USSR did not speak 'too softly' with the outside world (*Pravda*, 19 Sept. 1986). Georgy Arbatov has also stated that the Reagan administration wanted to provoke the Soviet leadership so that it would break off the US–Soviet dialogue (*Pravda*, 21 Nov. 1986). In response to the dispatch of US naval vessels into the 12-mile zone off the Black Sea coast, fleet admiral and deputy defence minister Chernavin claimed that 'The incident justifies stating with conviction that the activities of vessels of the US fleet were planned in advance and [that they] had a clearly provocative character (Interview in *Krasnaya zvezda*, 21 March 1987).

12. This was explicitly stated, for instance, by Aleksandr Bovin in *Izvestiya*, 20 July 1986. Similarly, in his speech to the French National Assembly, Gorbachev

said that 'We are realists and know how stable the historical, political, and economic relations are between Western Europe and the USA.' *Izvestiya*, 4 Oct. 1985.

13. *Izvestiya*, 25 Sept. 1985.

14. What is meant here are official visits by the foreign minister. Excluded here are stopovers (such as the two hours of discussion between Gromyko and his French counterpart in 1983) and the inclusion of the foreign minister as part of a larger, high-ranking delegation (such as in October 1985 when Sheverdnadze merely accompanied Gorbachev).

15. This chapter was completed in early 1989 and therefore does not take full account of these visits.

16. Chancellor Kohl at the press conference of 26 October, *Bulletin* (Press and Information Office of the Federal Government, Bonn), 141 (1 Nov. 1988).

17. An agreement on cultural exchanges had been in existence since 1973. Nothing had come of it in practical terms, however, because of Soviet–West German disagreements over the inclusion of participants from West Berlin.

18. *International Herald Tribune*, 28 Oct. 1988.

19. *Frankfurter Allgemeine Zeitung*, 5 Jan. 1989.

20. Credit compilation by Stiftung Wissenschaft und Politik (SWP), Ebenhausen.

21. This non-governmental agreement was signed during the Kohl visit to Moscow; see *Bulletin* (Press and Information Office of the Federal Government, Bonn), 141 (1 Nov. 1988).

22. See, for instance, A. Yu. Mel'vil', ' "Obraz vraga" i novoe politicheskoe myshlenie', *SShA*, 1 (Jan. 1988): 29–39; and V. Zhurkin, S. Karaganov and A. Kortunov, 'Vyzovy bezopasnosti – starye i novye', *Kommunist*, 1 (Jan. 1988): 47–8.

23. A recent example of this is Ilya Kremer, 'Esli khochesh' stat' drugom', *Moskovskie novosti*, 44 (30 Oct. 1988): 6, in response to an article by Rupert Scholz, the first article by a Federal German defence minister in the Soviet press, in the same issue of that journal.

24. Sergei Vybornov, Andrei Gusenkov and Vladimir Leontiev, 'Nothing is Simple in Europe', *International Affairs* (Moscow), 3 (March 1988): 41.

25. Igor Malaschenko, 'Warum bauen wir mehr Raketen ab?', *Neue Zeit* (Moscow), 7, (1988): 21.

26. *Pravda*, 1 Nov. 1988.

27. As summarized by the *Financial Times*, 9 Dec. 1988. Some of the details concerning the cuts and withdrawals were provided by Gorbachev, in mid-January 1989, in talks with members of the Trilateral Commission; see *Pravda*, 19 Jan. 1989. Other information is derived from communications to West German and American defence experts visiting the Soviet Union in February 1989.

28. This was explicitly stated in an editorial in *Izvestiya*, 22 July 1988.

29. In November 1981 in a dinner speech during his visit to Bonn; see *Pravda*, 24 Nov. 1981. A. Gromyko, the then foreign minister and Politburo member, had taken it up in January 1983 at a press conference in Bonn. 'The Federal Republic of Germany as well as the Soviet Union', he said, 'live in one common house, under one roof.' *Sowjetunion heute*, 2 (Feb. 1983): Supplement, p. xiii.

30. Concerning the military-political aspects of Western European integration, see, for instance, V.G. Baranovsky, *Zapadnaya Evropa: voenno-politicheskaya integratsiya* (Moscow: Mezhdunarodnye otnosheniya, 1988). The author is head of the Western European centre at IMEMO.

31. In a speech in Bucharest in May 1987.

32. At the dinner speech of 24 Oct. 1988; *Pravda*, 25 Oct. 1988.

33. The new machinery consists in the USSR agreeing that experts from West Berlin as members of West German delegations may participate in international conferences and meetings provided an asterisk appears behind their name. This asterisk is to point to a footnote which in turn states that the basis for their participation is the four-power status of Berlin. Invitations will not be sent to the street address of the institution in that city but to postal boxes.

34. See *Süddeutsche Zeitung*, 20 Sept. 1988.

35. *Süddeutsche Zeitung*, 17 Nov. 1988.

36. Published in *Izvestiya*, 21 Aug. 1988.

37. See *Pravda*, 8 Feb. 1988.

38. For the Warsaw Pact figures see *Pravda*, 30 Jan. 1989.

39. Concerning these issues see *The Gorbachev Challenge and European Security*, Report by the European Strategy Group (ESG) (Nomos: Baden-Baden, 1988), pp. 118–21.

40. In an interview with an Italian newspaper, Yurii Afanas'ev, the Director of the Institute of Historical Archives, said in response to a question as to what would happen if an Eastern-bloc country decided to 'get out of the empire' that the 'reaction [in Moscow] would be negative; there would not be fireworks in the Red Square to celebrate the development'. He continued that there were still 'many Soviet officials who remain faithful to the principles of that period . . . and to what in the West is called the "Brezhnev doctrine" ' (*La Stampa*, Milan, 1 Sept. 1988).

41. The Warsaw Pact proposed in July 1988 to cut the overall number of ground forces divisions in Central Europe in three stages from the current levels (NATO: 48 division equivalents; Warsaw Pact: 128 division equivalents) to 25–30 divisions. If these proposals were taken at face value, the Warsaw Pact would have to make cuts in the number of divisions amounting to approximately 80%. It is hardly likely that the Soviet military establishment would consent to such cuts with good grace.

Index